Spanish for Hospitality and Foodservice

Jennifer Thomas

Spanish Training
SERVICES

PEARSON
Prentice Hall

Upper Saddle River, New Jersey 07458

Library of Congress Cataloging-in-Publication Data

Thomas, Jennifer.
  Spanish for hospitality and foodservice / Jennifer Thomas.
    p. cm.
  ISBN 0-13-048261-7
    1. Spanish language–Conversation and phrase books (for restaurant and hotel personnel)
  2. Spanish language–Conversation and phrase books–English I. Title.
PC4120.R4T46 2003
468.3'421'024642—dc21

2003048733

Editor-in-Chief: Stephen Helba
Executive Editor: Vernon R. Anthony
Executive Assistant: Nancy Kesterson
Associate Editor: Marion Gottlieb
Editorial Assistant: Ann Brunner
Director of Manufacturing and Production: Bruce Johnson
Managing Editor: Mary Carnis
Production Liaison: Adele M. Kupchik
Creative Director: Cheryl Asherman
Design Coordinator: Christopher Weigand
Manufacturing Manager: Ilene Sanford

Manufacturing Buyer: Cathleen Petersen
Interior Design & Formatting: Pine Tree Composition, Inc.
Production Editor: Melissa Scott/Carlisle Communications, Inc.
Cover Design: Ruta Fiorino
Cover Image: Simon Watson, FoodPix/Getty Images
Senior Marketing Manager: Ryan DeGrote
Marketing Assistant: Elizabeth Farrell
Senior Marketing Coordinator: Adam Kloza
Printer/Binder: Banta, Harrisonburg
Cover Printer: Phoenix Color

Pearson Education LTD.
Pearson Education Australia PTY, Limited
Pearson Education Singapore, Pte. Ltd.
Pearson Education—North Asia Ltd.

Pearson Education, Canada, Ltd.
Pearson Education de Mexico, S.A. de C.V.
Pearson Educación—Japan
Pearson Education Malaysia, Pte. Ltd.

10 9 8 7 6 5 4 3 2
ISBN 0-13-048261-7

CONTENTS

PREFACE

PURPOSE

The *Spanish and English for Hospitality and Foodservice* training materials have been developed specifically for those who would like to work more productively and effectively with their diverse co-workers so that they can provide their guests with excellent service. The purpose of this course is to prepare you for that challenge. This training program will provide you with the necessary skills needed to be successful working in an organization with a diverse staff. You will learn:

- Industry specific vocabulary
- How to assign tasks, follow up, correct and praise behavior
- Key cultural differences
- Team building tips

Since the United States' service industries hire many Spanish-speaking employees, bilingual and bicultural employees are very needed and welcomed. The skills you learn in this training program will prove to be very practical and marketable for many years to come.

Benefits of Studying *Spanish* and *English for Hospitality and Foodservice*

- Improves service
- Improves supervisors' ability to communicate
- Increases productivity
- Improves safety
- Increases employee retention and referrals
- Builds teamwork, motivation, and rapport
- Improves cultural leadership skills of front line supervisors
- Increases confidence and comfort level working in a diverse setting
- Provides convenience and availability since it is an on-site class
- Provides consistency between university study and company training
- Oral proficiency in Spanish and English is a valuable skill to add to one's resume

SUPPORT MATERIALS

For the Student

The textbook includes Spanish and English word lists and corresponding pictures, interactive role play exercises, crossword puzzles, dialogues, review activities, and a Spanish/English dictionary. Each chapter contains a cultural reading as well as several team-building tips. A set of flashcards also allows students to review and practice the vocabulary together.

A pronunciation guide on CD is available.

For the Facilitator

The Facilitator's Guide offers many suggestions, teaching methods and instructions on how to implement the basic training program. It explains how to facilitate the learning activities and exciting games.

- **Overhead Transparencies** are provided to enhance the facilitator's presentation of the training program. There are popular games that help the participants review the material in an enjoyable atmosphere.
- **Flash Cards** are provided in two sizes. The large set is provided for the facilitator to introduce the vocabulary and to use with the review activities. The small sets allow the students to review and practice with one another in small groups.
- **Tests, Quizzes and Answer Keys** are provided for every chapter and activity in the textbook.

ACKNOWLEDGMENTS

A sincere thanks to Jacky and Jack Thomas, my parents, who introduced me to the game of golf as well as to the Spanish language. The combination of the two led to this training program. I love you.

A special thanks to my hardworking editors Vernon Anthony and Marion Gottlieb for recognizing the need for this training program

Thanks to my reviewers Jeffrey Conklin, Daytona Beach Community College; Roy Cook, Fort Lewis College; Diann Newman, Florida International University; and Joan Remington, Florida International University.

Thanks also to Chris Haserot, my illustrator; Melissa Scott, my project editor; Joe Drago, my business consultant, and to Larry Hickey for his spiritual advice.

Jennifer Thomas

Note: The term, Latino, is used through this text "generically," with the intent of encompassing all Spanish-speaking/Hispanic individuals. Different communities in areas of the country have different preferred terms. Further discussion can be found in the "Culture" section on page 18.

About Spanish Training Services

OUR STORY

Spanish Training Services provides industry-specific language and cultural training. The company has been written about in *Pro Magazine, Landscape Management, Nursery Management and Production, Grounds Maintenance,* and *Golfdome.*

Spanish Training Services is committed to offering quality language and cultural training to organizations in order to improve the skills of frontline managers and employees. The company specializes in training English- and Spanish-speaking employees to communicate more effectively and to work together more productively, so that they can provide excellent service to their guests.

While other companies and educational organizations are available for learning the Spanish and English language, their material is too broad, and cross-cultural management issues are not discussed. Spanish Training Services' unique training focus concentrates on and is organized around the specific vocabulary and leadership issues needed to carry out one's daily work responsibilities.

Spanish Training Services was founded in 1996 with the vision that the hardworking Latino labor force will continue to rise and that communication and effective leadership skills will play an increasingly important role in the relationships between the United States supervisor, the Latino employee, as well as the organizations' guests. Spanish Training Services is a privately-owned company, headquartered in Evanston, Illinois.

About the Author

Jennifer Thomas first noticed the need for managers to learn Spanish when she was speaking Spanish with a Latino employee at a golf club near Chicago. The employee lamented, " '¡Rápido!' That's the only Spanish word my boss knows! That's all he ever says!" They discussed how not knowing one another's language caused them to lose ten to fifteen minutes an hour in productivity trying to explain a task using just body language. The lack of communication had caused misunderstandings, mistakes, rework and poor service.

Shortly there after, Ms. Thomas developed and wrote *Spanish for Hospitality & Foodservice, English for Hospitality & Foodservice* as well as *Spanish for the Green Industry* and *English for the Green Industry*. She is a regular presenter at educational conferences, businesses, and university extension offices.

Her unique training methods and customized courses stem from her extensive educational background and experiences living and working in Mexico, Spain, and South America, as well as teaching high school Spanish for many years. Ms. Thomas holds a Master's degree in International Management from the American Graduate School for International Management.

As a former tennis teaching professional and junior golf instructor, Ms. Thomas has much experience training, coaching, and motivating in all walks of life. She lives in Evanston, Illinois and spends her summers in Green Lake, Wisconsin.

The Front Office

PART I—GREETINGS

Good morning.	**Buenos días.**
Good afternoon.	**Buenas tardes.**
Good night.	**Buenas noches.**
Welcome.	**Bienvenidos.**
Hi/Hello.	**Hola.**
How's it going?	**¿Qué tal?**
How are you?	**¿Cómo estás?**
Fine. And you?	**Bien. ¿Y tú?**
How's your family?	**¿Cómo está tu familia?**
What's your name?	**¿Cómo te llamas?**
My name is . . .	**Me llamo . . .**
See you later.	**Hasta luego.**
See you tomorrow.	**Hasta mañana.**
Goodbye.	**Adiós.**
Please.	**Por favor.**
Thank you.	**Gracias.**
You are very kind.	**Eres muy amable.**
I'm sorry.	**Lo siento.**
I'm studying Spanish.	**Estudio español.**
I speak Spanish a little.	**Hablo español un poco.**
Speak slowly, please.	**Habla más despacio, por favor.**
You are very patient.	**Eres muy paciente.**
Do you speak English?	**¿Hablas inglés?**
Do you understand English?	**¿Comprendes inglés?**

MATCHING EXERCISE

Write the letter of the Spanish phrase next to the English phrase it matches on the left.

1. _____ My name is . . .
2. _____ How's it going?
3. _____ Fine. And you?
4. _____ How's your family?
5. _____ See you tomorrow.
6. _____ Hi/Hello.
7. _____ See you later.
8. _____ Welcome.
9. _____ Please.
10. _____ Good morning.
11. _____ How are you?
12. _____ Thank you.
13. _____ Goodbye.

a. ¿Cómo estás?
b. ¿Qué tal?
c. Me llamo . . .
d. Bien. ¿Y tú?
e. Gracias.
f. Hasta luego.
g. Hola.
h. Buenos días.
i. ¿Cómo está tu familia?
j. Adiós.
k. Bienvenidos.
l. Por favor.
m. Hasta mañana.

CROSSWORD PUZZLES

Across

2. Do you speak English?
5. Good afternoon.
7. Hi/Hello.
8. How are you?
10. Please.
11. How's it going?

Down

1. Good night.
3. Good morning.
4. See you later.
6. Thank you.
9. Goodbye.

Across

1. Estudio español.
6. Buenas tardes.
7. ¿Cómo estás?
8. ¿Qué tal?
9. Hola.
11. Hasta luego.
13. Por favor.
14. ¿Cómo está tu familia?

Down

2. ¿Hablas inglés?
3. Buenos días.
4. Buenas noches.
5. Adiós.
10. Bienvenidos.
12. Gracias.

TRANSLATION EXERCISE

Translate the following to English:

1. Habla mas despacio, por favor. _____

2. Gracias. _____

3. Bienvenidos. _____

4. ¿Qué tal? _____

5. Hasta luego. _____

6. Hasta mañana. _____

7. ¿Cómo estás? _____

8. Bien. ¿Y tú? _____

9. Buenos días. _____

10. Lo siento. _____

Translate the following to Spanish:

1. Good morning. _____

2. How are you? _____

3. How's it going? _____

4. Fine, thanks. And you? _____

5. Good afternoon. _____

6. See you later. _____

7. Welcome. _____

8. I'm sorry. _____

9. Speak slowly, please. _____

10. Thank you. _____

MULTIPLE CHOICE

Circle the letter of the correct answer.

1. Please.
   a. Gracias.
   b. Buenos días.
   c. Adiós.
   d. Por favor.

2. Thank you.
   a. Gracias.
   b. Por favor.
   c. Bien.
   d. Hasta luego.

3. See you tomorrow.
   a. Buenos días.
   b. Hasta mañana.
   c. Adiós.
   d. Hasta luego.

4. How are you?
   a. ¿Qué tal?
   b. ¿Y tú?
   c. Bien, gracias.
   d. ¿Cómo estás?

5. How's it going?
   a. Bien. ¿Y tú?
   b. ¿Qué tal?
   c. ¿Cómo estás?
   d. Hasta luego.

6. See you later.
   a. Adiós.
   b. Hasta luego.
   c. Hasta mañana.
   d. Buenas noches.

7. I'm sorry.
   a. Buenos días.
   b. Hasta luego.
   c. Lo siento.
   d. Adiós.

8. Welcome.
   a. Buenos días.
   b. Adiós.
   c. Bienvenidos.
   d. Buenas tardes.

ROLE PLAY

A. **Good morning!** Pretend that you are at a hospitality conference and are in the registration line. In groups of four or five take turns greeting one another. The first student greets the person to the right and then that person greets to the right. Go around the circle two or three times using different phrases such as Hola, Buenos días, Bienvenidos, ¿Qué tal?, etc.

B. **Do you speak English?** Using the directions given in part A ask and answer about your language abilities. Also practice using goodbye phrases with one another.

PART II—INTRODUCTIONS

I'm . . .	Soy . . .
Argentine	**argentino (a)**
Bolivian	**boliviano (a)**
Chilean	**chileno (a)**
Costa Rican	**costarricense**
Cuban	**cubano (a)**
Dominican	**dominicano (a)**
Ecuadorian	**ecuatoriano (a)**
Guatemalan	**guatemalteco (a)**
Honduran	**hondureño (a)**
Mexican	**mexicano (a)**
Nicaraguan	**nicaragüense**
Panamanian	**panameño (a)**
Paraguayan	**paraguayo (a)**
Peruvian	**peruano (a)**
Puerto Rican	**puertorriqueño (a)**
Salvadoran	**salvadoreño (a)**
United States citizen	**estadounidense**
Uruguayan	**uruguayo (a)**
Venezuelan	**venezolano (a)**

WHERE ARE YOU FROM?

What's your name?	**¿Cómo te llamas?**
My name is Javier.	**Me llamo Javier.**
I'd like to introduce you to . . .	**Quiero presentarte a . . .**
Nice to meet you.	**Mucho gusto.**
Same to you.	**Igualmente.**
Where are you from?	**¿De dónde eres?**
I'm (from) . . .	**Soy (de) . . .**
Where is Carlos from?	**¿De dónde es Carlos?**
Carlos is (from) . . .	**Carlos es (de) . . .**
Where do you live?	**¿Dónde vives?**
I live in . . .	**Vivo en . . .**

MATCHING EXERCISE

Write the letter of the Spanish phrase next to the phrase it matches on the left.

1. _____ My name is
2. _____ I'm from
3. _____ Carlos is from
4. _____ Nice to meet you.
5. _____ Where is _____ from?
6. _____ What's your name?
7. _____ I'd like to introduce you to
8. _____ Same to you.
9. _____ Where are you from?
10. _____ Where do you live?

a. ¿Cómo te llamas?
b. Quiero presentarte a
c. Mucho gusto.
d. Soy de
e. Me llamo
f. Igualmente.
g. ¿De dónde es?
h. Carlos es de
i. ¿Dónde vives?
j. ¿De dónde eres?

CROSSWORD PUZZLES

Across

1. Same to you.
3. What's your name?
8. I'd like to introduce you to . . .

Down

2. Nice to meet you.
4. My name is
5. I'm from
6. Where are you from?
7. Where is _____ from?

Across

3. ¿Cómo te llamas?
8. ¿De dónde eres?

Down

1. Soy de
2. ¿De dónde es?
4. Igualmente.
5. Mucho gusto.
6. Me llamo
7. Carlos es de

RELATIONSHIP BUILDING TIP

Your employees are excited about their new job at your company. They have told their friends and family about it. Make their first week special by posting a big sign for them: "Welcome Carlos Martinez, Pete Black, and Kathy Smith!" If you have a group of employees traveling to your company on a two-day bus ride from the Mexican border, have a delicious welcome dinner for them upon their arrival. Music and decorations are always appreciated. Think about when you go to a state educational conference—you're handed a bag of goodies—i.e., t-shirts or baseball caps, notebooks, etc. It's the little things that make an impression.

TRANSLATION EXERCISE

Translate the following to English:

1. Carlos es de _____
2. Soy de _____
3. Mucho gusto _____
4. ¿Dónde vives? _____
5. ¿Cómo te llamas? _____
6. Hola. _____
7. Quiero presentarte a _____
8. ¿De dónde eres? _____
9. ¿De dónde es Carlos? _____
10. Me llamo Javier. _____

Translate the following to Spanish:

1. Where are you from? _____
2. Where is Maria from? _____
3. I'm from _____
4. Ana is from _____
5. Where do you live? _____
6. My name is Tomás. _____
7. I'd like to introduce you to _____
8. What's your name? _____
9. Pleased to meet you. _____
10. Same to you. _____

MULTIPLE CHOICE

Circle the correct answer.

1. Where are you from?
a. Mucho gusto.
b. ¿Cómo te llamas?
c. ¿De dónde eres?
d. ¿De dónde es?

2. My name is
a. Soy de
b. Me llamo
c. ¿De dónde es?
d. Mucho gusto

3. Nice to meet you.
a. Igualmente.
b. Me llamo
c. Soy de
d. Mucho gusto.

4. I'm from
a. Soy de
b. Carlos es de
c. ¿De dónde es?
d. ¿De dónde eres?

5. Same to you
a. Me llamo
b. Quiero presentarte a
c. Igualmente.
d. Mucho gusto.

6. Where do you live?
a. ¿De dónde eres?
b. ¿De dónde es?
c. ¿Cómo te llamas?
d. ¿Dónde vives?

7. I'd like to introduce you to
a. Igualmente.
b. Hola.
c. Mucho gusto.
d. Quiero presentarte a

8. I live in
a. ¿Cómo te llamas?
b. Me llamo
c. Mucho gusto.
d. Vivo en

ROLE PLAY

A. Work with a partner. Ask and answer: What's your name? My name is . . . etc. Follow the model.

(Pedro)

ESTUDIANTE A:	¿Cómo te llamas?
ESTUDIANTE B:	Me llamo Pedro.
ESTUDIANTE A:	Mucho gusto.
ESTUDIANTE B:	Igualmente.

1. José
2. Susan
3. Jack
4. Paco

5. Juan
6. Ana
7. Lola
8. Miguel

9. Pedro
10. Tomás

B. Work with a partner. Ask and answer: Where are you from? I'm from . . . Follow the model.

(Pedro / México / mexicano)

ESTUDIANTE A:	¿De dónde eres, Pedro?
ESTUDIANTE B:	Soy de México. Soy mexicano.

1. José / Guatemala
2. Susan / Chicago
3. Jack / los Estados Unidos
4. Paco / Colombia

5. Lola / Cuba
6. Juan / Tejas
7. Ana / Costa Rica
8. Miguel / Ecuador

9. Pedro / Panamá
10. Tomás / El Salvador
11. María / Honduras
12. Jorge / México

C. Work with a partner. Ask and answer: Where is . . . from? He's from . . . Follow the model.

(Javier/Chile)

ESTUDIANTE A:	¿De dónde es Javier?
ESTUDIANTE B:	Javier es de Chile. Es chileno.

1. José / Guatemala
2. Susan / Chicago
3. Jack / los Estados Unidos
4. Paco / Colombia

5. Lola / Cuba
6. Juan / Tejas
7. Ana / Costa Rica
8. Miguel / Ecuador

9. Pedro / Panamá
10. Tomás / El Salvador
11. María / Honduras
12. Jorge / México

PART III—LODGING AND ACCOMMODATIONS

bellman
el botones

taxi
el taxi

ice machine
la máquina de hielo

elevator
el ascensor

parking
el aparcamiento

vending machine
el distribuidor automático

airport transportation
el transporte al aeropuerto

restroom
el baño

MATCHING EXERCISE

Write the letter of each picture next to the Spanish word it matches below.

a.

b.

c.

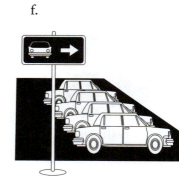

d.

e.

f.

g.

h.

1. _____ el transporte al aeropuerto

2. _____ el taxi

3. _____ el baño

4. _____ el aparcamiento

5. _____ el ascensor

6. _____ la máquina de hielo

7. _____ el botones

8. _____ el distribuidor automático

VOCABULARY EXERCISE

Write the Spanish word for each picture in the space provided.

1. _____

2. _____

3. _____

4. _____

5. _____

6. _____

7. _____

8. _____

MATCHING EXERCISE

Write the letter of the Spanish word next to the English word it matches on the left.

1. _____ elevator
2. _____ airport transportaton
3. _____ bellman
4. _____ restroom
5. _____ parking lot
6. _____ ice machine
7. _____ vending machine
8. _____ taxi

a. el ascensor
b. la máquina de hielo
c. el botones
d. el distribuidor automático
e. el baño
f. el taxi
g. el aparcamiento
h. el transporte al aeropuerto

CROSSWORD PUZZLES

Across

1. ascensor
4. transporte al aeropuerto
8. botones

Down

2. distribuidor automático
3. taxi
5. máquina de hielo
6. aparcamiento
7. baño

Across

2. bellman
4. ice machine
5. taxi
6. bathroom
7. vending machine
8. elevator

Down

1. parking lot
3. airport transportation

TRANSLATION EXERCISE

Translate the following to English:

1. el distribuidor automático _____
2. el baño_____
3. la máquina de hielo _____
4. el ascensor _____
5. el transporte al aeropuerto _____
6. el aparcamiento_____
7. el taxi_____
8. el botones _____

Translate the following to Spanish:

1. ice machine _____
2. vending machine _____
3. bellman _____
4. taxi_____
5. parking lot_____
6. restroom _____
7. elevator _____
8. airport transportation_____

MULTIPLE CHOICE

Circle the letter of the correct answer.

1. vending machine
   a. la máquina de hielo
   b. el aparcamiento
   c. el transporte al aeropuerto
   d. el distribuidor automático

2. elevator
   a. el taxi
   b. el baño
   c. el botones
   d. el ascensor

3. ice machine
   a. la máquina de hielo
   b. el aparcamiento
   c. el transporte al aeropuerto
   d. el distribuidor automático

4. bellman
   a. el taxi
   b. el baño
   c. el botones
   d. el ascensor

5. airport transportation
   a. la máquina de hielo
   b. el aparcamiento
   c. el transporte al aeropuerto
   d. el distribuidor automático

6. elevator
   a. el taxi
   b. el baño
   c. el botones
   d. el ascensor

7. parking lot
   a. la máquina de hielo
   b. el aparcamiento
   c. el transporte al aeropuerto
   d. el distribuidor automático

8. restroom
   a. el taxi
   b. el baño
   c. el botones
   d. el ascensor

9. taxi
   a. el taxi
   b. el baño
   c. el botones
   d. el ascensor

ROLE PLAY: FREQUENTLY ASKED QUESTIONS.

Pretend that you have just arrived at your hotel. You are looking forward to relaxing in your room but, you need to find out where a few things are first.

Ask *Where is_____?* Use *¿Dónde está_____?* Your partner will direct you to the left *(a la izquierda)* or to the right *(a la derecha).* Follow the model.

ESTUDIANTE A:	¿Dónde está el ascensor?
ESTUDIANTE B:	El ascensor está a la derecha.
ESTUDIANTE A:	Gracias.

1.

2.

3.

4.

5.

6.

LODGING TERMINOLOGY

Smoking	Fumadores
Non smoking	No fumadores
King	Tamaño King
Queen	Tamaño Queen
Double double	Doble matrimonial
Single —	Individual —
Room with one twin bed	Habitación con una sola cama gemela
Twin —	Doble —
Room with two twin beds	Habitación con dos camas gemelas
Double —	Doble —
Room with one double bed	Habitación con una cama matrimonial
Double Double —	Doble Doble —
Room with two double beds	Habitación con dos camas matrimoniales
Murphy —	Murphy —
Room with a bed that folds out of wall or closet	Habitación con una cama que se despliega desde una **a** pared o clóset
Suite —	Suite —
Room with one or more bedrooms and a living room	Habitación con uno o más dormitorios y una sala
Connecting —	Conexas —
Rooms that are side by side and have a door connecting the two rooms.	Habitaciones contiguas que tienen una puerta que las conecta.
Adjoining —	Adyacentes —
Rooms that are side by side but do not have a door connecting the two rooms.	Habitaciones contiguas que no tienen una puerta que las conecte.

REVIEW

Read the dialogue aloud with a partner and then translate it to English.	*Read the dialogue aloud with a partner and then translate it to Spanish.*
Mark: Hola. ¡Bienvenidos al *GOLDEN HOTEL!*	**Mark:** Hello. Welcome to the *GOLDEN HOTEL!*
Pablo: Gracias.	**Pablo:** Thank you.
Mark: ¿Cómo te llamas?	**Mark:** What's your name?
Pablo: Me llamo Pablo.	**Pablo:** My name is Pablo.

Mark:	¿De dónde eres?		**Mark:**	Where are you from?
Pablo:	Soy de Acapulco. Soy mexicano.		**Pablo:**	I'm from Acapulco. I'm Mexican.
Mark:	Pablo, quiero presentarte a Gloria.		**Mark:**	Pablo, I want to introduce you to Gloria.
Pablo:	Mucho gusto.		**Pablo:**	Nice to meet you.
Gloria:	Igualmente.		**Gloria:**	Same to you.
Pablo:	¿De dónde eres, Gloria?		**Pablo:**	Where are you from, Gloria?
Gloria:	Soy de Guatemala. Soy guatemalteca.		**Gloria:**	I'm from Guatemala. I'm Guatemalan.
Pablo:	¿Dónde vives?		**Pablo:**	Where do you live?
Gloria:	Vivo en Chicago.		**Gloria:**	I live in Chicago.
Mark:	¿Hablas inglés, Pablo?		**Mark:**	Do you speak English, Pablo?
Pablo:	No.		**Pablo:**	No.
Mark:	Estudio español.		**Mark:**	I'm studying Spanish.
Pablo:	Ah . . . sí . . .		**Pablo:**	Ah . . . yes . . .
Gloria:	. . . Pablo . . . ¡Mucho gusto!		**Gloria:**	. . . Pablo . . . Nice to meet you!
Pablo:	Gracias. Adiós.		**Pablo:**	Thank you. Goodbye.
Mark:	Hasta luego.		**Mark:**	See you later.
Gloria:	Hasta mañana.		**Gloria:**	See you tomorrow.
Huésped:	¿Dónde está elascensor?		**Guest:**	Where is the elevator?
Gloria:	A la derecha, senor.		**Gloria:**	To the right, sir.
Huésped:	¿y la máquina de hielo?		**Guest:**	And the ice machine?
Gloria:	A la izquierda.		**Gloria:**	To the left.
Huésped:	¡Gracias!		**Guest:**	Thank you!

Translate the following to Spanish:

1. Hi! How's it going? _____

2. Good morning!_____

3. Welcome! _____

4. What's your name? _____

5. Do you speak English? _____

6. Do you understand English?_____

7. I'm studying Spanish. _____

8. I speak Spanish a little. _____

9. How are you? Fine, and you? _____

10. Where are you from?_____

11. I'm from Guatemala. _____

12. Where do you live? _____

13. Nice to meet you. _____

14. I live in Atlanta._____

15. My name is Steve. _____

16. Where is the elevator? _____

17. Where is the ice machine?_____

18. Where is the vending machine? _____

19. Where is the bathroom? _____

20. Where is the parking lot? _____

CULTURE: NATIONALITIES AND TERMS

What's the best word to use when discussing your Spanish speaking employees? Hispanic? Latino? Mexican? Spanish? The best term to use would be the nationality of the person. If he is from Guatemala, he is Guatemalan. If she is from Mexico, she is Mexican.

The term "Hispanic" is an English word meaning "of or pertaining to ancient Spain." The United States Government, the United States Census Bureau, and Fortune 500 corporations use "Hispanic" as an umbrella term to refer to people from many different countries in Latin America and Europe. This term has become popular.

The term "Latinos" is also appropriate to use to refer to a group of Spanish speaking people from many different Latin American countries. It is used amongst the people. They refer to themselves as "Latinos." There is a popular women's magazine entitled *Latina*. Two articles in *USA Today* (January 15, 2001) support this term. One article is entitled "Get Rid of the Bogus 'Hispanic' Label" and the other, "It Should Be 'Latinos.'"

"Spanish people" is an incorrect term. People from the country of Spain are referred to as Spaniards.

A Spanish word for a United States citizen is "estadounidense." "Americans" (americanos) and "North Americans" (norteamericanos) are terms that refer to and encompass all people from all of North America including Canada, the United States, and Mexico.

TEAM BUILDING TIP

Latinos are very patriotic. Hang their country's flag next to the U.S. flag. Be sure and hang it high or secure it tightly. They are so popular they often disappear. Post a colorful map of Mexico or your employees' country. Show genuine interest in their town or village. Tack a piece of string into their exact city and attach it to a photo of them with their names.

Training, Praise, and Frequently Asked Questions

PART I—TRAINING PHRASES

Come with me.	**Ven conmigo.**
Watch me.	**Mírame.**
Do it like me.	**Házlo como yo.**
Try it.	**Trátalo.**
Keep trying.	**Continua tratando.**
Help me.	**Ayúdame.**
I'll help you.	**Te ayudo.**
It's necessary.	**Es necesario.**
It's important.	**Es importante.**
It's good.	**Está bien.**
It's bad.	**Está mal.**
It's so-so.	**Está así así.**
It's correct.	**Está correcto.**
It's not correct.	**No está correcto.**
Everything else is perfect.	**Todo lo demás está perfecto.**
Good work!	**¡Buen trabajo!**
You're very strong!	**¡Eres muy fuerte!**
You're a hard worker!	**¡Eres muy trabajador!**

MATCHING EXERCISE

Write the letter of the Spanish word next to the English word it matches on the left.

1. _____ Watch me.
2. _____ Do it like me.
3. _____ Try it.
4. _____ Come with me.
5. _____ Help me.
6. _____ It's necessary.
7. _____ It's important.
8. _____ It's good.
9. _____ It's bad.
10. _____ It's correct.
11. _____ It's not correct.
12. _____ Everything else is perfect.
13. _____ Good work!
14. _____ You're a hard worker!
15. _____ I'll help you.

a. Ayúdame.
b. Está bien.
c. Está correcto.
d. ¡Eres muy trabajador!
e. Mírame.
f. Ven conmigo.
g. Está mal.
h. Hazlo como yo.
i. Es importante.
j. Trátalo.
k. Te ayudo.
l. ¡Buen trabajo!
m. No está correcto.
n. Es necesario.
o. Todo lo demás está perfecto.

CROSSWORD PUZZLES

Across

1. ¡Buen trabajo!
3. Házlo como yo.
7. ¡Eres muy fuerte!
8. Está mal.
11. Está correcto.

Down

2. Mírame.
4. Es necesario.
5. ¡Eres muy trabajador!
6. Es importante.
8. Está bien.
9. Trátalo.
10. No está correcto.

Across

1. ¡Buen trabajo!
3. Házlo como yo.
7. ¡Eres muy fuerte!
8. Está mal.
10. Está bien.
11. ¡Eres muy trabajador!

Down

2. Mírame.
4. Es necesario.
5. Trátalo.
6. Es importante.
8. No está correcto.
9. Está correcto.

TRANSLATION EXERCISE

Translate the following to English:

1. Házlo como yo. _____

2. Es necesario. _____

3. Trátalo. _____

4. Continua tratando. _____

5. Está correcto. _____

6. Ayúdame. _____

7. Ven conmigo. _____

8. Mírame. _____

9. Es importante. _____

10. ¡Eres muy trabajador! _____

11. Está bien. _____

12. Te ayudo. _____

13. No está correcto. _____

14. Todo lo demás está perfecto. _____

15. ¡Buen trabajo! _____

Translate the following to Spanish:

1. Try it._____

2. Keep trying._____

3. It's important. _____

4. You're a hard worker! _____

5. Help me. _____

6. It's good. _____

7. I'll help you. _____

8. Come with me. _____

9. Watch me. _____

10. It's necessary. _____

11. Do it like me._____

12. It's not correct. _____

13. Everything else is perfect. _____

14. Good work! _____

15. You're very strong!_____

MULTIPLE CHOICE

Circle the letter of the correct answer.

1. Come with me.
  a. Está correcto.
  b. Ayúdame.
  c. Ven conmigo.
  d. Mírame.

2. It's not correct.
  a. Está correcto.
  b. Es importante.
  c. Está bien.
  d. No está correcto.

3. Try it.
  a. Házlo como yo.
  b. Trátalo.
  c. Continua tratando.
  d. Ayúdame.

4. Watch me.
  a. Está correcto.
  b. Ayúdame.
  c. Ven conmigo.
  d. Mírame.

5. Help me.
  a. Está correcto.
  b. Ayúdame.
  c. Ven conmigo.
  d. Mírame.

6. It's important.
  a. Está correcto.
  b. Es importante.
  c. Está bien.
  d. No está correcto.

7. You're a hard worker!
  a. ¡Eres muy trabajador!
  b. No está correcto.
  c. Todo lo demás está perfecto.
  d. ¡Buen trabajo!

8. Good work!
  a. No está correcto.
  b. ¡Eres muy fuerte!
  c. ¡Buen trabajo!
  d. ¡Eres muy trabajador!

9. Keep trying.
  a. Házlo como yo.
  b. Trátalo.
  c. Continua tratando.
  d. Ayúdame.

10. Do it like me.
  a. Házlo como yo.
  b. Trátalo.
  c. Continua tratando.
  d. Ayúdame.

PART II—PRAISING BEHAVIOR

Perfect!	**¡Perfecto!**	Fabulous!	**¡Fabuloso!**
Incredible!	**¡Increíble!**	Fantastic!	**¡Fantástico!**
Excellent!	**¡Excelente!**	Magnificent!	**¡Magnífico!**
Exceptional!	**¡Excepcional!**	Marvelous!	**¡Maravilloso!**

MATCHING EXERCISE

Write the letter of the Spanish word next to the English word it matches on the left.

1. _____ Perfect!   a. ¡Excepcional!
2. _____ Incredible!   b. ¡Fabuloso!
3. _____ Excellent!   c. ¡Fantástico!
4. _____ Exceptional!   d. ¡Perfecto!
5. _____ Fabulous!   e. ¡Maravilloso!
6. _____ Fantastic!   f. ¡Excelente!
7. _____ Magnificent!   g. ¡Increíble!
8. _____ Marvelous!   h. ¡Magnífico!

CROSSWORD PUZZLES

Across

1. Exceptional
5. Magnificent
7. Perfect

Down

1. Excellent
2. Fantastic
3. Incredible
4. Marvelous
6. Fabulous

Across

3. Excelente
6. Maravilloso
7. Fabuloso
8. Perfecto

Down

1. Excepcional
2. Increíble
4. Fantástico
5. Magnífico

PART III—MORE FREQUENTLY ASKED QUESTIONS

Where	**Dónde**
Where is	**Dónde está**
When is	**Cuándo es**
What	**Qué**
Who	**Quién**
With whom	**Con quién**
Why	**Por qué**
How	**Cómo**
How much, many	**Cuántos**
How much is the _____ ?	**¿Cuánto es _____ ?**
At what time is _____ ?	**¿A qué hora es _____ ?**
What are the hours of _____ ?	**¿Cuál es el horario de _____ ?**
Where is the _____ meeting?	**¿Dónde está la reunion de _____ ?**
I'd like to leave a message for _____ ?	**Quisiera dejar un recado para _____ .**
Are there any restaurants nearby?	**¿Hay unos restaurantes cerca?**

TEAM BUILDING TIP

Show your employees your appreciation of their hard work by awarding them training certificates. Make sure the whole group receives one. Many Latinos are group oriented and often do not like to be singled out. Shake hands with them, wish them congratulations, and snap a picture of them.

MATCHING EXERCISE

Write the letter of the word on the right next to the word it matches on the left.

1. _____ When

2. _____ What

3. _____ How many

4. _____ Where is

5. _____ Who

6. _____ Where

7. _____ With whom

8. _____ Why

9. _____ How

a. Cuántos

b. Quién

c. Con quién

d. Cómo

e. Qué

f. Cuándo

g. Por qué

h. Dónde

i. Dónde está

CROSSWORD PUZZLES

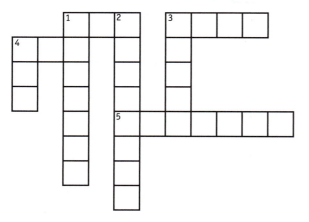

Across

1. Cómo
3. Cuándo
4. Quién
5. Dónde está

Down

1. Cuántos
2. Con quién
3. Dónde
4. Por qué

Across

2. How
4. Where
6. What
9. Where is

Down

1. Why
3. With whom
5. When
7. How many
8. Who

TRANSLATION EXERCISE

Translate the following to English:

1. Dónde _____

2. Cuándo es _____

3. Quién _____

4. Dónde está_____

5. Con quién _____

6. Por qué _____

7. Cuántos _____

8. Qué _____

9. Cómo _____

Translate the following to Spanish:

1. Who_____

2. Where _____

3. How many_____

4. When is _____

5. Where is_____

6. With whom _____

7. Why_____

8. How_____

9. What _____

MULTIPLE CHOICE

Circle the letter of the correct answer.

1. When is
   a. Dónde
   b. Quién
   c. Qué
   d. Cuándo es

2. Where is
   a. Con quién
   b. Por qué
   c. Dónde está
   d. Cómo

3. Who
   a. Cuántos
   b. Quién
   c. Qué
   d. Cuándo

4. With whom
   a. Con quién
   b. Por qué
   c. Dónde está
   d. Cómo

5. What
   a. Dónde
   b. Quién
   c. Qué
   d. Cuándo

6. How
   a. Con quién
   b. Por qué
   c. Dónde está
   d. Cómo

7. Where
   a. Dónde
   b. Quién
   c. Qué
   d. Cuándo

8. How many
   a. Quién
   b. Cuántos
   c. Qué
   d. Cuándo

9. Why
   a. Con quién
   b. Por qué
   c. Dónde está
   d. Cómo

Review

Read the dialogue aloud with a partner and then translate it to English.

Read the dialogue aloud with a partner and then translate it to Spanish.

Jacky:	¡Hola Pablo!
Pablo:	Buenos días.
Jacky:	¿Cómo estás?
Pablo:	Bien, gracias.
Jacky:	Por favor . . . Ven conmigo.
Pablo:	Okay.
Jacky:	Es importante . . . Mírame.
Pablo:	(mira a Jacky)
Jacky:	Trátalo.
Pablo:	(lo trata . . . pero no tiene mucha confianza)
Jacky:	Házlo como yo.
Pablo:	No está correcto . . .
Jacky:	Continua tratando.
Pablo:	(trata otra vez)
Jacky:	¡Excelente!
Pablo:	¿Está bien?
Jacky:	Sí. Todo lo demás está perfecto.
Pablo:	(tiene mucho orgullo)
Jacky:	Gracias. ¡Eres muy trabajador!

Jacky:	Hello Pablo!
Pablo:	Good morning.
Jacky:	How are you?
Pablo:	Fine, thank you.
Jacky:	Please . . . Come with me.
Pablo:	Okay.
Jacky:	It's important . . . Watch me.
Pablo:	(watches Jacky)
Jacky:	Try it.
Pablo:	(tries it . . . but is not very confident)
Jacky:	Do it like me.
Pablo:	It's not correct . . .
Jacky:	Keep trying.
Pablo:	(tries it again)
Jacky:	Excellent!
Pablo:	It's good?
Jacky:	Yes. Everything else is perfect.
Pablo:	(He is very proud)
Jacky:	Thank you. You're a hard worker!

Translate the following to Spanish:

1. It's important. _____

2. It's necessary. _____

3. Come with me. _____

4. Do it like me. _____

5. Perfect! _____

6. Fantastic! _____

7. Try it. _____

8. You're very strong! _____

9. It's good. It's bad. _____

10. It's correct. It's not correct. _____

11. Everything else is perfect. _____

12. You're a hard worker! _____

13. I'm sorry. _____

14. Help me. _____

15. Where is the elevator? _____

16. Who _____

17. With whom _____

18. How many _____

19. Where is the ice machine? _____

20. When _____

21. Please _____

22. Thank you _____

23. Welcome _____

24. How's it going? _____

25. What's your name? _____

26. Where is the vending machine? _____

27. Do you speak English? _____

28. I'm studying Spanish. _____

29. Where are you from? _____

30. You are very patient. _____

31. Nice to meet you. _____

32. Speak slowly, please. _____

33. Jesús is from Guadalajara. _____

34. I'd like to introduce you to _____

35. See you later. _____

CULTURE: CULTURAL SENSITIVITIES

Many times during childhood little boys have been told not to cry. "Don't be a cry baby!" and "Brush it off!" are common phrases young children hear. They learn to hide their emotions because they think it is a sign of weakness. They bring this attitude that they learned on the sports field into the business world. Males in business try to keep a "stiff upper lip." Toughness and a hard-nosed attitude are qualities that are respected and admired. It is generally understood that emotions and business do not mix; this enables managers from the United States to accept criticism of their work without taking it personally. A superior may reprimand a subordinate quite sternly for an error he or she had committed, but that afternoon they may be out playing a round of golf together. All is forgotten and they are laughing together once again. In short, emotions are considered to be personal, with no place in the tough world of business.

In the United States it is important to remember that in business your work may be criticized but not you personally. It is generally understood and accepted that one learns from his mistakes.

Latinos are highly sensitive to criticism. This includes criticism of their work. They are proud of their work and it shows. When their work is criticized it is taken personally. When they are criticized they are offended and will often shut the other person out. They often will stop speaking to him or give him the cold shoulder/silent treatment. Because of this sensitivity people often consider Latinos to be "thin-skinned." It is necessary to correct their mistakes, but one should also remember to build up their self esteem again by praising other parts of their work.

The Calendar, Numbers, and Time

PART I—NUMBERS

Cardinals

0	cero	13	trece	25	veinte y cinco	80	ochenta
1	uno	14	catorce	26	veinte y seis	90	noventa
2	dos	15	quince	27	veinte y siete	100	cien
3	tres	16	diez y seis	28	veinte y ocho	200	doscientos
4	cuatro	17	diez y siete	29	veinte y nueve	300	trescientos
5	cinco	18	diez y ocho	30	treinta	400	cuatrocientos
6	seis	19	diez y nueve	31	treinta y uno	500	quinientos
7	siete	20	veinte	32	treinta y dos	600	seiscientos
8	ocho	21	veinte y uno	40	cuarenta	700	setecientos
9	nueve	22	veinte y dos	50	cincuenta	800	ochocientos
10	diez	23	veinte y tres	60	sesenta	900	novecientos
11	once	24	veinte y cuatro	70	setenta	1000	mil
12	doce						

Ordinals

1st	primero	6th	sexto
2nd	segundo	7th	séptimo
3rd	tercero	8th	octavo
4th	cuarto	9th	noveno
5th	quinto	10th	décimo

MATCHING EXERCISE

Write the letter of the Spanish word next to the number it matches on the left.

1. _____ 6
2. _____ 14
3. _____ 8
4. _____ 10
5. _____ 15
6. _____ 0
7. _____ 7
8. _____ 18
9. _____ 2

10. _____ 3
11. _____ 12
12. _____ 11
13. _____ 1
14. _____ 16
15. _____ 9
16. _____ 17
17. _____ 13
18. _____ 4

a. trece
b. cero
c. diez
d. nueve
e. diez y siete
f. seis
g. cuatro
h. diez y seis
i. tres

j. diez y ocho
k. uno
l. quince
m. doce
n. catorce
o. ocho
p. dos
q. once
r. siete

MATCHING EXERCISE

Write the letter of the Spanish word next to the number it matches on the left.

1. _____ 20
2. _____ 70
3. _____ 10
4. _____ 80
5. _____ 100

6. _____ 40
7. _____ 90
8. _____ 30
9. _____ 60
10. _____ 50

a. treinta
b. noventa
c. sesenta
d. setenta
e. ochenta

f. diez
g. veinte
h. cien
i. cincuenta
j. cuarenta

MULTIPLE CHOICE

Circle the letter of the correct answer.

1. 80
a. ochocientos
b. ochenta
c. ocho
d. diez y ocho

2. 9
a. nueve
b. novecientos
c. noventa
d. diez y nueve

3. 100
a. diez
b. uno
c. cien
d. once

4. 2
a. dos
b. doce
c. cien
d. once

5. 300
a. treinta
b. tres
c. trece
d. trescientos

6. 50
a. catorce
b. cincuenta
c. cinco
d. quinientos

7. 3
a. tres
b. treinta
c. trece
d. trescientos

8. 18
a. ocho
b. diez y ocho
c. ochenta
d. ochocientos

9. 20
a. veinte y dos
b. nueve
c. veinte
d. treinta

10. 14
a. cuatro
b. catorce
c. cuarenta
d. cuatrocientos

ROLE PLAY

A. Telephone numbers. Your teacher will read off several of your telephone numbers. Raise your hand and answer "Hello" when you hear yours called!

B. My number is . . . Each student should ask the next student what his or her phone number is. One person should write the numbers on the chalkboard. If the recorder makes an error, the person whose number it is should correct it and then act as the recorder.

ESTUDIANTE A: ¿Cuál es tu número de teléfono / fax / celular?

ESTUDIANTE B: Mi número es_____.

C. Room numbers.

1. 324
2. 859
3. 767
4. 123
5. 930
6. 592
7. 1271
8. 1416
9. 1638
10. 2206

D. Addresses. Pretend your friend is looking for a new job. Using the business cards you have collected, read him the address and phone numbers of the organizations that have job openings. Have your partner write down the information you are giving him.

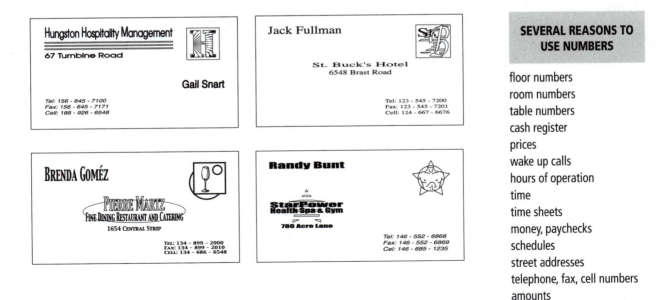

Hungston Hospitality Management
67 Turnbine Road
Gail Snart
Tel: 156 - 645 - 7100
Fax: 156 - 645 - 7171
Cell: 188 - 926 - 6548

Jack Fullman
St. Buck's Hotel
6548 Brast Road
Tel: 123 - 545 - 7200
Fax: 123 - 545 - 7201
Cell: 124 - 667 - 6676

BRENDA GOMÉZ
PIERRE MARTZ
FINE-DINING RESTAURANT AND CATERING
1654 CENTRAL STRIP
TEL: 134 - 899 - 2000
FAX: 134 - 899 - 2010
CELL: 134 - 686 - 6548

Randy Bunt
StarPower
Health Spa & Gym
786 Acre Lane
Tel: 146 - 552 - 6868
Fax: 146 - 552 - 6869
Cel: 146 - 685 - 1235

SEVERAL REASONS TO USE NUMBERS

floor numbers
room numbers
table numbers
cash register
prices
wake up calls
hours of operation
time
time sheets
money, paychecks
schedules
street addresses
telephone, fax, cell numbers
amounts

GRAMMAR: THERE IS, ARE

"Hay" can mean either "there is" or "there are."

There is a party.	**Hay una fiesta.**	There are ten pizzas.	**Hay diez pizzas.**

In a question, "Hay" can mean "Is there . . . ?" or "Are there . . . ?"

Is there beer?	**¿Hay cerveza?**	Are there CDs?	**¿Hay CDs?**

"No hay" means "there isn't any" or "there aren't any." In a question it means "Isn't there any?" or "Aren't there any?"

There isn't any music.	**No hay música.**
There aren't any pizzas.	**No hay pizzas.**
Isn't there any music?	**¿No hay música?**
Aren't there any pizzas?	**¿No hay pizzas?**

We use "¿Cuántos?" and "¿Cuántas?" to ask how many items there are. Sometimes "muchos" and "pocos" are used in the answer.

How many tacos are there?	**¿Cuántos tacos hay?**
There are thirty.	**Hay treinta.**
There are a lot.	**Hay muchos.**
How many pizzas are there?	**¿Cuántas pizzas hay?**
There are three.	**Hay tres.**
There are a few.	**Hay pocas.**

TRANSLATION EXERCISE

Translate the following to English:

1. Hay una fiesta._____
2. Hay pizza. _____
3. No hay cerveza. _____
4. No hay música. _____
5. ¿Cuántos tacos hay?_____
6. ¿Cuántos burritos hay? _____
7. ¿No hay pizza? _____
8. Hay seis._____
9. Hay pocos._____
10. Hay muchos. _____

Translate the following to Spanish:

1. There is a party._____
2. There is beer. _____
3. There is no pizza._____
4. There is no music. _____
5. How many tacos are there? _____
6. How many burritos are there?_____
7. There are eight. _____
8. There are a lot of parties._____
9. There are few pizzas. _____
10. Is there a lot of beer? _____

ROLE PLAY

A. Is there?/Are there? Your organization has asked you and a co-worker to help set things up for the welcome dinner they are having for its new employees. Tell your partner whether there are a lot or only a few of the items shown. (Consider anything under six as few.)

Hay muchos tacos.

tacos	hamburguesas
burritos	cervezas
pizzas	platos
ensaladas	sandwiches

B. How many are there? Using the picture in practice A, take turns asking and answering how many items of each picture there are on the table.

ESTUDIANTE A:	¿Cuántos burritos hay?
ESTUDIANTE B:	Hay ocho.

PART II—THE CALENDAR

Seasons—Las Estaciones

spring
la primavera

summer
el verano

fall
el otoño

winter
el invierno

Months of the Year—Los meses del año

January	**enero**	July	**julio**
February	**febrero**	August	**agosto**
March	**marzo**	September	**septiembre**
April	**abril**	October	**octubre**
May	**mayo**	November	**noviembre**
June	**junio**	December	**diciembre**

CHAPTER 3

Days of the Week—Los días de la semana

Sunday	**el domingo**	Thursday	**el jueves**
Monday	**el lunes**	Friday	**el viernes**
Tuesday	**el martes**	Saturday	**el sábado**
Wednesday	**el miércoles**		

Other Words—Otras palabras

day	**el día**	night	**la noche**
week	**la semana**	tomorrow morning	**mañana por la mañana**
month	**el mes**	tomorrow afternoon	**mañana por la tarde**
year	**el año**	tomorrow night	**mañana por la noche**
weekend	**el fin de semana**	every morning	**cada mañana**
today	**hoy**	every day	**cada día**
tonight	**esta noche**	every afternoon	**cada tarde**
tomorrow	**mañana**	every night	**cada noche**
yesterday	**ayer**	all the time	**todo el tiempo**
morning	**mañana**	only	**solamente**
afternoon	**tarde**	never	**nunca**

MATCHING EXERCISE

Write the letter of the Spanish word next to the English word it matches on the left.

1. _____ November
2. _____ July
3. _____ January
4. _____ August
5. _____ fall
6. _____ September
7. _____ June
8. _____ winter
9. _____ February
10. _____ October
11. _____ summer
12. _____ spring
13. _____ April
14. _____ May
15. _____ March
16. _____ December

a. mayo
b. febrero
c. invierno
d. junio
e. abril
f. octubre
g. noviembre
h. diciembre
i. agosto
j. julio
k. primavera
l. marzo
m. verano
n. otoño
o. enero
p. septiembre

CROSSWORD PUZZLES

Across

6. September
7. April
8. March
9. October
11. January
12. July

Down

1. November
2. August
3. December
4. February
5. May
10. June

Across

2. junio
3. marzo
5. abril
7. enero
9. septiembre
10. noviembre
11. octubre

Down

1. febrero
3. mayo
4. julio
6. agosto
8. diciembre

TRANSLATION EXERCISE

Translate the following to Spanish:

1. February _____

2. April _____

3. May _____

4. June _____

5. August _____

6. October _____

7. November _____

8. January _____

9. March _____

10. July _____

11. September _____

12. December _____

Translate the following to Spanish:

1. spring _____

2. summer _____

3. fall _____

4. winter _____

ROLE PLAY

A. **Payday!** For financial planning purposes your organization has given out a calendar of paydays. Working with a partner give the dates. Follow the model.

(May 5, May 15)

ESTUDIANTE A: el cinco de mayo

ESTUDIANTE B: el quince de mayo

1. January 10, 24
2. February 8, 22
3. March 2, 13
4. April 6, 19
5. May 10, 24
6. June 16, 30

7. July 12, 28
8. August 8, 31
9. September 17, 29
10. October 9, 19
11. November 4, 14
12. December 3, 13

B. When is . . . ? Working in groups of four or five, ask and answer when each other's birthdays are. Follow the model.

ESTUDIANTE A:	¿Cuándo es tu cumpleaños?
ESTUDIANTE B:	Mi cumpleaños es el 3 de mayo.

C. What's the date? Work with the entire class. Stand up and ask one another: "¿Cuándo es tu cumpleaños?" ("When is your birthday?") and wait for the response "mi cumpleaños es . . ."(my birthday is . . .) Form a line according to the order of your birthdays starting with January 1 and ending with December 31. See if you did it correctly by having the first January birthday call off his/her date in Spanish until the line ends.

MATCHING EXERCISE

Write the letter of the Spanish word next to the English word it matches on the left.

1. _____ Friday
2. _____ Tuesday
3. _____ Saturday
4. _____ Thursday
5. _____ Sunday
6. _____ Wednesday
7. _____ Monday
8. _____ day

9. _____ month
10. _____ week
11. _____ year
12. _____ today
13. _____ tomorrow
14. _____ weekend
15. _____ yesterday

a. hoy
b. lunes
c. sábado
d. miércoles
e. año
f. martes
g. viernes
h. ayer

i. fin de semana
j. jueves
k. domingo
l. semana
m. mañana
n. día
o. mes

CROSSWORD PUZZLES

Across

3. Sunday
5. Friday
6. Saturday
7. Wednesday

Down

1. Monday
2. Thursday
4. Tuesday

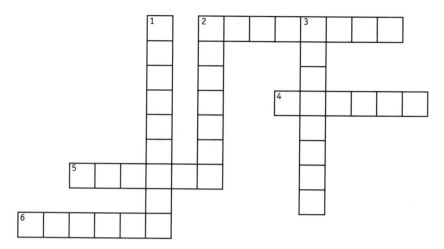

Across

2. jueves
4. domingo
5. lunes
6. viernes

Down

1. miércoles
2. martes
3. sábado

TRANSLATION EXERCISE

Translate the following to Spanish:

1. Sunday_____
2. Friday _____
3. Thursday_____
4. Monday_____
5. Saturday _____
6. Tuesday _____
7. Wednesday _____

Translate the following to Spanish:

1. today _____
2. tomorrow _____
3. morning _____
4. afternoon_____
5. day_____
6. weekend_____
7. every day _____
8. every afternoon _____
9. every morning_____
10. only _____

MULTIPLE CHOICE

Circle the letter of the correct answer.

1. **Sunday**
   a. domingo
   b. sábado
   c. jueves
   d. viernes

2. **Friday**
   a. martes
   b. jueves
   c. viernes
   d. domingo

3. **Wednesday**
   a. sábado
   b. lunes
   c. jueves
   d. miércoles

4. **Tuesday**
   a. domingo
   b. jueves
   c. viernes
   d. martes

5. **Monday**
   a. sábado
   b. lunes
   c. jueves
   d. miércoles

6. **Thursday**
   a. domingo
   b. jueves
   c. viernes
   d. martes

7. **Saturday**
   a. sábado
   b. lunes
   c. domingo
   d. miércoles

ROLE PLAY

Can you work on Tuesday? Pretend it's spring break and your hotel is preparing for the big rush of college students who will be arriving soon! Working with a partner, ask him or her: *Can you work on . . . ? ¿Puedes trabajar el. . . ?* To express 'on' use 'el'. Follow the model.

(Tuesday and Thursday)

ESTUDIANTE A: ¿Puedes trabajar el martes y el jueves?

ESTUDIANTE B: Sí puedo.

No, no puedo.

1. Wednesday and Friday
2. Monday and Tuesday
3. Saturday and Sunday
4. Tuesday and Thursday
5. Friday and Saturday
6. Tuesday, Friday and Sunday
7. Monday, Wednesday and Friday
8. Saturday, Sunday and Monday
9. Thursday, Friday and Saturday
10. Wednesday, Saturday and Sunday

PART III—TIME

In expressing the time of day, "It is" is expressed by "Es la una" ("It's one o'clock"), and "Son las dos, tres" . . . for the plural hours ("It's two o'clock, three o'clock," etc.).

| It is one o'clock. | **Es la una.** |
| It is two (three, etc.) o'clock. | **Son las dos (tres, etc.).** |

Time after the Hour is Expressed by the Hour + y, Followed by the Number of Minutes. Half Past is Expressed by "y Media" and a Quarter Past is Expressed by "y Cuarto."

It's 1:10.	**Es la una y diez.**
It's 2:20.	**Son las dos y veinte.**
It's 3:15.	**Son las tres y cuarto. (or Son las tres y quince.)**
It's 5:30.	**Son las cinco y media. (or Son las cinco y treinta.)**

At 8:00 . . . At 9:00, etc., would be A Las Ocho . . . A Las Nueve, etc.

At what time is . . .	**¿A qué hora es . . . ?**
At what time is the party?	**¿A qué hora es la fiesta?**
The party is at 6:00.	**La fiesta es a las seis.**

TIME EXPRESSIONS

What time is it?	**¿Qué hora es?**	pm at night	**por la noche**
It's five o'clock.	**Son las cinco.**	on time	**a tiempo**
At what time is . . .	**¿A qué hora es . . . ?**	exactly, sharp	**en punto**
At 2:00, 3:00 . . .	**A las dos, tres . . .**	late	**tarde**
am in the morning	**por la mañana**	early	**temprano**
pm in the afternoon	**por la tarde**	all the time	**todo el tiempo**

MATCHING EXERCISE

Write the letter of the Spanish phrase, on the right, next to the English phrase it matches on the left.

1. _____ It's 2:00.
2. _____ At 2:00
3. _____ It's 10:00.
4. _____ At 10:00
5. _____ What time is it?
6. _____ It's 6:30.
7. _____ At 6:30

8. _____ At what time is?
9. _____ in the morning
10. _____ in the afternoon
11. _____ early
12. _____ late
13. _____ on time
14. _____ exactly, sharp

a. temprano
b. A las dos
c. Son las diez.
d. A tiempo
e. ¿Qué hora es?
f. Son las dos.
g. tarde

h. en punto
i. Son las seis y media.
j. A las diez
k. de la tarde
l. ¿A qué hora es?
m. de la mañana
n. A las seis y media

CROSSWORD PUZZLES

Across

5. por la mañana
6. por la noche
8. temprano
9. tarde

Down

1. ¿Qué hora es?
2. por la tarde
3. a tiempo
4. en punto
7. todo el tiempo

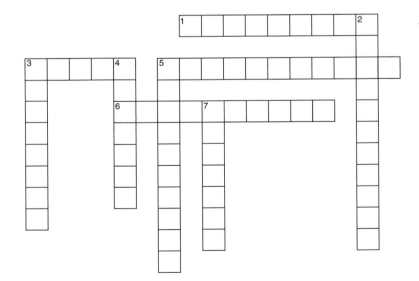

Across

1. What time is it?
3. late
5. in the morning
6. at night

Down

2. It's five o'clock.
3. early
4. exactly
5. in the afternoon
7. on time

MULTIPLE CHOICE

Circle the letter of the correct answer.

1. all the time
   a. todo el tiempo
   b. en punto
   c. tarde
   d. temprano

2. It's 7:00.
   a. A las seis.
   b. Son las seis.
   c. Son las siete.
   d. A las siete.

3. It's 8:00.
   a. Son las dos.
   b. Son las ocho.
   c. A las dos.
   d. A las ocho.

4. at 9:00
   a. son las nueve y diez
   b. a las nueve y doce
   c. son las nueve y once
   d. a las nueve

5. at 6:30
   a. son las siete y media
   b. a las seis y media
   c. son las seis y media
   d. a las siete y media

6. What time is it?
   a. ¿Qué hora es?
   b. ¿A qué hora?
   c. ¿Cómo estás?
   d. ¿Qué tal?

7. It's 3:00.
   a. Son las cinco.
   b. Son las tres.
   c. Son las tres y media.
   d. Son las dos.

8. exactly, sharp
   a. tarde
   b. de nada
   c. temprano
   d. en punto

9. It's 1:00.
   a. Es la una.
   b. Son las once.
   c. A las once.
   d. A la una.

10. late
   a. temprano
   b. tarde
   c. tiempo
   d. ahora

ROLE PLAY

A. What time is it? Working with a partner, ask and answer what time it is. Follow the model.

| **ESTUDIANTE A:** | ¿Qué hora es? |
| **ESTUDIANTE B:** | Son las tres y media. |

1. 2:00
2. 5:00
3. 7:00
4. 11:00

5. 9:30
6. 8:30
7. 4:30
8. 11:30

9. 7:45
10. 5:45
11. 3:45
12. 6:45

B. **At what time is . . . ?** Pretend it's the first day of classes and seminars. Take turns asking and answering at what time the courses take place. Follow the model.

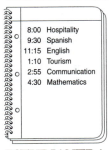

8:00 Hospitality
9:30 Spanish
11:15 English
1:10 Tourism
2:55 Communication
4:30 Mathematics

| ESTUDIANTE A: | ¿A qué hora es la clase de arte? |
| ESTUDIANTE B: | A las dos. |

8:00 Hospitalidad   1:10 Turismo

9:30 Español   2:55 Comunicación

11:15 Inglés   4:30 Matemáticas

ROLE PLAY

Wake Up Calls Travelers depend on the hotel to wake them up. This is an extremely important guest need that must be taken care of correctly. Working with a partner practice asking and answering in Spanish about wake up calls.

ESTUDIANTE A:	¿Quiseria una llamada?
ESTUDIANTE B:	Sí. . . at 7:30.
ESTUDIANTE A:	¿Por la mañana, tarde o noche?
ESTUDIANTE B:	Por la mañana.

1. 8:00 am
2. 6:00 pm
3. 9:30 am
4. 7:10 am
5. 5:15 pm
6. 4:20 pm
7. 11:00 am
8. 10:45 pm
9. 3:30 am
10. 2:15 pm

RELATIONSHIP TIP

Just as people in the United States would not like to work on holidays or on Super Bowl Sunday, for example, your Spanish-speaking employees don't want to work on their special holidays either. Find out which ones they celebrate and don't forget to recognize them with a greeting card or a bouquet of flowers. Examples: La Virgen de Guadalupe, World Cup Soccer, Independence Days (see Chapter 12 for other important days). Mark your calendar and plan a celebration!

REVIEW

Translate the following to Spanish:

1. There are seven days in a week._____

2. There are four weeks in a month. _____

3. There are four seasons in a year. _____

4. When is your birthday?_____

5. My birthday is May 24. _____

6. Can you work on Saturday? _____

7. Can you work on Sunday? _____

8. Can you work on Monday?_____

9. Yes, I can. _____

10. No, I cannot. _____

11. What time is it? _____

12. It's 2:00. It's 5:30._____

13. At what time is the party (*la fiesta*)? _____

14. The party is at 7:30. _____

15. The party is on Saturday! _____

Translate the following to Spanish:

1. How's it going? _____

2. How are you? _____

3. Welcome. _____

4. How's your family? _____

5. Where is the elevator? _____

6. See you later. _____

7. I'd like to introduce you to _____

8. Where are you from?_____

9. Do you speak English? _____

10. Come with me. _____

11. Where is the ice machine?_____

12. Do it like me. _____

13. Help me. _____

14. It's important. _____

15. You're a hard worker! _____

Read the dialogue aloud with a partner and then translate it to English.

¡Bienvenidos!	¡Fiesta!
Qué:	¡Una Celebración!
Cuándo:	sábado, el 3 de marzo
	A las seis de la noche
Dónde:	1620 Highland
Quién:	Mark
Oficina:	770-845-6293
Cell:	770-292-5856

Gloria: ¡Hay una fiesta!

Pablo: ¡Fantástico! ¿Cuándo es?

Gloria: El sábado . . . el 3 de marzo.

Pablo: ¿Dónde está la fiesta?

Gloria: 1620 Highland.

Pablo: ¿A qué hora?

Gloria: A las seis.

(El sábado a la fiesta . . . hay mucha música . . .)

Mark: Hola. ¡Bienvenidos!

Gloria: Gracias.

Pablo: ¿Qué tal?

Mark: ¡Magnífico!

Mark: Quiero presentarte a Octavio.

Gloria: Mucho gusto.

Octavio: Igualmente.

Gloria: ¿De dónde eres, Octavio?

Octavio: Soy de Oaxaca. Soy mexicano.

Gloria: ¿Hablas inglés?

Octavio: Sí. ¿Hablas inglés, Gloria?

Gloria: Estudio inglés.

Mark: Estudio español.

Octavio: ¡Perfecto! *¿Dónde está la cerveza?*
(los dirige a la cocina)

Gloria: ¡Increíble!

Pablo: Hay pizza y ensalada.

Gloria: Sí . . . ¡Y hay muchos tacos y burritos!

Octavio: Primero . . . ¡Una cerveza!

Read the dialogue aloud with a partner and then translate it to Spanish.

Welcome!	Party!
What:	A Celebration!
When:	Saturday, March 3
	At 6:00 pm
Where:	1620 Highland
Who:	Mark
Office:	770-845-6293
Cell:	770-292-5856

Gloria: There is a party!

Pablo: Fantastic! When is it?

Gloria: On Saturday . . . March 3.

Pablo: Where is the party?

Gloria: 1620 Highland.

Pablo: At what time?

Gloria: At 6:00.

(On Saturday at the party . . . there is a lot of music . . .)

Mark: Hello. Welcome!

Gloria: Thank you.

Pablo: How's it going?

Mark: Magnificent!

Mark: I want to introduce you to Octavio.

Gloria: Nice to meet you.

Octavio: Same to you.

Gloria: Where are you from, Octavio?

Octavio: I'm from Oaxaca. I'm Mexican.

Gloria: Do you speak English?

Octavio: Yes. Do you speak English, Gloria?

Gloria: I'm studying English.

Mark: I'm studying Spanish.

Octavio: Perfect! *¿Dónde está la cerveza?*
(directs them to the kitchen)

Gloria: Incredible!

Pablo: There is pizza and salad.

Gloria: Yes . . . And there are many tacos and burritos!

Octavio: First . . . A beer!

CULTURE: TIME MANAGEMENT

When people from the United States and Latin American countries work together, one of the greatest difficulties is time management. Cultures treat time very differently. For employees coming from another country where time is looked upon differently, the pace of life in the United States may be quite difficult to adapt to.

Since "time is money" in the United States and since money is what business is concerned with—everything is controlled by the clock. Employees are always under pressure to meet time commitments. Being late is thought to be a disgrace. Not only business but social events as well progress by the clock. United States citizens are often said to be "slaves to nothing but the clock."

People in the United States place a high value on arriving at each meeting at exactly the designated hour. Punctuality is equated with reliability and efficiency, both meaningful values in U.S. culture, whereas late arrival and tardiness suggest the opposite.

In other countries many people live their lives without a daily and hourly calendar. Scheduling each day's exact activities hour by hour in an appointment book or hand held computer is still unfamiliar to many people. This would probably not allow for a natural flow of events in their opinion.

If a United States citizen has to wait more than four or five minutes in a line for service he is often very irritated because of it. A Latino would most likely be talking with a friend or just waiting patiently and politely. From the Latino perspective, impatient United States citizens may seem impolite or even obnoxious.

Among modern Latino professionals this relaxed feeling toward time has begun to change. As people's lives become more complex and pressures for improved productivity increase, people are starting to feel more concern for punctuality, and time appointments are more often met. But this is a gradual process, and the general feeling still is "what we don't get done today will keep until *mañana*." Such extreme awareness of the clock does not come naturally to most Latinos, who favor a more easygoing approach to life.

RELATIONSHIP TIP

Paychecks! This is why Latinos have come to work in the United States. Explain to them exactly how to get their paychecks as well as how to cash them or send money home. Be aware that they probably do not have much cash with them when they arrive. If possible do not make them wait for two weeks before receiving their first paycheck.

Many financial institutions in Latin American countries are not as safe and trusted as those in the United States. U.S. citizens are confident in their banks and know that their money is safe there. This is not true of many Latino financial institutions, where rampant corruption exists. As a result, many Latinos who come to work in the United States keep way too much cash in their wallets and homes.

As the Latino population in Lexington, Kentucky grew so did the knowledge that Latinos kept a lot of cash in their homes. Robberies increased. It would be a good idea to bring in a Spanish speaking bank employee to your organization to explain the United States' banking system.

Family and Work Personnel

PART I—FAMILY

family
la familia

grandparents
los abuelos

parents
los padres

mother
la madre

father
el padre

son
el hijo

daughter
la hija

children
los hijos

brother
el hermano

sister
la hermana

wife
la esposa

husband
el esposo

aunt
la tía

uncle
el tío

cousin
el (la) primo (a)

GROUP I

family	**la familia**
mother	**la madre**
father	**el padre**
children	**los hijos**
brother	**el hermano**
sister	**la hermana**
grandparents	**los abuelos**
grandchildren	**los nietos**

GROUP II

husband	**el esposo**
wife	**la esposa**
parents	**los padres**
son	**el hijo**
daughter	**la hija**
uncle	**el tío**
aunt	**la tía**
cousin	**el (la) primo(a)**

GRAMMAR
THE ARTICLE "THE"

In English, there is only one word for the word "the." In Spanish, there are four forms: "la," "las," "el," and "los." They are the singular and plural, feminine and masculine forms. In English we do not have the concept of feminine and masculine nouns; things are neuter.

	Singular	Plural
Feminine	la	las
Masculine	el	los

Write the correct form of the article "the." The ending of the following words should match with one of the four forms you choose: "la," "las," "el" or "los."

1. ____ tacos
2. ____ salsa
3. ____ burritos
4. ____ cervezas
5. ____ amigos
6. ____ fiestas
7. ____ patio
8. ____ margarita

GROUP I

MATCHING EXERCISE

Write the letter of each picture next to the Spanish word it matches below.

a.

b.

c.

d.

e.

f.

g.

h.

1. _____ los nietos
2. _____ la madre
3. _____ el hermano
4. _____ la familia
5. _____ los abuelos
6. _____ la hermana
7. _____ el padre
8. _____ los hijos

VOCABULARY EXERCISE

Write the Spanish word for each picture in the space provided.

1. _____

2. _____

3. _____

4. _____

5. _____

6. _____

7. _____

8. _____

MATCHING EXERCISE

Write the letter of the Spanish word next to the English word it matches on the left.

1.	_____ grandparents	a.	la hermana
2.	_____ children	b.	la madre
3.	_____ father	c.	la familia
4.	_____ family	d.	los nietos
5.	_____ grandchildren	e.	el hermano
6.	_____ sister	f.	el padre
7.	_____ mother	g.	los abuelos
8.	_____ brother	h.	los hijos

TRANSLATION EXERCISE

Translate the following to English:

1. los nietos _____

2. los abuelos _____

3. los hijos _____

4. el hermano _____

5. la familia _____

6. la madre _____

7. la hermana _____

8. el padre _____

Translate the following to English:

1. el hermano _____

2. la madre _____

3. los abuelos _____

4. los hijos _____

5. la hermana _____

6. la familia _____

7. el padre _____

8. los nietos _____

GROUP II

MATCHING EXERCISE

Write the letter of each picture next to the Spanish word it matches below.

a.

b.

c.

d.

e.

f.

g.

h.

1. _____ el hijo
2. _____ los padres
3. _____ la tía
4. _____ el primo
5. _____ la hija
6. _____ el esposo
7. _____ el tío
8. _____ la esposa

VOCABULARY EXERCISE

Write the Spanish word for each picture in the space provided.

1. _____

2. _____

3. _____

4. _____

5. _____

6. _____

7. _____

8. _____

MATCHING EXERCISE

Write the letter of the Spanish word next to the English word it matches on the left.

1. _____ daughter   a. la esposa
2. _____ aunt   b. los primos
3. _____ husband   c. el hijo
4. _____ parents   d. la tía
5. _____ uncle   e. el esposo
6. _____ son   f. la hija
7. _____ cousins   g. los padres
8. _____ wife   h. el tío

TRANSLATION EXERCISE

Translate the following to English:

1. el tío _____

2. los padres _____

3. la hija _____

4. el esposo _____

5. el primo_____

6. la tía _____

7. el hijo _____

8. la esposa _____

Translate the following to Spanish:

1. aunt _____

2. son _____

3. wife _____

4. cousin _____

5. parents _____

6. uncle _____

7. daughter _____

8. husband _____

MULTIPLE CHOICE

Circle the letter of the correct answer.

1. father
a. el hermano
b. el primo
c. la madre
d. el padre

2. husband
a. el hermano
b. el esposo
c. el hijo
d. el tío

3. cousin
a. el hermano
b. el primo
c. la madre
d. el padre

4. mother
a. la madre
b. la tía
c. la hermana
d. la hija

5. grandparents
a. los hermanos
b. los primos
c. los abuelos
d. los hijos

6. aunt
a. la hija
b. la madre
c. la hermana
d. la tía

7. family
a. los abuelos
b. los primos
c. la familia
d. la madre

8. brother
a. el hermano
b. el primo
c. la madre
d. el padre

9. son
a. la hija
b. el hijo
c. el hermano
d. la hermana

CROSSWORD PUZZLES

Across

5. family
6. brother
7. father
8. wife
9. aunt
10. grandparents

Down

1. mother
2. daughter
3. son
4. parents
6. sister
8. husband
9. uncle

Across

1. esposo
2. hija
3. hijo
6. tía
7. esposa
8. primo
9. madre

Down

2. hermano
4. abuelos
9. tío

ROLE PLAY

mother / Margarita, 43

brother / Guillermo, 18

daughter / Raquel, 8

sister / Cristina, 22

son / Raul, 6

uncle / Samuel, 39

father / Ignacio, 55

grandfather / Ricardo, 69

A. What's your son's name? In Chapter 1 you learned how to ask co-workers their names and state yours. Now, working with partners ask them the names of their family members in the photo. "Tu" means "your." "Mi" means "my." Follow the model.

(son / Raul)

| **ESTUDIANTE A:** | ¿Cómo se llama tu hijo? |
| **ESTUDIANTE B:** | Mi hijo se llama Raul. |

B. How old is he? Working with a partner ask and answer how old the people are in the family photo. Follow the model.

(Raul, 6)

| **ESTUDIANTE A:** | ¿Cuántos años tiene Raul? |
| **ESTUDIANTE B:** | Raul tiene seis años. |

C. How old are you? Take turns asking and answering: How old are you? I am. . . Follow the model.

(Adam, 20)

| **ESTUDIANTE A:** | ¿Cuántos años tiene, Adam? |
| **ESTUDIANTE B:** | Tengo 20 años. |

1. Marta, 18
2. Rodolfo, 72
3. Bob, 34
4. Frank, 45

5. Nancy, 50
6. Gustavo, 61
7. Enrique, 83
8. Sonia, 29

PART II—WORK PERSONNEL

1. _____

2. _____

3. _____

4. _____

5. _____

6. _____

7. _____

8. _____

9. _____

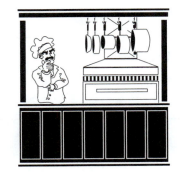

10. _____

11. _____

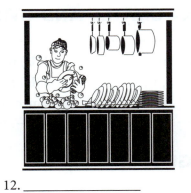

12. _____

13. _____

14. _____

15. _____

GROUP 1

boss	**el (la) jefe**	guest	**el (la) huésped**
supervisor	**el (la) supervisor**	man	**el hombre**
housekeeper	**la camarista**	woman	**la mujer**
bellman	**el botones**	child	**el (la) niño(a)**

GROUP 2

server (waiter, waitress)	**el (la) mesero(a)**	chef	**el (la) chef**
cook	**el (la) cocinero(a)**	dishwasher	**el lavaplatos**
bartender	**el (la) cantinero(a)**	manager	**el (la) gerente**
groundskeeper	**el jardinero**		

COGNATES AND OTHER WORDS

receptionist	**el (la) recepcionista**	busboy	**el busboy**
cliente	**el (la) cliente**	host/hostess	**la hostess**
mechanic	**el mecánico**		

GROUP I

MATCHING EXERCISE

Write the letter of each picture next to the Spanish word it matches below.

a.

b.

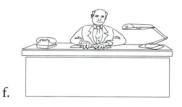

c.

d.

e.

f.

g.

h.

1. _____ la camarista

2. _____ el (la) jefe

3. _____ el (la) niña

4. _____ el (la) huésped

5. _____ el hombre

6. _____ la mujer

7. _____ el botones

8. _____ el (la) supervisor

VOCABULARY EXERCISE

Write the Spanish word for each picture in the space provided.

1. _____

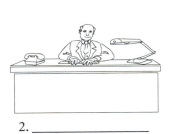

2. _____

3. _____

4. _____

5. _____

6. _____

7. _____

8. _____

MATCHING EXERCISE

Write the letter of the Spanish word next to the English word it matches on the left.

1. _____ housekkeeper
2. _____ guest
3. _____ supervisor
4. _____ man
5. _____ bellman
6. _____ boss
7. _____ child
8. _____ woman

a. el, la huésped
b. la mujer
c. el jefe
d. la camarista
e. el, la niña
f. el botones
g. el, la supervisor
h. el hombre

TRANSLATION EXERCISE

Translate the following to English:

1. el hombre _____
2. el, la huésped _____
3. la camarista _____
4. la mujer _____
5. el botones _____
6. el (la) jefe _____
7. el (la) niño (a) _____
8. el (la) supervisor (a) _____

Translate the following to Spanish:

1. guest _____
2. man _____
3. housekeeper _____
4. bellman _____
5. woman _____
6. child _____
7. boss _____
8. supervisor _____

GROUP II

MATCHING EXERCISE

Write the letter of each picture next to the Spanish word it matches below.

a.

b.

c.

d.

e.

f.

g.

1. _____ el jardinero

2. _____ el (la) cantinero (a)

3. _____ el (la) mesero (a)

4. _____ el (la) concinero (a)

5. _____ el (la) gerente

6. _____ el lavaplatos

7. _____ el (la) chef

VOCABULARY EXERCISE

Write the Spanish word for each picture in the space provided.

1. _____

2. _____

3. _____

4. _____

5. _____

6. _____

7. _____

MATCHING EXERCISE

Write the letter of the Spanish word next to the English word it matches on the left.

1._____ groundskeeper
2._____ cook
3._____ bartender
4._____ manager
5._____ dishwasher
6._____ server
7._____ chef

a. el lavaplatos
b. el (la) cocinero (a)
c. el (la) mesero (a)
d. el (la) cantinero (a)
e. el jardinero
f. el (la) chef
g. el (la) gerente

TRANSLATION EXERCISE

Translate the following to English:

1. el jardinero _____
2. el (la) cocinero (a) _____
3. el (la) chef _____
4. el lavaplatos _____
5. el (la) gerente _____
6. el (la) cantinero (a) _____
7. el (la) mesero _____

Translate the following to Spanish:

1. chef _____
2. server _____
3. cook _____
4. manager _____
5. bartender _____
6. groundskeeper _____
7. dishwasher _____

MULTIPLE CHOICE

Circle the letter of the correct answer.

1. guest
a. el gerente
b. el hombre
c. el mesero
d. el huésped

2. housekeeper
a. el cocinero
b. el lavaplatos
c. la camarista
d. la mujer

3. cook
a. el jardinero
b. el cocinero
c. el botones
d. el gerente

4. manager
a. el gerente
b. el hombre
c. el mesero
d. el huésped

5. bellman
a. el lavaplatos
b. el jefe
c. el botones
d. el hombre

6. man
a. el gerente
b. el hombre
c. el mesero
d. el huésped

7. woman
a. el cocinero
b. el lavaplatos
c. la camarista
d. la mujer

8. dishwasher
a. el cocinero
b. el lavaplatos
c. la camarista
d. el mesero

9. server
a. el gerente
b. el hombre
c. el mesero
d. el huésped

CROSSWORD PUZZLES

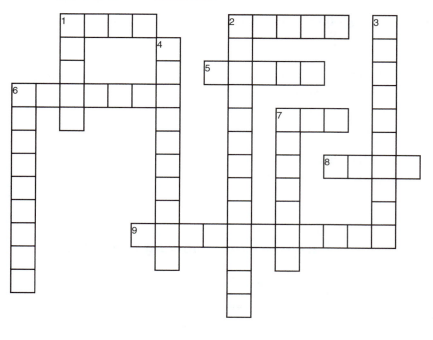

Across

1. chef
2. húesped
5. mujer
6. botones
7. hombre
8. jefe
9. camarista

Down

1. niño
2. jardinero
3. lavaplatos
4. supervisor
6. cantinero
7. gerenle

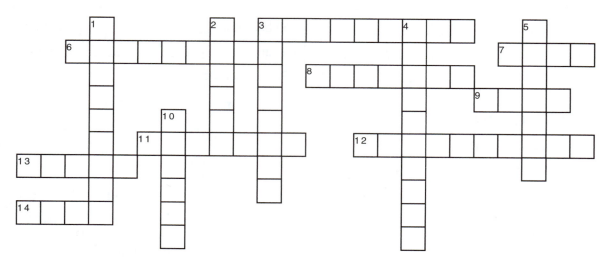

Across

3. housekeeper
6. bartender
7. boss
8. guest
9. chef
11. bellhop
12. dishwasher
13. woman
14. child

Down

1. gardener
1. server
3. cook
4. supervisor
5. manager
10. man

ROLE PLAY

Where is. . . ? Pretend there is a problem at the reception desk where you work and you need to find one of your co-workers to fix it. Working with a partner ask and answer where the person is. Follow the model.

Use the following locations:

La oficina   El bar

El restaurante   El hotel

ESTUDIANTE A: ¿Dónde está el botones?
ESTUDIANTE B: El botones está en el hotel.

1.

2.

3.

4.

5.

6.

7.

8.

9.

10.

11.

12.

13.

14.

15.

PART III—PERSONALITY TYPES AND EMOTIONS
ADJECTIVES AND COGNATES

Cognates are adjectives that are the same or very similar in both English and Spanish. An adjective is a word that describes a noun, in this case, people. (For men the words end in -o and for women they end in -a.)

aggressive	**agresivo (a)**	intellectual	**intelectual**
ambitious	**ambicioso (a)**	intelligent	**inteligente**
comical	**cómico (a)**	introverted	**introvertido (a)**
cooperative	**cooperativo (a)**	materialistic	**materialista**
cruel	**cruel**	organized	**organizado (a)**
extroverted	**extrovertido (a)**	patient	**paciente**
generous	**generoso (a)**	responsible	**responsable**
fair	**justo (a)**	romantic	**romántico (a)**
hardworking	**trabajador (a)**	sensitive	**sensitivo (a)**
honest	**honesto (a)**	sincere	**sincero (a)**
impatient	**impaciente**	sociable	**sociable**
impulsive	**impulsivo (a)**	superstitious	**supersticioso (a)**
independent	**independiente**	timid	**tímido (a)**

VOCABULARY EXERCISE

A. Write your initials next to the characteristics that describe you.

agresivo (a) _____

ambicioso (a) _____

cómico (a) _____

cooperativo (a) _____

cruel _____

extrovertido (a) _____

generoso (a) _____

justo (a) _____

trabajador (a) _____

honesto (a) _____

impaciente _____

impulsivo (a) _____

independiente _____

intelectual _____

inteligente _____

introvertido (a) _____

materialista _____

organizado (a) _____

paciente _____

responsable _____

romántico (a) _____

sensitivo (a) _____

sincero (a) _____

sociable _____

supersticioso (a) _____

tímido (a) _____

B. Next, write the initials of one of your classmates or co-workers near the characteristics that describe him or her.

C. Now write the initials of your significant other near the characteristics that describe him or her.

GRAMMAR: THE VERB "SER"

Ser	to be
Soy	I am
Eres	You are
Es	He, she is

1. The verb "**ser**" means "to be". In Chapter 1 you learned three forms of "**ser**" to tell from where someone is.

Soy de California.	I am from California.
¿De dónde eres?	Where are you from?
Juan es de Honduras.	Juan is from Honduras.

2. We also use the verb "**ser**" to describe what someone is like.

Soy cómica.	I am comical.
Eres ambicioso.	You are ambitious.
María es inteligente.	María is intelligent.

HOW MUCH

muy	very
no muy	not very
un poco	a little
un poquito*	a very little

*Poco and poquito are used for amounts. Pequeño, chico, and chiquito are used with sizes.

ROLE PLAY

A. I am. . . Tell the following: 1) a characteristic you have a lot of, 2) one you have a little of, and 3) one you don't have.

1. Soy muy . . .
2. Soy un poco . . .
3. No soy muy . . .

B. You are. . .

1. Eres muy. . .
2. Eres un poco. . .
3. No eres muy. . .

C. He is. . .

1. Mi jefe es muy. . .
2. Mi supervisor es un poco. . .
3. Mi amigo no es muy. . .

D. Pretend this is a want ad. List the characteristics you need and want in an employee.

_____   _____

_____   _____

Fill in the blank with one of the cognate / characteristics.

1. El jefe es _____

2. La camarista es_____

3. El cocinero es _____

4. El supervisor es _____

5. La chef es _____

6. El lavaplatos es _____

7. La gerente es_____

8. El botones es _____

9. El cantinero es _____

10. El mesero es _____

EMOTIONS

¿Cómo estás?	How are you?
Estoy. . .	I am. . .
cansado (a)	tired
confundido (a)	confused
contento (a)	content
enojado (a)	angry
furioso (a)	furious
nervioso (a)	nervous
ocupado (a)	busy
preocupado (a)	worried
triste	sad
feliz	happy
enfermo	sick
de buen humor	good mood
de mal humor	bad mood

MATCHING EXERCISE

Write the letter of the Spanish word next to the English word it matches on the left.

1. _____ good mood
2. _____ content
3. _____ happy
4. _____ sick
5. _____ tired
6. _____ sad
7. _____ angry
8. _____ busy

9. _____ worried
10. _____ bad mood
11. _____ furious
12. _____ nervous
13. _____ confused
14. _____ How are you?
15. _____ I am. . .

a. Estoy. . .
b. preocupado, a
c. triste
d. ¿Cómo estás?
e. feliz
f. de buen humor
g. de mal humor
h. confundido, a

i. contento, a
j. cansado, a
k. enojado, a
l. nervioso, a
m. furioso, a
n. enfermo, a
o. ocupado, a

CROSSWORD PUZZLES

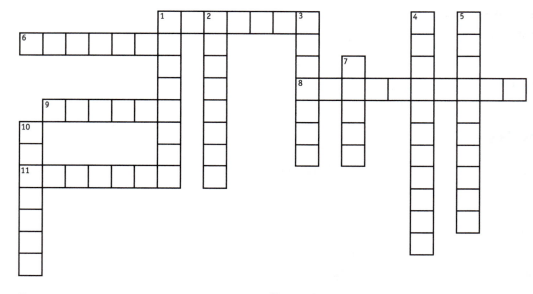

Across

1. tired
6. angry
8. worried
9. sad
11. furious

Down

1. content
2. nervous
3. busy
4. good mood
5. bad mood
7. happy
10. sick

Across

2. nervioso
5. de mal humor
6. enfermo
8. enojado
11. cansado
12. ocupado

Down

1. de buen humor
3. feliz
4. preocupado
7. contento
9. furioso
10. triste

GRAMMAR: THE VERB "ESTAR"

ESTAR	to be
Estoy	I am
Estás	You are
Está	He, she is

As you know, when we want to ask how someone is feeling, we ask *¿Cómo estas?* When we want to say how someone is feeling we also use the verb "estar".

Estoy preocupado.	I am worried.
¿Estás nervioso?	Are you nervous?
¡La cliente está enojada!	The client is angry!

TRANSLATION EXERCISE

Translate the following to English:

1. Estoy enfermo. _____
2. ¿Estás preocupado? _____
3. ¿Está enojado? _____
4. Estoy triste. _____
5. ¡Está furiosa! _____
6. Está ocupada. _____
7. ¿Estás de mal humor? _____
8. Estoy confundido. _____
9. Estoy cansado. _____
10. ¿Está feliz? _____
11. ¡Estás de buen humor! _____
12. ¿Estás contenta? _____

Translate the following to Spanish:

1. Are you sick? _____
2. Is she angry? _____
3. I am worried. _____
4. Are you confused? _____
5. You're in a good mood! _____
6. I am fine. _____
7. Are you busy? _____
8. He is happy. _____
9. Are you tired? _____
10. He is in a bad mood. _____
11. She is furious! _____
12. I am nervous. _____

MULTIPLE CHOICE

Circle the correct answer.

1. Are you sick?
   a. Está triste.
   b. ¿Estás enfermo?
   c. Está mal.
   d. Estás bien.

2. She is in a good mood.
   a. Está bien.
   b. Está de buen humor.
   c. Está contenta.
   d. Estoy contenta.

3. Is he angry?
   a. ¿Estás enojado?
   b. ¿Estás cansado?
   c. ¿Está enojado?
   d. ¿Estoy enojado?

4. Are you sad?
   a. ¿Estás triste?
   b. ¿Estás enojado?
   c. ¿Estás mal?
   d. ¿Estás enfermo?

5. I am worried.
   a. Estoy preocupado.
   b. Estoy ocupado.
   c. Estoy enojado.
   d. Estoy triste.

6. He is in a bad mood.
   a. Está enojado.
   b. Estoy mal.
   c. Estoy enojado.
   d. Está de mal humor.

7. Are you tired?
   a. ¿Estás contento?
   b. Estoy cansado.
   c. ¿Estás cansado?
   d. ¿Estás confundido?

8. Are you nervous?
   a. ¿Estás nervioso?
   b. Estoy nervioso.
   c. ¿Está nervioso.
   d. ¿Estás enojado?

9. She is furious!
   a. ¡Está furioso!
   b. ¡Está furiosa!
   c. ¡Estoy furiosa!
   d. ¡Estoy furioso!

10. Are you confused?
   a. Estoy cansada.
   b. Estoy confundida.
   c. ¿Estás confundida?
   d. ¿Estás contenta?

REVIEW

Translate to Spanish:

1. There are five children in my family. _____

2. There are four brothers. _____

3. What's your uncle's name? _____

4. What's your son's name? _____

5. How old is your daughter? _____

6. Cristina is five years old. _____

7. My son is responsible and cooperative. _____

8. My manager is comical and organized. _____

9. The crew is hardworking. _____

10. The client is furious! _____

11. Are there problems? _____

12. I am nervous and worried. _____

13. My boss is angry! _____

14. The supervisor is in a good mood. _____

15. Are you sick? Sad? Confused? _____

Read and translate the story.

The Royalty Hotel

Hola. Me llamo Octavio. Soy de Oaxaca, México. Soy mexicano. Tengo veinte y dos años. Hay doce personas en mi familia. Tengo cuatro hermanos, dos hermanas, mis padres y cuatro abuelos. Estoy triste porque* mi familia está en México y estoy en los Estados Unidos. Hablo español. . . no hablo inglés. Soy el lavaplatos en *The Royalty Hotel*.

*porque – because

En los Estados Unidos tengo muchos amigos buenos. Tengo muchas amigas buenas. ¡Gloria es la mujer que me interesa* !Gloria es la camarista en el hotel. Es generosa, sincera, cómica y muy romantica. Es de Guanajuato, México. Gloria habla inglés un poco. Es inteligente. Tiene diez y nueve años.

*Me interesa – interests me

La familia de Gloria es grande. Gloria tiene tres hermanos en los Estados Unidos. Su hermano es el recepcionista. Se llama Manuel. Manuel tiene veinte y cinco años y es muy responsable y organizado. Manual habla inglés y español. Es bilingue. Su hermano, Luis, tiene veinte y tres años y es cooperativo, trabajador, y muy frágil. Luis es el botones. Su hermano, Raimundo, es el cocinero. Raimundo es cómico y siempre está de buen humor.

El señor David Kane es el gerente general. El supervisa las actividades de las camaristas, los cocineros, los lavaplatos, los botones, los meseros y los jardineros porque el servicio es muy importante para los clientes.

The Royalty Hotel

Hello. My name is Octavio. I'm from Oaxaca, Mexico, I'm Mexican. I'm twenty two years old. There are twelve people in my family. I have four brothers, two sisters, my parents and my four grandparents. I am sad because* my family is in Mexico and I am in the United States. I speak Spanish. . . I don't speak English. I am the dishwasher at The Royalty Hotel.

*because – porque

In the United States I have many good friends. I have many good girl friends. Gloria is the woman who most interests* me! Gloria is the housekeeper in the hotel. She is generous, sincere, comical, and very romantic. She is from Guanajuato, Mexico. Gloria speaks English a little. She is intelligent. She is nineteen years old.

*interests me – Me interesa

Gloria's family is large. Gloria has three brothers in the United States. Her brother is the receptionist at The Royalty Hotel. His name is Manuel. Manuel is twenty five years old and is very responsible and organized. Manual speaks English and Spanish. He is bilingual. Her brother, Luis, is twenty three years old and is cooperative, hard working, and very sensitive. Luis is the bellman. Her brother, Raimundo, is the cook. Raimundo is comical and always in a good mood.

Mr. David Kane is the general manager. He supervises the activities of the housekeepers, cooks, dishwashers, bellmen, servers, and gardeners because service is very important to the clients.

Translate the following to Spanish:

1. Monday, Wednesday, Friday _____

2. Tuesday, Thursday, Saturday _____

3. March, June, August _____

4. January, December, September _____

5. There is salad, pizza, and beer. _____

6. Is there music? _____

7. Speak slowly, please. _____

8. I'm sorry. _____

9. I'd like to introduce you to _____

10. Where are you from? _____

11. Come with me. _____

12. Do it like me. _____

13. Try it. Continue trying. _____

14. You're a hard worker! _____

15. I'll help you. _____

16. It's important. It's necessary. _____

17. It's good. It's bad. It's so-so. _____

18. Everything else is perfect. _____

19. Where is the manager? _____

20. How many? _____

CULTURE: THE FAMILY

A common Spanish phrase "La familia sobre todo" addresses the importance given to the Latino family. It means "The family above all." Family takes priority over work and all other areas of life.

The strength of the Latino society is the family unit. It is often referred to as the "extended family" since it includes not only parents and children but aunts, uncles, cousins and grandparents as well.

Within the traditional family, the father is the undisputed authority figure and disciplinarian. All important decisions are made by him. Traditionally, the mother is subordinate. She is valued as a devoted mother and dutiful wife. The parents are devoted to their children and they are protected and loved. The typical weekend entertainment consists of the entire family, including grandparents, aunts, uncles, and cousins. Raised in these circumstances, children feel protected but are also very dependent on the help and support of their families.

When a child begins school, he normally goes along with the thinking of others. He now believes his teacher to be the undisputed authority. Because of this upbringing and education, when young latino employees arrive at the workplace, they seem submissive to their supervisor and accept instructions unquestioningly. Since they believe that their supervisor has complete authority, the employees' responsibility is simply to complete the boss's instructions and the job assignments.

The word "family" in the United States traditionally refers to simply parents and their children. In the typical United States family, the mother and father are considered equal partners and are co-authority figures.

In the United States, work often has more importance than the family. Family life and activities must fit in around work schedules. Employees are also counted upon to transfer their families to another city if they get a job promotion. Families often relocate many times during their careers. Family members become scattered and live in many different parts of the United States. Parents and siblings often only see one another a few times a year.

Divorce is common. The present family condition and the loss of traditional family values (for example, home-cooked family dinners every night) has caused a lot of controversy over the years. The situation that has developed has placed extra burdens on the single parent who now has even less time available for the children because of the need to work full-time outside of the home.

A child brought up in this type of family or where both parents work full time has had to do many tasks on his/her own. They have been responsible for many things at an early age. This type of person becomes self-sufficient, independent, and individualistic—characteristics that are considered positive in the United States. Because of this upbringing, young people arrive at a business organization full of self-confidence. They have many of the characteristics that are admired in an employee. They are independent thinkers, aggressive and competitive. They are not afraid to say "no," disagree with their boss, or share their opinions with him. Many employees look forward to taking on positions that require more responsibility.

Many organizations in the United States have begun to understand the importance of a good, stable family life. They have begun to implement flexible work schedules as well as providing child care facilities at the workplace.

RELATIONSHIP TIP

Many of your Latino co-workers may be miles from their families while working here in the United States. They are here to make money for their families. Many will be homesick. You have now become their new family. Ask for and post a picture of their families near the map and flag of their countries. Show interest in their children. Ask their names and how old they are. Bring a picture of your family and continue your conversations!

RELATIONSHIP TIP

Rent the movie, *La Familia*, from your local video store. It stars Jimmy Smits and it is a funny yet sad story about a Latino family. Enjoy a Mexican dinner while you watch it and don't forget a box of Kleenex. F.Y.I: There are only subtitles for the first five minutes!

5

Sports and Activities

PART I—SPORTS

to play baseball
jugar al béisbol

to play basketball
jugar al básquetbol

to play football
jugar al fútbol americano

to play soccer
jugar al fútbol

to play tennis
jugar al tenis

to play golf
jugar al golf

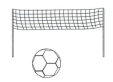

to play volleyball
jugar al volibol

to play sports
jugar a los deportes

to play billiards
jugar al billar

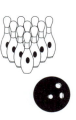

to bowl
jugar al boliche

to fish
pescar

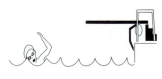

to swim
nadar

VOCABULARY EXERCISE

Write the Spanish word for each picture in the space provided.

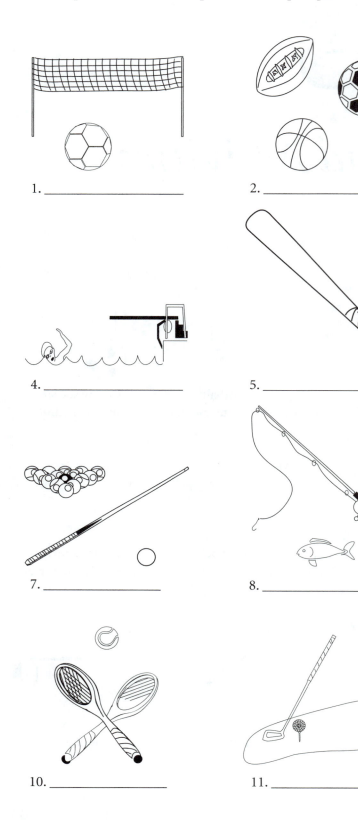

1. _____

2. _____

3. _____

4. _____

5. _____

6. _____

7. _____

8. _____

9. _____

10. _____

11. _____

12. _____

MATCHING EXERCISE

Write the letter of the Spanish phrase next to the English phrase it matches on the left.

1. _____ to play basketball
2. _____ to bowl
3. _____ to fish
4. _____ to play baseball
5. _____ to swim
6. _____ to play sports
7. _____ to play golf
8. _____ to play volleyball
9. _____ to play billiards
10. _____ to play soccer

a. jugar al volibol
b. jugar a los deportes
c. jugar al fútbol
d. pescar
e. jugar al boliche
f. jugar al básquetbol
g. jugar al béisbol
h. jugar al golf
i. nadar
j. jugar al billar

CROSSWORD PUZZLES

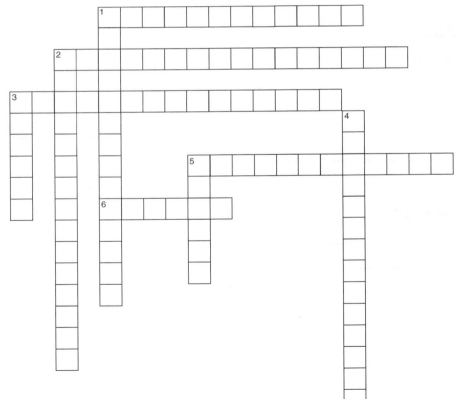

Across

1. jugar al fútbol
2. jugar al volibol
3. jugar al billar
5. jugar a los deportes
6. pescar

Down

1. jugar al fútbol americano
2. jugar al básquetbol
3. jugar al boliche
4. jugar al béisbol
5. nadar

TRANSLATION EXERCISE

Translate the following to Spanish:

1. to play golf _____
2. to play sports _____
3. to play pool _____
4. to play soccer _____
5. to swim _____

6. to fish _____
7. to bowl _____
8. to play volleyball _____
9. to play basketball _____
10. to play tennis _____

GRAMMAR: DO YOU LIKE TO. . . ? / ¿TE GUSTA. . . ?

To ask someone's likes and dislikes, simply ask *¿Te gusta?* before the sports and activities you have learned.

Do you like to play soccer?	**¿Te gusta jugar al fútbol?**
Do you like to play baseball?	**¿Te gusta jugar al béisbol?**
Do you like to play golf?	**¿Te gusta jugar al golf?**
Yes, I like to go to parties.	**Sí, me gusta ir a las fiestas.**
No, I do not like to go to parties.	**No, no me gusta ir a las fiestas.**

One does not need to repeat the whole sentence. *Sí, me gusta* or *No, no me gusta* is also a correct way to respond in Spanish.

TRANSLATION EXERCISE

Translate the following to English:

1. ¿Te gusta jugar al volibol? _____
2. ¿Te gusta pescar? _____
3. ¿Te gusta nadar? _____
4. ¿Te gusta jugar a los deportes? _____
5. ¿Te gusta jugar al golf? _____

Translate the following to Spanish:

1. Do you like to play volleyball? _____
2. Do you like to swim? _____
3. Do you like to play tennis? _____
4. Do you like to fish? _____
5. Do you like to play sports? _____
6. Do you like to play basketball? _____
7. Do you like to play baseball? _____
8. Do you like to play soccer? _____
9. Do you like to play billiards? _____
10. Do you like to bowl? _____

ROLE PLAY

A. **I like to . . .** Pretend you are working at a university campus which has sports fields. Say whether you love (me encanta), like (me gusta), or don't like (no me gusta) to play the sport shown. Use one of the following phrases.

I love to play soccer.	**Me encanta jugar al fútbol.**
I like to play soccer.	**Me gusta jugar al fútbol.**
I do not like to play soccer.	**No me gusta jugar al fútbol.**

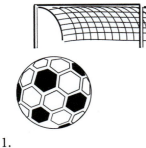

1.

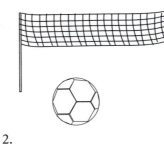

2.

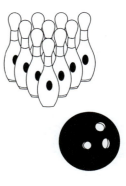

3.

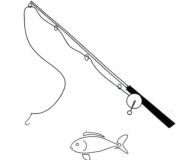

4.

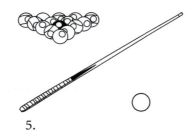

5.

6.

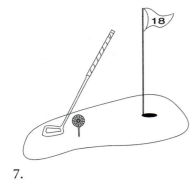

7.

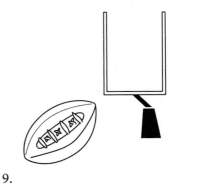

8.

9.

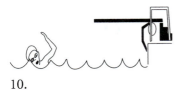

10.

B. **What do you like to do?** Working with a partner, ask what activities he/she likes and does not like to do in each season. Follow the model.

ESTUDIANTE A: ¿Qúe te gusta hacer en la primavera?
ESTUDIANTE B: Me gusta jugar al béisbol pero no me gusta nadar.

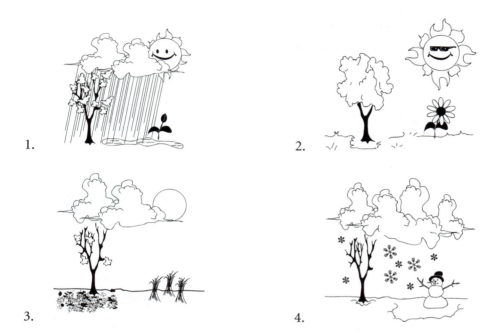

1.

2.

3.

4.

C. **With whom?** Working with a partner tell when and with whom you like to play these sports. Follow the model.

summer/volleyball/friends   En el verano me gusta jugar al volibol con mis amigos.

1. baseball/brothers   2. football/supervisors   3. swim/children   4. basketball/uncle

5. soccer/cook   6. fish/boss   7. billiards/father   8. bowling/family

PART II—ACTIVITIES

to read
leer

to dance
bailar

to go to parties
ir a las fiestas

to be with family
estar con la familia

to play cards
jugar cartas

to drink
tomar, beber

to eat
comer

to listen to music
escuchar música

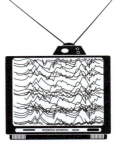

to watch television
mirar la televisión

MATCHING EXERCISE

Write the letter of each picture next to the Spanish word it matches below.

a.

b.

c.

d.

e.

f.

g.

h.

i.

1. _____ bailar
2. _____ leer
3. _____ comer
4. _____ tomar, beber
5. _____ ir a las fiestas

6. _____ mirar la televisión
7. _____ escuchar música
8. _____ jugar cartas
9. _____ estar con la familia

VOCABULARY EXERCISE

Write the Spanish word for each picture in the space provided.

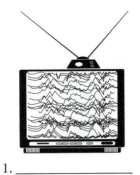

1. _____

2. _____

3. _____

4. _____

5. _____

6. _____

7. _____

8. _____

9. _____

MATCHING EXERCISE

Write the letter of the Spanish phrase next to the English phrase it matches on the left.

1. _____ to listen to music
2. _____ to read
3. _____ to dance
4. _____ to play cards
5. _____ to be with family
6. _____ to watch television
7. _____ to eat
8. _____ to drink
9. _____ to go to parties

a. tomar, beber
b. jugar cartas
c. ir a las fiestas
d. mirar la televisión
e. leer
f. estar con la familia
g. escuchar música
h. comer
i. bailar

CROSSWORD PUZZLES

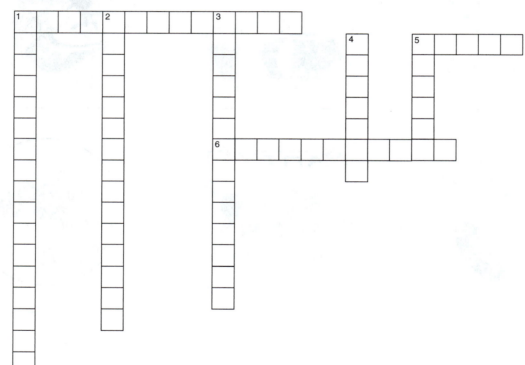

Across

1. ir a las fiestas
5. comer
6. jugar cartas

Down

1. mirar la televisión
2. escuchar música
3. estar con la familia
4. bailar
5. leer

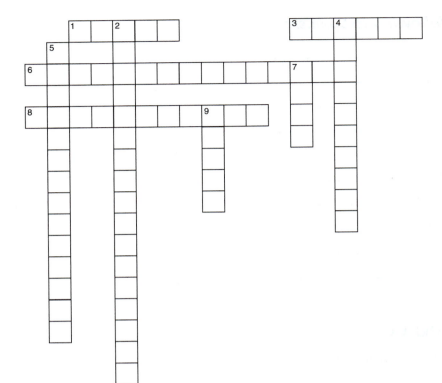

Across

1. to eat
3. to dance
6. to be with family
8. to play cards

Down

2. to watch television
4. to go to parties
5. to listen to music
7. to read
9. to drink

TRANSLATION EXERCISE

Translate the following to English:

1. ir a las fiestas _____

2. mirar la televisión _____

3. bailar _____

4. estar con la familia _____

5. tomar _____

6. comer _____

7. jugar cartas _____

8. escuchar música _____

9. leer _____

10. jugar al béisbol _____

Translate the following to Spanish:

1. to listen to music _____
2. to read _____
3. to dance _____
4. to drink _____
5. to eat _____
6. to go to parties _____
7. to watch television _____
8. to be with family _____
9. to play cards _____
10. to play soccer _____

MULTIPLE CHOICE

Circle the letter of the correct answer.

1. to listen to music
   a. mirar la televisión
   b. escuchar la radio
   c. escuchar música
   d. ir a las fiestas

2. to dance
   a. nadar
   b. pescar
   c. jugar cartas
   d. bailar

3. to play cards
   a. jugar al billar
   b. jugar al volibol
   c. jugar al boliche
   d. jugar cartas

4. to fish
   a. pescar
   b. nadar
   c. tomar
   d. ir a las fiestas

5. to read
   a. comer
   b. tomar
   c. bailar
   d. leer

6. to bowl
   a. nadar
   b. bailar
   c. jugar al boliche
   d. jugar al billar

7. to play billiards
   a. jugar al billar
   b. jugar al boliche
   c. comer
   d. bailar

8. to swim
   a. bailar
   b. comer
   c. nadar
   d. pescar

GRAMMAR: EXPRESSING I . . . AND DO YOU . . . ?

You have learned to express your likes and dislikes using the verb *gustar*. To express that you actually take part in the activity, take off the *–ar, -er,* or *–ir* ending and add *'o'* to the word. Study the model.

I like to listen to music.	**Me gusta escuchar música.**
I listen to jazz.	**Escucho jazz.**

To say that you do not take part in the activities, add "no" before the word.

I dance.	**Bailo.**
I do not dance.	**No bailo.**

To ask someone about what activities he/she participates in, take off the *–ar-er,* or *–ir* ending and add *"as"* to the word.

Do you like to watch television?	**¿Te gusta mirar la televisión?**
Do you watch *Friends?*	**¿Miras *Friends?***
Yes, I watch *Friends.*	**Sí, miro *Friends.***

Jugar "to play" is irregular.

I play golf.	**Juego al golf.**
Do you play volleyball?	**¿Juegas al volibol?**

TRANSLATION EXERCISE

Translate the following to Spanish:

1. I dance. _____
2. I swim. _____
3. I fish. _____
4. I drink. _____
5. I listen to music. _____
6. I play billiards. _____
7. I watch television. _____
8. I read. _____
9. I do not dance. _____
10. I do not swim. _____
11. I do not fish. _____
12. I do not drink. _____
13. I do not listen to music. _____
_____

14. I do not play billiards. _____
15. I do not watch television. _____
16. I do not read. _____
17. Do you dance? _____
18. Do you swim? _____
19. Do you fish? _____
20. Do you drink? _____
21. Do you listen to music? _____
_____
22. Do you play billiards? _____
23. Do you watch television? _____
_____
24. Do you read? _____
25. Do you dance? _____

ROLE PLAY

A. **Do you . . . ?** Always talking about work gets boring! Find out more about your co-workers interests by asking if he/she participates in these activities. Follow the model.

	ESTUDIANTE A:	¿Juegas al tenis?
	ESTUDIANTE B:	Sí, juego al tenis. (No, no juego al tenis.)

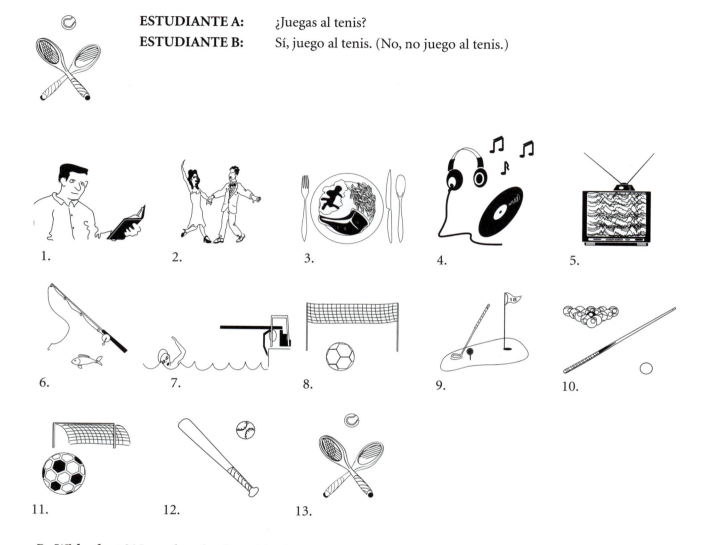

1.   2.   3.   4.   5.

6.   7.   8.   9.   10.

11.   12.   13.

B. **With whom?** Now ask each other with whom (*Con quién*) they do the activities. Follow the model.

ESTUDIANTE A:	¿Con quién juegas al tenis?
ESTUDIANTE B:	Juego al tenis con mi amigo.

C. **When?** Working with a partner, ask and answer when (*¿Cuándo?*) he/she does these activities. Follow the model.

ESTUDIANTE A:	¿Cuándo juegas al tenis?
ESTUDIANTE B:	Juego al tenis en el verano.

REVIEW

Translate the following to Spanish:

1. I like to read. _____

2. I like to be with my family. _____

3. I do not like to go to parties. _____

4. Do you like to play sports? _____

5. Do you like to watch television? _____

6. Do you like to play billiards? _____

7. I listen to music. Do you listen to music? _____

8. I do not watch television. _____

9. I watch golf with my father on Sundays. _____

10. I dance with my wife on Saturdays. _____

11. I play soccer with my supervisors in the fall. _____

12. I fish on the weekends with my friends. _____

13. I play golf in the summer with my boss. _____

14. When do you play volleyball? _____

15. When do you play baseball? _____

Read the dialogue aloud with a partner and then translate it to English.

(viernes, 22 de abril)

Gloria:	¡Hola, Octavio!
Octavio:	Hola. ¿Qué tal?
Gloria:	¡Fantástico! ¡Es viernes!
Octavio:	¿Qué te gusta hacer los sábados?
Gloria:	Me gusta estar con familia.
Octavio:	Ah . . . ¿Te gusta jugar al fútbol?
Gloria:	No . . . no me gusta.
Octavio:	¿Te gusta jugar al volibol?
Gloria:	No . . . no me gusta jugar deportes.
Octavio:	Ah . . . ¿Te gusta jugar al billar?
Gloria:	Sí . . . un poco. ¿Hay música?

Read the dialogue aloud with a partner and then translate it to Spanish.

(Friday, April 22)

Gloria:	Hello, Octavio!
Octavio:	Hello. How's it going?
Gloria:	Fantastic! It's Friday!
Octavio:	What do you like to do on Saturdays?
Gloria:	I like to be with my family.
Octavio:	Ah . . . Do you like to play soccer?
Gloria:	No . . . I don't like to.
Octavio:	Do you like to play volleyball?
Gloria:	No . . . I do not like to play sports.
Octavio:	Ah . . . Do you like to play billiards?
Gloria:	Yes . . . A little. Is there music?

(el sábado, 23 de abril en el bar)

Octavio:	Primero . . . ¿Tomas una margarita?
Gloria:	No, gracias. No tomo.
Octavio:	Me gusta tomar. Una margarita, por favor. . .
Gloria:	¿Hay pizza? ¡ Me encanta comer!
Sergio:	¡Hola! ¿Qué tal?
Octavio:	¡Sergio! ¡Hola! ¿Como estás?
Sergio:	¡Magnífico!
Octavio:	¿Cómo está la familia?
Sergio:	¡Excelente! Gracias.
Octavio:	¿Y tus hermanos?
Sergio:	Bien, gracias.
Octavio:	Quiero presentarte a Gloria.
Sergio:	Mucho gusto.
Gloria:	Igualmente.
Octavio:	¡Hasta luego!

(Octavio y Gloria van a jugar al billar)

Octavio:	Ven conmigo, Gloria. . .
Gloria:	Estoy nerviosa.
Octavio:	Mírame.
Gloria:	(lo mira)
Octavio:	Trátalo.
Gloria:	(golpea mal la bola)
Octavio:	No está correcto. . . Házlo como yo.
Gloria:	Ayúdame, Octavio.
Octavio:	Está así así.
Gloria:	¡No me gusta jugar al billar!
Octavio:	Continua tratando. . . ¡Fabuloso!
Gloria:	Eres paciente, Octavio.
Octavio:	Todo lo demás está correcto.
Gloria:	Muchas gracias. Octavio. . . ¿Te gusta bailar?

(On Saturday, April 23 at the bar)

Octavio:	First . . . Do you want to drink a margarita?
Gloria:	No, thank you. I do not drink.
Octavio:	I like to drink. A margarita, please. . .
Gloria:	Is there pizza? I love to eat!
Sergio:	Hello! How's it going?
Octavio:	Sergio! Hello! How are you?
Sergio:	Magnificent!
Octavio:	How's the family?
Sergio:	Excellent! Thank you.
Octavio:	And your brothers?
Sergio:	Fine, thank you.
Octavio:	I want to introduce you to Gloria.
Sergio:	Nice to meet you.
Gloria:	Same to you.
Octavio:	See you later!

(Octavio and Gloria go to play billiards)

Octavio:	Come with me, Gloria. . .
Gloria:	I'm nervous.
Octavio:	Watch me.
Gloria:	(she watches him)
Octavio:	Try it.
Gloria:	(she hits the ball poorly)
Octavio:	It's not correct. . . Do it like me.
Gloria:	Help me, Octavio.
Octavio:	It's so-so.
Gloria:	I don't like to play billiards!
Octavio:	Keep trying. . . Fabulous!
Gloria:	You are patient, Octavio.
Octavio:	Everything else is correct.
Gloria:	Thank you very much. Octavio. . . Do you like to dance?

CULTURE: INDIVIDUALISTIC CULTURES VS. COOPERATIVE GROUP CULTURES

In the United States people speak of "healthy competition." Children begin competing with one another from a very early age. School activities such as spelling bees, relay races, soccer and Little League baseball continue to be popular. As they grow older, the games change, but not their competitive nature. It continues as they make bets on the golf course and gamble while playing cards. As adults they compete for jobs. The United States thrives on the stimulus of competition. The people enjoy a competitive environment and feel that it does, for the most part, make for quality performance, a healthy business, improved products and services, and a strong economy.

The phrases "play to win" and compete "head to head" and "one on one" are commonly heard. The United States is an individualistic society. In the United States, rewards are for individual achievement. Common awards presented are "Employee of the Month," "Teacher of the Year" and "Most Valuable Player." Companies feel the need to hire in business consultants to facilitate "Team Building" seminars for their employees so that they learn to work together better as a group.

Working as a group comes naturally to many other cultures. People are born into collectives and groups that may be their extended family. People are very involved in and gain their identity from the group. They feel loyalty to the group should be highly rewarded. Most Latinos are very cooperative and work well with one another in the group. (The saying "It takes a village to raise a child" is now being realized as an important concept in the United States.) They are protective of the group as a whole and will often tell a supervisor they do not want a person in their group because he/she makes the group look bad.

The majority of Latino employees are not strongly competitive in terms of wanting to surpass the performance of their co-workers. In a soccer game, yes, they are competitive, but at work they value a more friendly, relaxed atmosphere free of conflict and confrontation. They find it unpleasant to step over a co-worker so that they can look good.

They would like to be in agreement with one another with no outright winners and losers. Latinos usually avoid competitions or volunteering for an assignment which may show them in a negative light. What if they fail? In a close-knit and group-oriented Latino society, one's standing with friends and co-workers is very important.

TEAM BUILDING TIP

In Chapter 13 you will read about the H2B government immigrant labor program. One of the top five reasons H2B employees quit is the lack of evening entertainment. They are miles from their family and friends, and these activities would give them something to look forward to, rather than just working all the time.

Put up a basketball hoop and a volleyball net near your facility. Outline the boundaries with spray paint. You may not be able to communicate with your employees in Spanish well right now, but until you can communicate better with them in Spanish, at least you can play with them. Organize a soccer or a volleyball league with other organizations near you. Have them go out bowling or to a pool hall twice a month. Go to a baseball game together. Have you ever lived in a foreign country and felt the loneliness? Show your employees you care about them, and they will return year after year.

6

The Housekeeping Department

PART I—PLACES

lobby
el vestíbulo

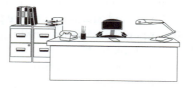

office
la oficina

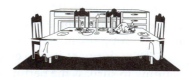

dining room
el comedor

restaurant
el restaurante

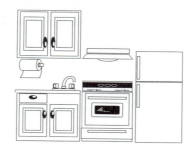

kitchen
la cocina

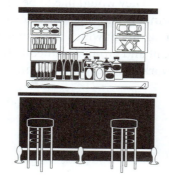

bar
el bar

bedroom
el cuarto

bathroom
el baño

laundry room
la lavandería

basement
el sótano

hallway
el pasillo

floor
el piso

carpet
la alfombra

stairs
la escalera

windows
las ventanas

GROUP I

lobby	**el vestíbulo**	bar	**el bar**
office	**la oficina**	bedroom	**el cuarto**
dining room	**el comedor**	bathroom	**el baño**
restaurant	**el restaurante**	laundry room	**la lavandería**
kitchen	**la cocina**	basement	**el sótano**

GROUP II

hallway	**el pasillo**	stairs	**la escalera**
floor	**el piso**	windows	**las ventanas**
carpet	**la alfombra**		

GROUP I

MATCHING EXERCISE

Write the letter of each picture next to the Spanish word it matches below.

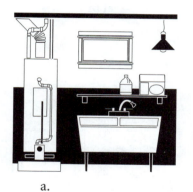

a.

b.

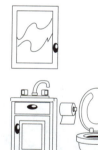

c.

d.

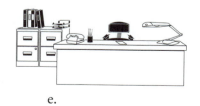

e.

f.

g.

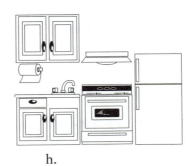

h.

i.

j.

1. _____ el sótano

2. _____ la lavandería

3. _____ el baño

4. _____ el cuarto

5. _____ el bar

6. _____ la cocina

7. _____ el restaurante

8. _____ el comedor

9. _____ la oficina

10. _____ el vestíbulo

VOCABULARY EXERCISE

Write the Spanish word for each picture in the space provided.

1. _____

2. _____

3. _____

4. _____

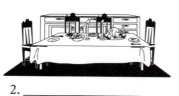

5. _____

6. _____

7. _____

8. _____

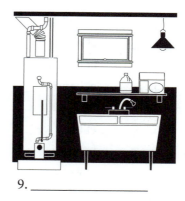

9. _____

10. _____

MATCHING EXERCISE

Write the letter of the Spanish word next to the English word it matches on the left.

1. _____ bathroom	a. el cuarto
2. _____ basement	b. el vestíbulo
3. _____ kitchen	c. la oficina
4. _____ laundry room	d. el comedor
5. _____ dining room	e. la cocina
6. _____ restaurant	f. el baño
7. _____ bedroom	g. el bar
8. _____ bar	h. el restaurante
9. _____ office	i. el sótano
10. _____ lobby	j. la lavandería

TRANSLATION EXERCISE

Translate the following to Spanish:

1. bedroom _____
2. kitchen _____
3. bar _____
4. bathroom _____
5. office _____
6. dining room _____
7. lobby _____
8. basement _____
9. restaurant _____
10. laundry room _____

Translate the following to English:

1. el vestíbulo _____
2. el comedor _____
3. la cocina _____
4. el cuarto _____
5. el baño _____
6. la oficina _____
7. la lavandería _____
8. el sótono _____
9. el bar _____
10. el restaurante _____

GROUP II

MATCHING EXERCISE

Write the letter of each picture next to the Spanish word it matches below.

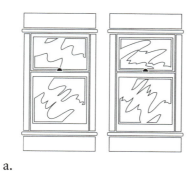

a.

b.

c.

d.

e.

1. _____ el piso
2. _____ el corredor
3. _____ la alfombra
4. _____ las ventanas
5. _____ la escalera

VOCABULARY EXERCISE

Write the Spanish word for each picture in the space provided.

1. _____

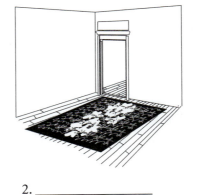

2. _____

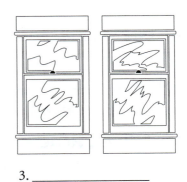

3. _____

4. _____

5. _____

MATCHING EXERCISE

Write the letter of the Spanish word next to the English word it matches on the left.

1. _____ windows   a. el piso

2. _____ stairs   b. la escalera

3. _____ carpet   c. la alfombra

4. _____ floor   d. el corredor

5. _____ hallway   e. las ventanas

TRANSLATION EXERCISE

Translate the following to English:

1. el corredor _____

2. las ventanas _____

3. la escalera _____

4. la alfombra _____

5. el piso _____

Translate the following to Spanish:

1. carpet _____

2. floor _____

3. hallway _____

4. windows _____

5. stairs _____

MULTIPLE CHOICE

Circle the letter of the correct answer.

1. kitchen
   a. el corredor
   b. el cuarto
   c. la cocina
   d. el comedor

2. stairs
   a. la escalera
   b. el corredor
   c. las ventanas
   d. la alfombra

3. basement
   a. el piso
   b. la lavandería
   c. el baño
   d. el sótano

4. floor
   a. el piso
   b. el baño
   c. el bar
   d. el sótano

5. bedroom
   a. la cocina
   b. el cuarto
   c. el corredor
   d. el comedor

6. windows
   a. la escalera
   b. el corredor
   c. las ventanas
   d. la alfombra

7. hallway
   a. la cocina
   b. el cuarto
   c. el corredor
   d. el comedor

8. carpet
   a. la escalera
   b. el corredor
   c. las ventanas
   d. la alfombra

9. bathroom
   a. el piso
   b. la lavandería
   c. el baño
   d. el sótano

10. lobby
   a. el vestíbulo
   b. la lavandería
   c. la oficina
   d. la alfombra

11. dining room
   a. el corredor
   b. el comedor
   c. la cocina
   d. el cuarto

12. laundry room
   a. el vestíbulo
   b. la lavandería
   c. la alfombra
   d. el comedor

CROSSWORD PUZZLES

Across

2. baño
5. sótano
6. piso
7. escalera
9. ventanas
10. lavandería

Down

1. cocina
2. cuarto
3. corredor
4. alfombra
8. bar
10. vestíbulo
11. comedor
12. restaurante
13. oficina

Across

4. laundryroom
8. basement
9. dining room
11. bar
13. office
14. windows

Down

1. bathroom
2. bedroom
3. floor
5. carpet
6. bar
7. lobby
10. stairs
12. kitchen

GRAMMAR: WHERE IS. . . ?

To ask where someone or something is located use the expression, *¿Dónde está?* Study the examples.

Where is Javier?	**¿Dónde está Javier?**
Javier is in the office.	**Javier está en la oficina.**
Where is Matt?	**¿Dónde está Matt?**
Matt is in the bar.	**Matt está en el bar.**
Where is María?	**¿Dónde está María?**
María is in the restaurant.	**María está en el restaurante.**

ROLE PLAY

Where is. . . ? Pretend that there is a problem and you need to find one of your employees to fix it. Working with a partner ask and answer where the following employees are. Follow the model.

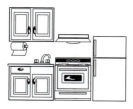

Juan

ESTUDIANTE A   ¿Dónde está Juan?

ESTUDIANTE B   Juan está en la cocina.

1. Beth

2. Arturo

3. José Angel

4. Jennifer

5. Lupe

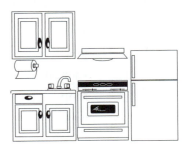

6. Roberto

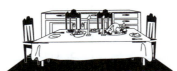

7. Bill

8. Steve

9. Jesús

10. Kathy

PART I—ACTIONS TO USE WITH PLACES

vacuum	**aspira**		sweep	**barre**
mop	**trapea**		polish	**pule**
wax	**cera**			

MATCHING EXERCISE

Write the letter of the Spanish word next to the English word it matches on the left.

1. _____ sweep   a. cera
2. _____ polish   b. trapea
3. _____ vacuum   c. pule
4. _____ mop   d. aspira
5. _____ wax   e. barre

TRANSLATION EXERCISE

Translate the following to Spanish:

1. mop _____
2. sweep _____
3. wax _____
4. vacuum _____
5. polish _____

Translate the following to English:

1. pule _____
2. trapea _____
3. barre _____
4. aspira _____
5. cera _____

MULTIPLE CHOICE

Circle the letter of the correct answer.

1. polish
- a. cera
- b. trapea
- c. pule
- d. aspira

2. mop
- a. pule
- b. trapea
- c. barre
- d. aspira

3. sweep
- a. barre
- b. aspira
- c. trapea
- d. pule

4. wax
- a. trapea
- b. barre
- c. aspira
- d. cera

5. vacuum
- a. trapea
- b. aspira
- c. barre
- d. cera

TRANSLATION EXERCISE

Translate the following to English:

1. Barre la oficina. _____

2. Aspira el cuarto. _____

3. Pule el piso. _____

4. Trapea la lavandería. _____

5. Barre el bar. _____

6. Aspira el comedor. _____

7. Pule la escalera. _____

8. Trapea la cocina. _____

9. Cera el corredor. _____

10. Aspira el vestíbulo. _____

11. Pule el comedor. _____

12. Barre el restaurante. _____

13. Trapea el sótano. _____

14. Cera el piso. _____

15. Aspira la alfombra. _____

Translate the following to Spanish:

1. Vacuum the dining room. _____

2. Sweep the floor. _____

3. Mop the kitchen. _____

4. Wax the hallway. _____

5. Polish the stairway. _____

6. Vacuum the lobby. _____

7. Mop the basement. _____

8. Wax the floor. _____

9. Sweep the bar. _____

10. Vacuum the carpet. _____

11. Polish the windows. _____

12. Mop the laundry room. _____

13. Polish the floor. _____

14. Vacuum the bedroom. _____

15. Sweep the office. _____

PART II—THE BEDROOM AND BATHROOM

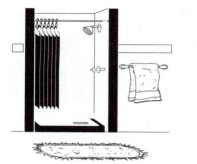

shower
la ducha

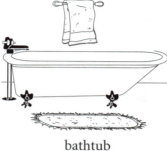

bathtub
la tina

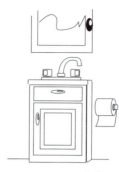

sink
la lavamanos

mirror
el espejo

toilet
el inodoro

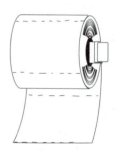

toilet paper
el papel de baño

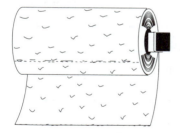

paper towels
las toallas de papel

furniture
los muebles

closet
el closet

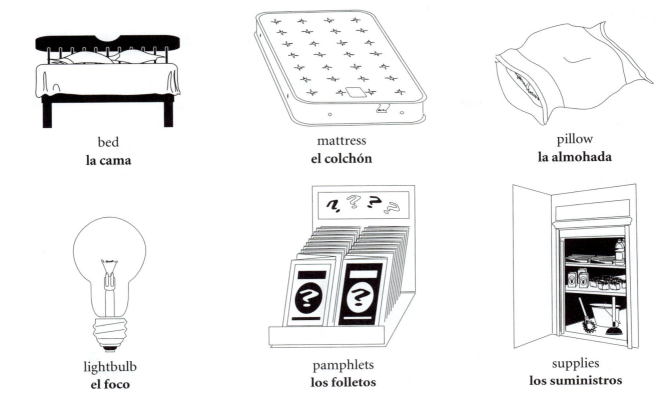

bed
la cama

mattress
el colchón

pillow
la almohada

lightbulb
el foco

pamphlets
los folletos

supplies
los suministros

GROUP I

shower	**la ducha**	toilet	**el inodoro**
bathtub	**la tina**	toilet paper	**el papel de baño**
sink	**la lavamanos**	paper towels	**las toallas de papel**
mirror	**el espejo**		

GROUP II

furniture	**los muebles**	pillow	**la almohada**
closet	**el closet**	lightbulb	**el foco**
bed	**la cama**	pamphlets	**los folletos**
mattress	**el colchón**	supplies	**los suministros**

COGNATES

Bible	**La Biblia**	lamp	**la lámpara**
shampoo	**el champú**	television	**la televisión**
conditioner	**el condicionador**	radio	**la radio**
lotion	**la loción**	directory	**el directorio**

GROUP I

MATCHING EXERCISE

Write the letter of each picture next to the Spanish word it matches below.

a.

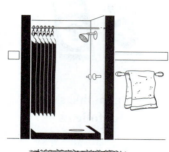
b.

c.

d.

e.

f.

g.

1. _____ las toallas de papel
2. _____ el papel de baño
3. _____ el inodoro
4. _____ el espejo
5. _____ la lavamanos
6. _____ la tina
7. _____ la ducha

VOCABULARY EXERCISE

Write the Spanish word for each picture in the space provided.

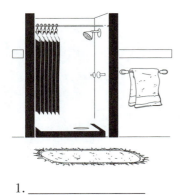

1. _____

2. _____

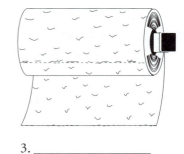

3. _____

4. _____

5. _____

6. _____

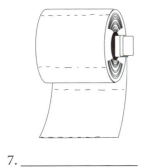

7. _____

MATCHING EXERCISE

Write the letter of the Spanish word next to the English word it matches on the left.

1. _____ mirror
2. _____ toilet
3. _____ shower
4. _____ bathtub
5. _____ toilet paper
6. _____ sink
7. _____ paper towels

a. la tina
b. la lavamanos
c. el inodoro
d. las toallas de papel
e. el papel de baño
f. el espejo
g. la ducha

TRANSLATION EXERCISE

Translate the following to English:

1. las toallas de papel_____
2. la ducha _____
3. el papel de baño_____
4. la tina _____
5. el inodoro _____
6. el espejo_____
7. la lavamanos _____

Translate the following to Spanish:

1. paper towels _____
2. sink _____
3. shower _____
4. bathtub _____
5. toilet _____
6. toilet paper _____
7. mirror _____

GROUP II

MATCHING EXERCISE

Write the letter of each picture next to the Spanish word it matches below.

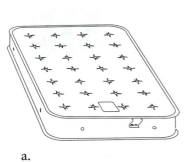

a.

b.

c.

d.

e.

f.

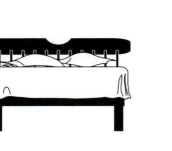

g.

h.

1. _____ los suministros
2. _____ la cama
3. _____ el colchón
4. _____ los folletos
5. _____ el foco
6. _____ la almohada
7. _____ el closet
8. _____ los muebles

VOCABULARY EXERCISE

Write the Spanish word for each picture in the space provided.

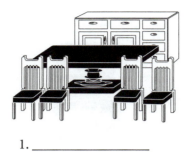

1. _____

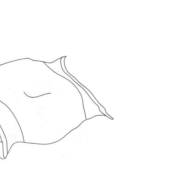

2. _____

3. _____

4. _____

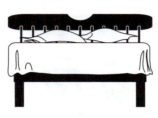

5. _____

6. _____

7. _____

8. _____

MATCHING EXERCISE

Write the letter of the Spanish word next to the English word it matches on the left.

1. _____ furniture
2. _____ closet
3. _____ supplies
4. _____ pamphlets
5. _____ light bulb
6. _____ pillow
7. _____ mattress
8. _____ bed

a. la cama
b. los folletos
c. el foco
d. la almohada
e. el colchón
f. los muebles
g. el closet
h. los suministros

TRANSLATION EXERCISE

Translate the following to English:

1. la almohada _____
2. el foco _____
3. los suministros _____
4. el colchón _____
5. la cama _____
6. los folletos _____
7. el closet _____
8. los muebles _____

Translate the following to Spanish:

1. supplies _____
2. light bulb _____
3. furniture _____
4. pamphlets _____
5. closet _____
6. bed _____
7. mattress _____
8. pillow _____

MULTIPLE CHOICE

Circle the letter of the correct answer.

1. paper towels
   a. las toallas de papel
   b. los suministros
   c. los folletos
   d. los muebles

2. toilet
   a. la ducha
   b. el espejo
   c. la tina
   d. el inodoro

3. bed
   a. la almohada
   b. la cama
   c. el foco
   d. el colchón

4. furniture
   a. la almohada
   b. los suministros
   c. los folletos
   d. los muebles

5. bathtub
   a. la ducha
   b. el espejo
   c. la tina
   d. el inodoro

6. toilet paper
   a. el papel de baño
   b. las toallas de papel
   c. los suministros
   d. la tina

7. **supplies**
   a. los folletos
   b. los muebles
   c. los suministros
   d. las toallas de papel

8. **light bulb**
   a. el foco
   b. la tina
   c. la cama
   d. la lavamanos

9. **sink**
   a. el foco
   b. la tina
   c. la cama
   d. la lavamanos

10. **shower**
    a. la ducha
    b. el espejo
    c. la tina
    d. el inodoro

11. **pamphlets**
    a. los folletos
    b. los muebles
    c. las toallas de papel
    d. los suministros

12. **mirror**
    a. la ducha
    b. el espejo
    c. la tina
    d. el inodoro

CROSSWORD PUZZLES

Across

1. suministros
9. papel de baño
11. inodoro
12. espejo
14. muebles

Down

2. toallas de papel
3. ducha
4. colchón
5. foco
6. cama
7. closet
8. tina
10. folletos
13. lavamanos

Across

4. mirror
6. paper towels
11. toilet
12. bed
14. pamphlets

Down

1. sink
2. pillow
3. toilet paper
5. supplies
6. bathtub
7. shower
8. closet
9. mattress
10. light bulb
13. furniture

PART II—ACTIONS TO USE WITH THE BEDROOM AND BATHROOM

wash	lava	dust	desempolva
clean	limpia	put (arrange)	coloca
scrub	restrega		

MATCHING EXERCISE

Write the letter of the Spanish word next to the English word it matches on the left.

1. _____ wash   a. limpia
2. _____ scrub   b. desempolva
3. _____ clean   c. coloca
4. _____ put, arrange   d. lava
5. _____ dust   e. restrega

TRANSLATION EXERCISE

Translate the following to English:

1. coloca _____
2. desempolva _____
3. lava _____
4. restrega _____
5. limpia _____

Translate the following to Spanish:

1. dust _____
2. scrub _____
3. wash _____
4. put, arrange _____
5. clean _____

MULTIPLE CHOICE

Circle the letter of the correct answer.

1. dust
   a. restrega
   b. lava
   c. desempolva
   d. coloca

2. put, arrange
   a. limpia
   b. coloca
   c. restrega
   d. lava

3. wash
   a. lava
   b. limpia
   c. coloca
   d. restrega

4. scrub
   a. restrega
   b. lava
   c. desempolva
   d. coloca

5. clean
   a. desempolva
   b. coloca
   c. lava
   d. limpia

CROSSWORD PUZZLES

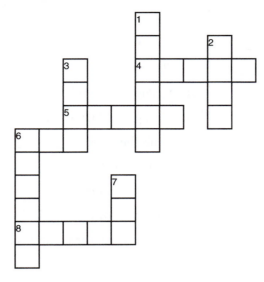

Across

4. limpia
5. restrega
6. pon
8. barre

Down

1. aspira
2. lava
3. desempolva
6. pule
7. trapea

Across

1. vacuum
5. polish
7. dust
9. sweep

Down

2. put
3. scrub
4. mop
6. clean
8. wash

Translate the following to English:

1. Restrega la ducha. _____

2. Desempolva el espejo. _____

3. Coloca los suministros. _____

4. Lava la lavamanos. _____

5. Coloca el papel de baño. _____

6. Restrega el inodoro. _____

7. Coloca los folletos. _____

8. Desempolva los muebles. _____

9. Restrega la tina. _____

10. Lava el espejo. _____

11. Coloca el colchón. _____

12. Limpia el closet. _____

13. Desempolva la cama. _____

14. Restrega la lavamanos. _____

15. Coloca las toallas de papel. _____

Translate the following to Spanish:

1. Dust the furniture. _____

2. Wash the mirror. _____

3. Clean the sink. _____

4. Arrange the supplies. _____

5. Arrange the furniture. _____

6. Scrub the toilet. _____

7. Dust the bed. _____

8. Clean the closet. _____

9. Put paper towels. _____

10. Put (arrange) the pamphlets. _____

11. Scrub the bathtub. _____

12. Dust the mirror. _____

13. Put toilet paper. _____

14. Put the lightbulb. _____

15. Scrub the shower. _____

ROOM STATUS CODES

CÓDIGOS DEL ESTADO DE LAS HABITACIONES

VR	Vacant and Ready	**Libre y lista**
VC	Vacant and Clean	**Libre y limpia**
VD	Vacant and Dirty	**Libre y sucia**
OR	Occupied and Ready	**Ocupada y lista**
OC	Occupied and Clean	**Ocupada y limpia**
OD	Occupied and Dirty	**Ocupada y sucia**
CO	Check-Out	**Salida del hotel**
OO	Out of Order	**Fuera de servicio**
DND	Do Not Disturb	**No molestar**
V/O OR O/V	Status Unclear	**Estado indefinido**

vacant	**libre**		Check-Out	**Salida del hotel**
occupied	**ocupada**		Out of Order	**Fuera de servicio**
ready	**lista**		Do Not Disturb	**No molestar**
clean	**limpia**		Status Unclear	**Estado indefinido**
dirty	**sucia**			

MATCHING EXERCISE

Write the letter of the Spanish word next to the English word it matches on the left.

1. _____ occupied
2. _____ dirty
3. _____ ready
4. _____ Check-Out
5. _____ vacant
6. _____ Out of Order
7. _____ clean
8. _____ Do Not Disturb
9. _____ Status Unclear

a. limpia
b. Fuera de servicio
c. libre
d. No molestar
e. ocupada
f. Estado indefinido
g. lista
h. sucia
i. Salida del hotel

TRANSLATION EXERCISE

Translate the following to English:

1. Fuera de servicio _____
2. lista _____
3. ocupada _____
4. Salida del hotel _____
5. sucia _____
6. No molestar _____
7. libre _____
8. Fuera de servicio _____
9. limpia _____

Translate the following to Spanish:

1. vacant _____
2. occupied _____
3. out of order _____
4. Do Not Disturb _____
5. clean _____
6. dirty _____
7. Status Unclear _____
8. Check-Out _____
9. ready _____

DIALOGUE

Read the dialogue aloud. Then translate it to English.

Recepcionista:	¡Bienvenidos al Royalty Hotel!
Sra. Baker:	Gracias.
Recepcionista:	¿Es su familia?
Sra. Baker:	Sí. Quiero presentarle a mi esposa, Barbara.
Recepcionista:	Mucho gusto.
Sra. Baker:	Igualmente.
Recepcionista:	¿Y sus hijos?
Sr. Baker:	Sí. . . Bobby tiene trece años y Beth tiene diez y seis años.
Beth:	Hola. ¿Hay champú, condicionador y loción en el cuarto?
Recepcionista:	Sí. Y un teléfono. Y hay una televisión para su hermano.
Carlos:	Hola, soy Carlos, el botones. ¿Puedo ayudarles?
Sr. Baker:	¡Fantastico! Sí. . . ayúdeme, por favor.
Carlos:	Ven conmigo, Señor Baker.
Sr. Baker:	¡Usted. es muy fuerte!
Carlos:	El cuarto número 523 está al final del corredor.
Sr. Baker:	¿Para el jueves, viernes y sábado?
Carlos:	Sí, está correcto . . . tres días y dos noches.
Sr. Baker:	Buen trabajo, Carlos.
(Le da una propina)	
Carlos:	Gracias, Señor Baker. Hasta luego.
Sra. Baker:	¡A la cama! Estoy muy cansada.
Bobby:	¡Excelente! Hay muchas almohadas.
Beth:	¡Y muchos suministros en el baño!
Sra. Baker:	¿Qué hay?
Beth:	Hay champú, condicionador, loción . . .
Sr. Baker:	Aquí es la Biblia y hay folletos y el directorio del hotel.
Sra. Baker:	Me gusta leer y no hay un foco en la lámpara.
Bobby:	¡Pero todo lo demás está perfecto!
Sr. Baker:	Hay muchas actividades en el directorio.
Bobby:	¿Qué deportes hay?
Sr. Baker:	Puedes nadar, pescar, jugar volibol, tennis . . .
Beth:	¡Me encanta jugar al volibol! ¿Cuándo es?
Sr. Baker:	El viernes por la noche y el sábado y el domingo por las tardes.
Sra. Baker:	Primero . . . ¡al restaurante!
Mr. Baker:	¿Dónde está?

Mrs. Baker:	Está al final del corredor al lado del bar.
Alberto:	Buenos días. Soy Alberto, el supervisor.
Juana:	Buenos días, señor. Mucho gusto.
Alberto:	¿Es su primer día en el Royalty Hotel?
Juana:	Mi segundo. ¡Estoy nerviosa y preocupada!
Alberto:	Primero, Juana, quiero presentarle a muchas personas en el hotel.
Juana:	Está bien.
Alberto:	Ven conmigo a la cocina y al restaurante.

(En la cocina)

Alberto:	Mike, quiero presentarle a la camarista.
Mike:	Hola. ¿Cómo te llamas?
Juana:	Me llamo Juana.
Mike:	*¿Juana, La Cubana?*
Juana:	¡Eres cómico! ¡Es una canción! Soy mejicana.
Raul:	Hola, soy Raúl, el lavaplatos.
Roberto:	Hola, Juana. Bienvenido. Soy Roberto, el cocinero.
Alberto:	¿Dónde está el cantinero?
Roberto:	Kevin está en el comedor con los meseros.
Alberto:	Muy bien. Ven conmigo, Juana.

(Un poco más tarde)

Alberto:	Primero, limpia el baño, por favor.
Juana:	Increíble. . .
Alberto:	Sí es horrible, ¿no? Lava la ducha . . .
Juana:	¿Y la tina y la lavamanos?
Alberto:	Sí. . . y restrega el inodoro.
Juana:	Está bien.
Alberto:	Segundo, limpia el cuarto y desempolva los muebles.
Juana:	¿Y la televisión, la lámpara, y el teléfono?
Alberto:	Sí, aspira la alfombra, por favor.
Juana:	Está bien.
Alberto:	Coloca los folletos y suministros.
Juana:	¿Y limpio las ventanas y los espejos?
Alberto:	Sí gracias, Juana. Eres muy trabajadora.
Juana:	Hasta luego, señor.

(Alberto sale.)

Juana:	¡Estoy cansada! . . . Una cama. . . una almohada. . .

Read the dialogue aloud. Then translate it to Spanish.

Receptionist:	Welcome to the Royalty Hotel!
Mr. Baker:	Thank you.
Receptionist:	Is this your family?
Mr. Baker:	Yes. I'd like to introduce you to my wife, Barbara.
Receptionist:	Nice to meet you.
Barbara:	Same to you.
Receptionist:	And your children?
Mr. Baker:	Yes. . . Bobby is thirteen years old and Beth is sixteen.
Beth:	Hi. Is there shampoo, conditioner, and lotion in the room?
Receptionist:	Yes. And a telephone. And there is a television for your brother.
Carlos:	Hello, I'm Carlos, the bellhop. ¿Can I help you?
Mr. Baker:	Fantastic! Yes. . . help me, please.
Carlos:	Come with me, Mr. Baker.
Mr. Baker:	You are very strong!
Carlos:	Room number 523 is at the end of the corridor.
Mr. Baker:	For Thursday, Friday, and Saturday?
Carlos:	Yes, correct. . . three days and two nights.
Mr. Baker:	Good work, Carlos.
(He gives him a tip)	
Carlos:	Thank you, Mr. Baker. See you later.
Barbara:	To bed! I'm very tired.
Bobby:	Excellent! There are many pillows.
Beth:	And many supplies in the bathroom!
Mrs. Baker:	What is there?
Beth:	There is shampoo, conditioner, lotion. . .
Mr. Baker:	Here is the Bible and there are pamphlets and the hotel directory.
Barbara:	I like to read and there is no light bulb in the lamp.
Bobby:	But everything else is perfect!
Mr. Baker:	There are many activities in the hotel directory.
Bobby:	What sports are there?
Mr. Baker:	You can swim, fish, play volleyball, tennis. . .
Beth:	I love to play volleyball! When is it?
Mr. Baker:	Friday night and Saturday and Sunday afternoons.
Barbara:	First. . . to the restaurant.
Mr. Baker:	Where is it?

Barbara:	At the end of the hallway next to the bar.
Alberto:	Good morning. I'm Alberto, the supervisor.
Juana:	Good morning, sir. Nice to meet you.
Alberto:	Is this your first day at the Royalty Hotel?
Juana:	My second. I'm nervous and worried.
Alberto:	First, Juana, I want to introduce you to many people at the hotel.
Juana:	Okay.
Alberto:	Come with me to the kitchen and to the restaurant.

(In the kitchen)

Alberto:	Mike, I want to introduce you to the housekeeper.
Mike:	Hello. What's your name?
Juana:	My name is Juana.
Mike:	*Juana, La Cubana*?
Juana:	You are comical. It's a song! I'm Mexican.
Raul:	Hi, I'm Raul, the dishwasher.
Roberto:	Hi, Juana. Welcome. I'm Roberto, the cook.
Alberto:	Where is the bartender?
Roberto:	Kevin is in the dining room with the servers.
Alberto:	Very good. Come with me, Juana.

(A little later)

Alberto:	First, clean the bathroom, please.
Juana:	Incredible. . .
Alberto:	Yes, it's horrible, isn't it? Wash the shower. . .
Juana:	And the bathtub and sink?
Alberto:	Yes. . . and scrub the toilet.
Juana:	Okay.
Alberto:	Second, clean the bedroom and dust the furniture.
Juana:	And the television, lamp, and telephone?
Alberto:	Yes, vacuum the carpet, please.
Juana:	Okay.
Alberto:	Arrange the pamphlets and the supplies.
Juana:	And clean the windows and the mirrors?
Alberto:	Yes, thank you, Juana. You are a hard worker!
Juana:	See you later, sir.

(Alberto leaves.)

Juana:	I'm tired! . . . a bed. . . a pillow. . .

REVIEW

Translate the following to Spanish.

1. Sunday, Monday, Tuesday _____

2. April, May, June _____

3. You are very kind. _____

4. It's five o'clock. _____

5. There is pizza _____

6. There is no salad. _____

7. Where are you from? _____

8. I'd like to introduce you to _____

9. Come with me. _____

10. Watch me. _____

11. You're a hard worker! _____

12. Good work! _____

13. The manager is in a good mood. _____

14. The cook is furious! _____

15. Where is the housekeeper? _____

16. Where, When, With whom _____

17. I like to play golf. _____

18. I do not like to watch televison. _____

19. Do you like to swim? _____

20. Do you like to play soccer? _____

CULTURE: COMMUNICATION STYLES

In Latino cultures, yes may mean yes, maybe or even no. Latinos do not always say what they mean or mean precisely what they say. Latinos tend to hint, suggest or recommend rather than come out and say what they think. One can't always tell it like it is and be so blunt because that may upset the other person. In the Latino culture, as in many other cultures, saving face is important. All answers are given in order to avoid hurt feelings. As a result of this, evasive, half answers and "white lies" are common responses. These answers can be very confusing and problematic to a United States supervisor who has been raised to be open, direct, and above all honest, in workplace situations.

Maintaining harmony and saving face are key issues in the Latino society. The truth, if it would harm a relationship or cause a person to lose face, should be changed a bit. Often a Latino tells his supervisor what he thinks his supervisor wants to hear. It's not always appropriate to disagree, challenge, or say no to one's supervisor. Protecting and reinforcing the personal relationship and bond is the goal of the communication process.

In the United States, yes means yes and no means no. Supervisors say what they mean and mean what they say. One does not need to read into what is said. In the United States it's important to "tell it like it is." Supervisors are less likely to imply and tend to state specifically what they think. A Latino woman interested in the communication field considers people in the United States blunt.

In the United States telling, the truth is valued more highly than sparing a person's feelings. The phrase "Honesty is the best policy" is so common in the United States society that it was the easiest $100 question on the television show, *Who Wants to be a Millionaire*! Giving and receiving information efficiently is the main goal of the communication process. It's okay in the United States to disagree and to challenge your boss or coworkers.

If Latinos make a mistake, it is important for them to understand that they do not lose face with their supervisor, if they admit the truth. More likely, they will lose that respect if they don't admit it and the mistake is found out later.

In order to get at the truth, it is important to have a good, trusting relationship with your Latino coworkers. A United States supervisor must be aware that a Latino will not open up to people with whom he is not close. Once that bond exists, supervisors find that their Latino coworkers become more open and direct with their answers.

RELATIONSHIP TIP

In order for Spanish speaking employees to keep current with the news in their countries, it would be good to order them a subscription to their countries' daily newspapers. The Mexican newspaper, *La Prensa,* can be found at www.laprensa.com.

7

The Laundry Room

PART I—LINENS

linens
la ropa

soiled linens
la ropa sucia

sheet
la sábana

pillowcase
la funda

towel
la toalla

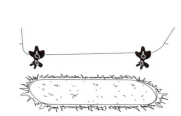

bathmats
el tapete de baño

tablecloth
el mantel

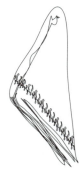

napkin
las servilleta

blanket
la manta

mattress pad
el protector de colchón

spread
la colcha

stain
la mancha

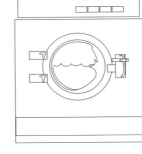

washer
la máquina

dryer
la secadora

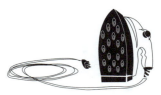

iron
la plancha

GROUP I

linens	la ropa	**towel**	la toalla
soiled linens	la ropa sucia	**bathmats**	el tapete de baño
sheet	la sábana	**tablecloth**	el mantel
pillowcase	la funda	**napkin**	las servilleta

GROUP II

blanket	la manta	**washer**	la máquina
mattress pad	el protector de colchón	**dryer**	la secadora
spread	la colcha	**iron**	la plancha
stain	la mancha		

GROUP I

MATCHING EXERCISE

Write the letter of each picture next to the Spanish word it matches below.

a.

b.

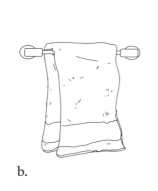

c.

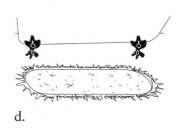

d.

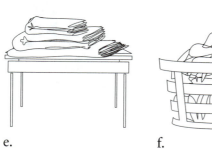

e.

f.

g.

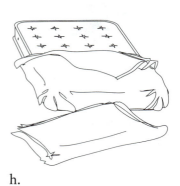

h.

1. _____ la ropa

2. _____ la toalla

3. _____ la funda

4. _____ la ropa sucia

5. _____ el tapete de baño

6. _____ el mantel

7. _____ la servilleta

8. _____ la sábana

VOCABULARY EXERCISE

Write the Spanish word for each picture in the space provided.

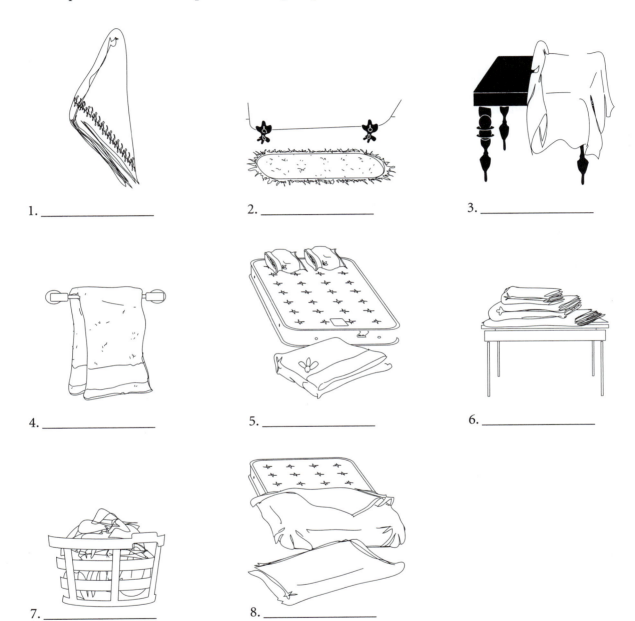

1. _____

2. _____

3. _____

4. _____

5. _____

6. _____

7. _____

8. _____

MATCHING EXERCISE

Write the letter of the Spanish word next to the English word it matches on the left.

1. _____ pillowcase
2. _____ sheet
3. _____ linens
4. _____ towel
5. _____ soiled linens
6. _____ bathmat
7. _____ tablecloth
8. _____ napkin

a. la toalla
b. el tapete de baño
c. la servilleta
d. el mantel
e. la sábana
f. la funda
g. la ropa
h. la ropa sucia

TRANSLATION EXERCISE

Translate the following to English:

1. la toalla _____
2. la servilleta _____
3. la ropa sucia _____
4. la funda _____
5. la ropa _____
6. el tapete de baño _____
7. el mantel _____
8. la sábana _____

Translate the following to Spanish:

1. linens _____
2. soiled linens _____
3. sheet _____
4. pillowcase _____
5. napkin _____
6. tablecloth _____
7. bathmat _____
8. towel _____

GROUP II

MATCHING EXERCISE

Write the letter of each picture next to the Spanish word it matches below.

a.

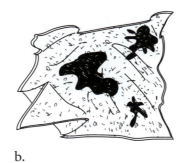

b.

c.

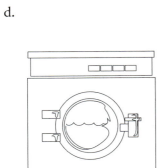

d.

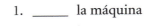

e.

f.

g.

1. _____ la máquina

2. _____ la manta

3. _____ la colcha

4. _____ la secadora

5. _____ la plancha

6. _____ la mancha

7. _____ el protector de colchón

VOCABULARY EXERCISE

Write the Spanish word for each picture in the space provided.

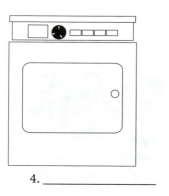

1. _____

2. _____

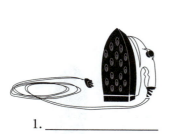

3. _____

4. _____

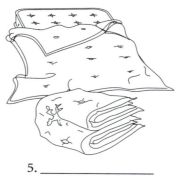

5. _____

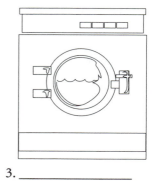

6. _____

7. _____

MATCHING EXERCISE

Write the letter of the Spanish word next to the English word it matches on the left.

1. _____ spread   a. la secadora
2. _____ mattress pad   b. la colcha
3. _____ blanket   c. la manta
4. _____ stain   d. el protector de colchón
5. _____ iron   e. la mancha
6. _____ washer   f. la plancha
7. _____ dryer   g. la máquina

TRANSLATION EXERCISE

Translate the following to English:

1. la mancha _____
2. la máquina _____
3. la manta _____
4. la secadora _____
5. la plancha _____
6. el protector de colchón _____
7. la colcha _____

Translate the following to Spanish:

1. dryer _____
2. spread _____
3. blanket _____
4. washer _____
5. iron _____
6. stain _____
7. mattress pad _____

CROSSWORD PUZZLE

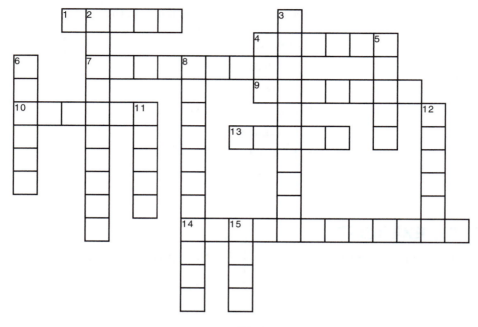

Across

1. mancha
4. ropa
7. tapete de baño
9. manta
10. colcha
13. toalla
14. ropa sucia

Down

2. mantel
3. funda
5. sábana
6. máquina
8. protector de colchón
11. secadora
12. servilleta
15. plancha

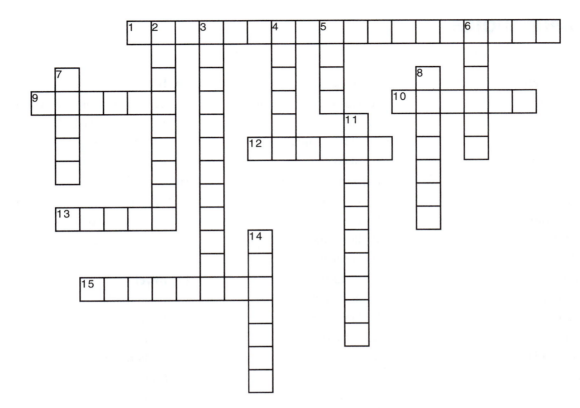

Across

1. mattress pad
9. sheet
10. stain
12. tablecloth
13. pillowcase
15. dryer

Down

2. soiled linens
3. bathmat
4. towel
5. linen
6. spread
7. blanket
8. washer
11. napkin
14. iron

MULTIPLE CHOICE

Circle the letter of the correct answer.

1. soiled linens
   a. la ropa
   b. la mancha
   c. la ropa sucia
   d. la máquina

2. sheet
   a. la sábana
   b. la secadora
   c. la funda
   d. la servilleta

3. pillowcase
   a. la manta
   b. la plancha
   c. la ropa
   d. la funda

4. stain
   a. la mancha
   b. la plancha
   c. la ropa
   d. la funda

5. mattress pad
   a. el protector de colchón
   b. el tapete de baño
   c. la ropa sucia
   d. la colcha

6. napkin
   a. la sábana
   b. la secadora
   c. la funda
   d. la servilleta

7. tablecloth
   a. la mancha
   b. la manta
   c. la máquina
   d. la funda

8. linens
   a. la sábana
   b. la ropa
   c. la funda
   d. la plancha

9. bathmat
   a. el protector de colchón
   b. el tapete de baño
   c. la ropa sucia
   d. la colcha

10. spread
   a. el protector de colchón
   b. el tapete de baño
   c. la ropa sucia
   d. la colcha

11. towel
   a. la toalla
   b. la funda
   c. la colcha
   d. la manta

12. blanket
   a. la funda
   b. la mancha
   c. la manta
   d. la colcha

GRAMMAR

To express the plural (more than one item) add 's' or 'es' to the end of the word. If the word ends in 'o' or 'a' add 's'. If the word ends in any other letter add 'es'. Study the examples.

the towel	**la toalla**
the towels	**las toallas**
the tablecloth	**el mantel**
the tableclothes	**los manteles**

Make the following words plural.

1. la funda _____

2. la colcha _____

3. el protector _____

4. la manta _____

5. la servilleta _____

6. el mantel _____

7. la sábana _____

8. el tapete _____

9. la toalla _____

10. la secadora _____

PART I—ACTIONS TO USE WITH THE LAUNDRY ROOM

check	checa	**dry**	seca
fold	dobla	**iron**	plancha
wash	lava		

MATCHING EXERCISE

Write the letter of the Spanish word next to the English word it matches on the left.

1. _____ dry   a. dobla
2. _____ wash   b. checa
3. _____ fold   c. seca
4. _____ iron   d. plancha
5. _____ check   e. lava

TRANSLATION EXERCISE

Translate the following to English:

1. lava _____
2. checa _____
3. dobla _____
4. seca _____
5. plancha _____

Translate the following to Spanish:

1. fold _____
2. dry _____
3. iron _____
4. check _____
5. wash _____

MULTIPLE CHOICE

Circle the letter of the correct answer.

1. fold
   a. seca
   b. checa
   c. plancha
   d. dobla

2. wash
   a. lava
   b. dobla
   c. seca
   d. checa

3. iron
   a. seca
   b. checa
   c. plancha
   d. dobla

4. check
   a. lava
   b. dobla
   c. seca
   d. checa

5. dry
   a. seca
   b. checa
   c. plancha
   d. dobla

Translate the following to English:

1. Lava la ropa sucia. _____
2. Checa las manchas. _____
3. Seca las colchas. _____
4. Plancha los manteles. _____
5. Lava las sábanas. _____
6. Dobla las servilletas. _____
7. Seca las toallas. _____
8. Checa los protectores de colchón. _____
9. Plancha las fundas. _____
10. Seca la ropa. _____
11. Dobla las colchas. _____
12. Checa la secadora. _____
13. Lava las toallas. _____
14. Plancha las servilletas. _____
15. Dobla la ropa. _____

Translate the following to Spanish:

1. Wash the towels. _____
2. Fold the napkins. _____
3. Dry the bathmats. _____
4. Check the stains. _____
5. Dry the linens. _____
6. Iron the tablecloths. _____
7. Wash the mattress pad. _____
8. Check the dryers. _____
9. Fold the napkins. _____
10. Wash the pillowcases. _____
11. Check the iron. _____
12. Fold the blanket. _____
13. Dry the spreads. _____
14. Wash the soiled linens. _____
15. Fold the sheets. _____

PART II—CLEANING SUPPLIES

broom
la escoba

bucket
la cubeta

bag
la bolsa

sponge
la esponja

vacuum
la aspiradora

spray
la rociada

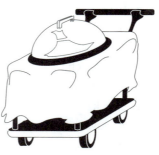

cart
el carrito

gloves
los guantes

rag
el trapo

mop
el trapeador

garbage can
el basurero

scrub brush
el cepillo

scouring pad
el estropajo

polish
el lustrador

bleach
el blanqueador

GROUP I

broom	la escoba	**vacuum**	la aspiradora
bucket	la cubeta	**spray**	la rociada
bag	la bolsa	**cart**	el carrito
sponge	la esponja	**gloves**	los guantes

GROUP II

rag	el trapo	**scouring pad**	el estropajo
mop	el trapeador	**polish**	el lustrador
garbage can	el basurero	**bleach**	el blanqueador
scrub brush	el cepillo		

COGNATE

detergent   detergente

GROUP I

MATCHING EXERCISE

Write the letter of each picture next to the Spanish word it matches below.

 a.

 b.

 c.

 d.

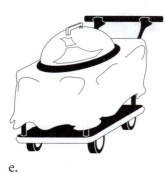 e.

 f.

 g.

h.

1. _____ la esponja
2. _____ los guantes
3. _____ la rociada
4. _____ la bolsa
5. _____ la aspiradora
6. _____ la escoba
7. _____ el carrito
8. _____ la cubeta

VOCABULARY EXERCISE

Write the Spanish word for each picture in the space provided.

1. _____

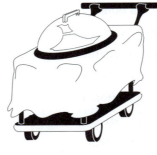

2. _____

3. _____

4. _____

5. _____

6. _____

7. _____

8. _____

MATCHING EXERCISE

Write the letter of the Spanish word next to the English word it matches on the left.

1. _____ gloves
2. _____ cart
3. _____ spray
4. _____ broom
5. _____ bucket
6. _____ sponge
7. _____ bag
8. _____ vacuum

a. la bolsa
b. la aspiradora
c. los guantes
d. la rociada
e. la esponja
f. el carrito
g. la cubeta
h. la escoba

TRANSLATION EXERCISE

Translate the following to English:

1. el carrito _____
2. la rociada _____
3. la esponja _____
4. la cubeta _____
5. la aspiradora _____
6. la bolsa _____
7. los guantes _____
8. la escoba _____

Translate the following to Spanish:

1. gloves _____
2. cart _____
3. bucket _____
4. bag _____
5. broom _____
6. vacuum _____
7. spray _____
8. sponge _____

GROUP II

MATCHING EXERCISE

Write the letter of each picture next to the Spanish word it matches below.

a.   b.   c.   d.

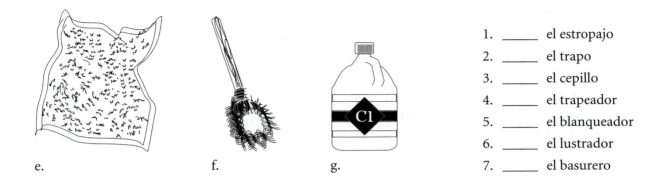

1. _____ el estropajo
2. _____ el trapo
3. _____ el cepillo
4. _____ el trapeador
5. _____ el blanqueador
6. _____ el lustrador
7. _____ el basurero

e.

f.

g.

VOCABULARY EXERCISE

Write the Spanish word for each picture in the space provided.

1. _____

2. _____

3. _____

4. _____

5. _____

6. _____

7. _____

MATCHING EXERCISE

Write the letter of the Spanish word next to the English word it matches on the left.

1. _____ mop
2. _____ scrub brush
3. _____ rag
4. _____ bleach
5. _____ garbage can
6. _____ scouring pad
7. _____ polish

a. el trapo
b. el basurero
c. el lustrador
d. el cepillo
e. el estropajo
f. el trapeador
g. el blanqueador

TRANSLATION EXERCISE

Translate the following to English:

1. el cepillo _____
2. el trapo _____
3. el blanqueador _____
4. el lustrador _____
5. el basurero _____
6. el trapeador _____
7. el estropajo _____

Translate the following to Spanish:

1. mop _____
2. bleach _____
3. polish _____
4. scouring pad _____
5. scrub brush _____
6. rag _____
7. garbage can _____

MULTIPLE CHOICE

Circle the letter of the correct answer.

1. bag
a. la escoba
b. la bolsa
c. la cubeta
d. el trapeador

2. broom
a. la escoba
b. la bolsa
c. la cubeta
d. el trapeador

3. vacuum
a. la aspiradora
b. la rociada
c. el blanqueador
d. el lustrador

4. mop
a. la escoba
b. la bolsa
c. la cubeta
d. el trapeador

5. bleach
a. la aspiradora
b. la rociada
c. el blanqueador
d. el lustrador

6. cart
a. los guantes
b. el carrito
c. el basurero
d. el cepillo

7. bucket
a. la escoba
b. la bolsa
c. la cubeta
d. el trapeador

8. gloves
a. los guantes
b. el carrito
c. el basurero
d. el cepillo

9. rag
a. el trapo
b. el trapeador
c. la escoba
d. el cepillo

10. scrub brush
   a. el trapo
   b. el trapeador
   c. la escoba
   d. el cepillo

11. garbage can
   a. los guantes
   b. el carrito
   c. el basurero
   d. el cepillo

12. spray
   a. el lustrador
   b. la rociada
   c. la aspiradora
   d. el estropajo

CROSSWORD PUZZLES

Across

   2. trapo
   4. trapeador
   5. lustrador
   7. cepillo
   9. esponja
   10. aspiradora
   11. bolsa
   12. carrito
   13. basurero

Down

   1. blanqueador
   3. guantes
   6. rociada
   7. estropajo
   8. escoba
   11. cubeta

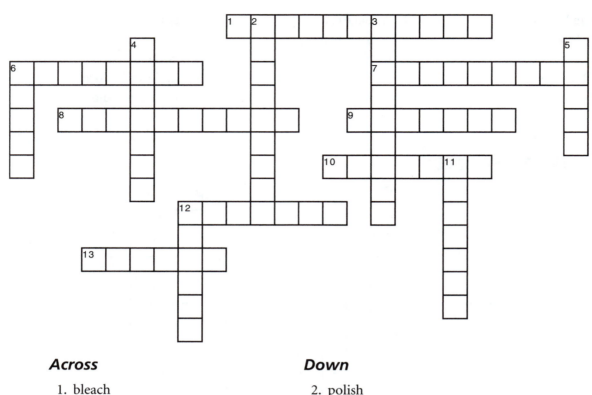

Across

1. bleach
6. garbage can
7. mop
8. vacuum
9. spray
10. gloves
12. cart
13. broom

Down

2. polish
3. scouring pad
4. scrub brush
5. rag
6. bag
11. sponge
12. bucket

GRAMMAR

To express 'Give me' use the Spanish word 'Dame.' Study the examples.

| Give me the bucket. | **Dame la cubeta.** |
| Give me the mop. | **Dame el trapo.** |

To express 'Give it to me' use the following Spanish word:

| Give it to me. | **Dámelo.** (if the item you are referring to ends in-'o') |
| Give it to me. | **Dámela.** (if the item ends in 'a') |

Don't worry too much about if the word ends in –o or –a. Your Latino co-worker will understand what you mean if you use *Dámelo* all the time.

ROLE PLAY

A. Give me the. . . Pretend that there was a big rain storm and the basement in your facility has flooded. Many employees are helping to clean it. Ask your partner to give you a cleaning item using the words '*Dámelo*' or '*Dámela*.' Follow the model.

ESTUDIANTE A:	Dame la cubeta.
ESTUDIANTE B:	¿La cubeta?
ESTUDIANTE A:	Sí. Dámela. Gracias.

1.

2.

3.

4.

5.

6.

7.

8.

9.

10.

PART II—ACTIONS TO USE WITH CLEANING SUPPLIES

bring	trae
get	consigue
use	usa
fill	llena
empty	vacia
give me	dame
give him, her	dale

MATCHING EXERCISE

Write the letter of the Spanish word next to the English word it matches on the left.

1. _____ use
2. _____ empty
3. _____ bring
4. _____ fill
5. _____ get
6. _____ give me

a. trae
b. consigue
c. dame
d. usa
e. llena
f. vacia

TRANSLATION EXERCISE

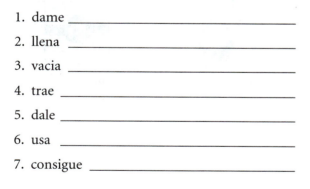

Translate the following to English:

1. dame _____
2. llena _____
3. vacia _____
4. trae _____
5. dale _____
6. usa _____
7. consigue _____

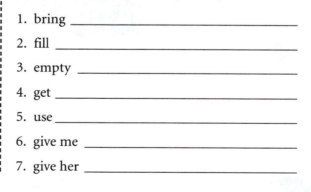

Translate the following to Spanish:

1. bring _____
2. fill _____
3. empty _____
4. get _____
5. use _____
6. give me _____
7. give her _____

MULTIPLE CHOICE

Circle the letter of the correct answer.

1. bring
   a. consigue
   b. vacia
   c. trae
   d. llena

2. give her
   a. dame
   b. dale
   c. vacia
   d. usa

3. fill
   a. usa
   b. vacia
   c. trae
   d. llena

4. get
   a. vacia
   b. consigue
   c. trae
   d. dame

5. empty
   a. usa
   b. vacia
   c. trae
   d. llena

Translate the following to English:

1. Llena la cubeta. _____

2. Usa la escoba. _____

3. Vacia la bolsa. _____

4. Dame la esponja. _____

5. Trae la aspiradora. _____

6. Llena el basurero. _____

7. Consigue el carrito. _____

8. Trae el trapeador. _____

9. Usa los guantes. _____

10. Vacia el basurero. _____

11. Dame el trapo. _____

12. Dale el trapeador. _____

13. Usa el estropajo. _____

14. Trae el blanqueador. _____

15. Consigue el lustrador. _____

Translate the following to Spanish:

1. Bring the cart. _____

2. Give me the vacuum. _____

3. Use the spray. _____

4. Empty the garbage can. _____

5. Bring the broom. _____

6. Get the mop. _____

7. Fill the bucket. _____

8. Give her the scouring pad. _____

9. Get the bucket. _____

10. Give me the gloves. _____

11. Bring the polish. _____

12. Empty the bag. _____

13. Get the bleach. _____

14. Use the polish. _____

15. Fill the cart. _____

DIALOGUE

Read the dialogue aloud. Then translate it to English.

Ana:	Hola. Buenos días.
Marta:	Buenos días, Ana.
Ana:	Hay mucha ropa sucia.
Marta:	¿Dónde?
Ana:	La ropa sucia está por aquí.
Marta:	¿Hay muchas manchas en las servilletas?
Ana:	Sí, y en los manteles.
Marta:	Primero, lava los manteles.
Ana:	¿Y las servilletas?
Marta:	Sí, está correcto.
Ana:	Segundo, checa las sábanas para las manchas.
Marta:	¿Y las fundas?
Ana:	Sí. Y lava las colchas y los protectores de colchón.
Marta:	¿Y las toallas y los tapetes de baño?
Ana:	Sí. . . y por la tarde, seca la ropa.
Marta:	¿Las sábanas, las fundas y las colchas?
Ana:	Sí. . . y plancha las servilletas y los manteles.
Marta:	Está bien.
Ana:	Es importante. Hay una fiesta en el comedor.
Marta:	¿Cuándo es?
Ana:	Mañana. . . El sábado. . . el 24 de mayo.
Marta:	¿A qué hora es la fiesta?
Ana:	A las 6:30 por la noche.
Marta:	Ana, eres muy organizada.
Ana:	No, soy muy nerviosa.
Marta:	Eres muy trabajadora.
Ana:	Marta, por favor, dobla 70 servilletas.
Marta:	¿60?
Ana:	No está correcto. . . 70. ¿Dónde está Peter?
Marta:	¿Quién es Peter? ¿El mesero?

Read the dialogue aloud. Then translate it to Spanish.

(English translation)

Ana:	Hello. Good morning.
Marta:	Good morning, Ana.
Ana:	There are a lot of soiled linens.
Marta:	Where?
Ana:	The soiled linens are around here.
Marta:	Are there a lot of stains on the napkins?
Ana:	Yes, and on the tablecloths.
Marta:	First, wash the tablecloths.
Ana:	And the napkins?
Marta:	Yes, that's correct.
Ana:	Second, check the sheets for stains.
Marta:	And the pillowcases?
Ana:	Yes. And wash the spreads and mattress pads.
Marta:	And the towels and the bathmats?
Ana:	Yes. And in the afternoon, dry the linens.
Marta:	The sheets, pillowcases and the spreads?
Ana:	Yes. . . and iron the napkins and the tablecloths.
Marta:	Okay.
Ana:	It's important. There is a party in the dining room.
Marta:	When is it?
Ana:	Tomorrow. . . Saturday. . . May 24th.
Marta:	What time is the party?
Ana:	6:30 at night.
Marta:	Ana, you are very organized.
Ana:	No, I am very nervous.
Marta:	You are a hard worker.
Ana:	Marta, please, fold 70 napkins.
Marta:	60?
Ana:	That's not correct. . . 70. Where is Peter?
Marta:	Who is Peter? The server?

Ana:	Sí. Dale las servilletas y los manteles.		**Ana:**	Yes. Give him the napkins and the tablecloths.
Marta:	Está bien.		**Marta:**	Okay.
Ana:	Angel es el cantinero y está en el comedor. Dale las toallas.		**Ana:**	Angel is the bartender and is in the dining room. Give him the towels.
Marta:	Hay muchas preparaciónes, ¿no?		**Marta:**	There are a lot of preparations, right?
(Despues de la fiesta)			(After the party)	
Marta:	¡Qué fiesta ayer!		**Marta:**	What a party yesterday!
Ana:	¡Sí! A muchas personas les gustan bailar y escuchar música!		**Ana:**	Yes! Many people like to dance and listen to music.
Marta:	Sí. Y comer y tomar.		**Marta:**	Yes. And eat and drink.
Ana:	¿Te gusta bailar?		**Ana:**	Do you like to dance?
Marta:	Sí. Bailo con mi esposo los sábados por la noche.		**Marta:**	Yes. I dance with my husband on Saturday nights.
Ana:	¿Dónde?		**Ana:**	Where?
Marta:	En un bar con buena música. Se llama *El Club*.		**Marta:**	At a bar with good music. It's called *El Club*.
Ana:	Marta, por favor, primero barre. . .		**Ana:**	Marta, please, first sweep. . .
Marta:	¿El piso y la escalera?		**Marta:**	The floor and the staircase?
Ana:	Sí. La escoba está en el carrito.		**Ana:**	Yes. The broom is on the cart.
Marta:	Segundo, trapea el piso y la escalera.		**Marta:**	Second, mop the floor and the stairs.
Ana:	¿Dónde está el trapeador?		**Ana:**	Where is the mop?
Marta:	En el carrito. Llena la cubeta con el blanquedor y agua.		**Marta:**	On the cart. Fill the bucket with bleach and water.
Ana:	Limpio el baño.		**Ana:**	I am cleaning the bathroom.
Marta:	Está bien. Usa los guantes.		**Marta:**	Okay. Use gloves.
Ana:	Me gusta escuchar música. ¿Hay un radio?		**Ana:**	I like to listen to music. Is there a radio?
Marta:	Sí. ¿Qué programa escuchas?		**Marta:**	Yes. What program do you listen to?
Ana:	Me gusta la música tradicional.		**Ana:**	I like traditional music.

REVIEW

Translate the following to Spanish.

1. Good morning. _____

2. How's it going? _____

3. See you later. _____

4. Wednesday, Thursday, Friday _____

5. There is. . . _____

6. The guest is furious! _____

7. The dishwasher is tired. _____

8. The bellboy is in a bad mood. _____

9. You're very strong! _____

10. It's not correct. _____

11. Everything else is perfect. _____

12. When? Where? With whom? _____

13. How many? _____

14. I like to dance. _____

15. Do you like to play billiards? _____

16. light bulb _____

17. toilet paper _____

18. Wash the mirror. _____

19. Dust the furniture. _____

20. Scrub the shower. _____

CULTURE: TRAINING

Effective training is one of the most crucial and important matters in any organization. In Latin American countries it is highly theoretical and there are few structured training programs. In the United States, however, training programs are organized, specific and very practical. Structured training programs are widely used in successful companies.

When conducting training, an issue to consider is an employee's attitude toward uncertainty. This varies in different cultures. In the United States people do not fear taking a risk or failing. When asked to volunteer in front of a group, many often do. They learn and improve their skills, products and services by trying different techniques and procedures. Training is very practical and hands on.

For the most part, Latinos are receptive and eager to learn new methods and appreciate the opportunity for training very much. During training sessions it is important to remember that in many Latin cultures taking a risk and failing in front of others is to be avoided if at all possible. Ask for a volunteer from a group of Latinos and the majority of heads look down. One doesn't try something new unless he/she knows it works. He/she may feel very unsure of his/her abilities. If a volunteer fails, he/she may not try again. Latinos are very resourceful and have excellent skills. They can, however, become discouraged if they feel that they are being told the only way to do a task is the "American way".

When training and developing an unsure employee in any culture, it is important to build his/her self esteem. Praise the employee every small step of the way so that he/she becomes more self confident in his/her abilities. He/she will perform the task better if he/she is not nervous about making a mistake.

RELATIONSHIP TIP

Have a coat drive at your company—better yet, have a warm clothes drive. In many regions of the United States it is still very cold in March, April, and May, and your employees may not own good, warm winter coats, hats, and gloves.

The Restaurant and Locations

PART I—CHINA AND FLATWARE

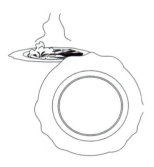

dinner plate
el plato

salad plate
el plato para ensalada

bread plate
el plato para pan

coffee cup
la taza

saucer
el platillo

bowl
el tazón

glass
el vaso

wine glass
la copa

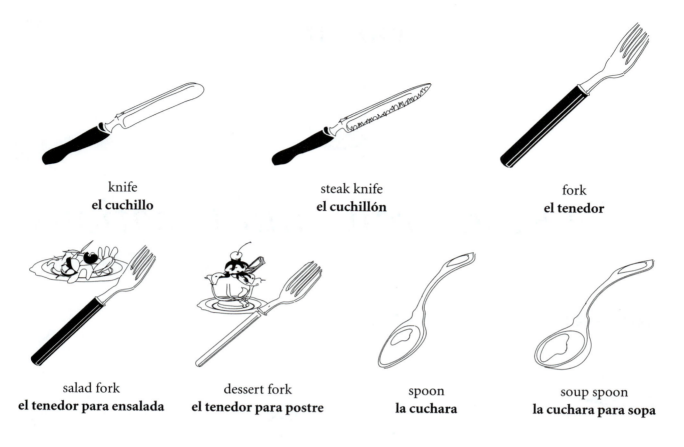

knife
el cuchillo

steak knife
el cuchillón

fork
el tenedor

salad fork
el tenedor para ensalada

dessert fork
el tenedor para postre

spoon
la cuchara

soup spoon
la cuchara para sopa

GROUP I

dinner plate	el plato	**saucer**	el platillo
salad plate	el plato para ensalada	**bowl**	el tazón
bread plate	el plato para pan	**glass**	el vaso
coffee cup	la taza	**wine glass**	la copa

GROUP II

knife	el cuchillo	**dessert fork**	el tenedor para postre
steak knife	el cuchillón	**spoon**	la cuchara
fork	el tenedor	**soup spoon**	la cuchara para sopa
salad fork	el tenedor para ensalada		

ADDITIONAL WORDS

china   la loza
silverware   la cubertería
glassware   la cristalería
linen   la mantelería

GROUP I

MATCHING EXERCISE

Write the letter of each picture next to the Spanish word it matches below.

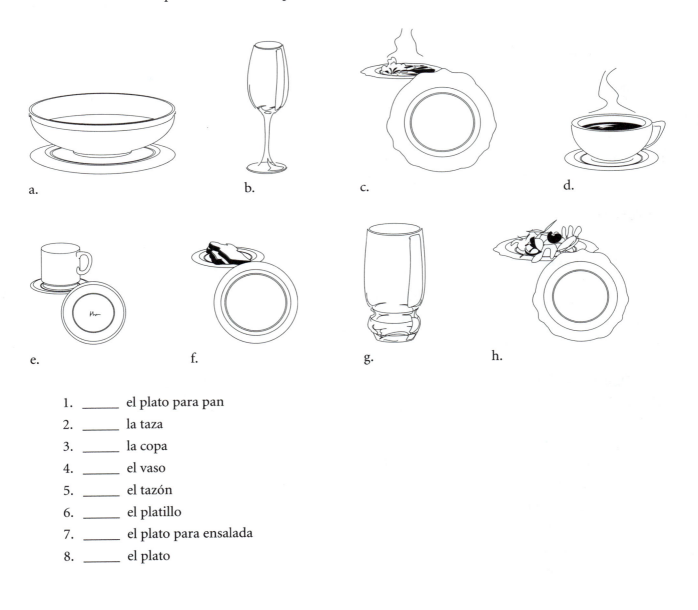

a.   b.   c.   d.

e.   f.   g.   h.

1. _____ el plato para pan
2. _____ la taza
3. _____ la copa
4. _____ el vaso
5. _____ el tazón
6. _____ el platillo
7. _____ el plato para ensalada
8. _____ el plato

VOCABULARY EXERCISE

Write the Spanish word for each picture in the space provided.

1. _____

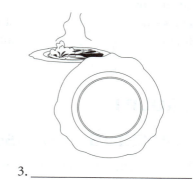

2. _____

3. _____

4. _____

5. _____

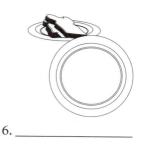

6. _____

7. _____

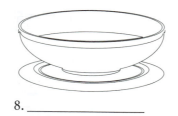

8. _____

MATCHING EXERCISE

Write the letter of the Spanish word next to the English word it matches on the left.

1. _____ wine glass
2. _____ bowl
3. _____ coffee cup
4. _____ salad plate
5. _____ dinner plate
6. _____ saucer
7. _____ glass
8. _____ bread plate

a. el plato
b. la taza
c. el plato para ensalada
d. el platillo
e. el vaso
f. la copa
g. el plato para pan
h. el tazón

TRANSLATION EXERCISE

Translate the following to English:

1. el plato _____

2. el platillo _____

3. el vaso _____

4. la taza _____

5. el plato para pan _____

6. el tazón _____

7. la copa _____

8. el plato para ensalada _____

Translate the following to Spanish:

1. wine glass _____

2. glass _____

3. dinner plate _____

4. bowl _____

5. bread plate _____

6. salad plate _____

7. coffee cup _____

8. saucer _____

GROUP II

MATCHING EXERCISE

Write the letter of each picture next to the Spanish word it matches below.

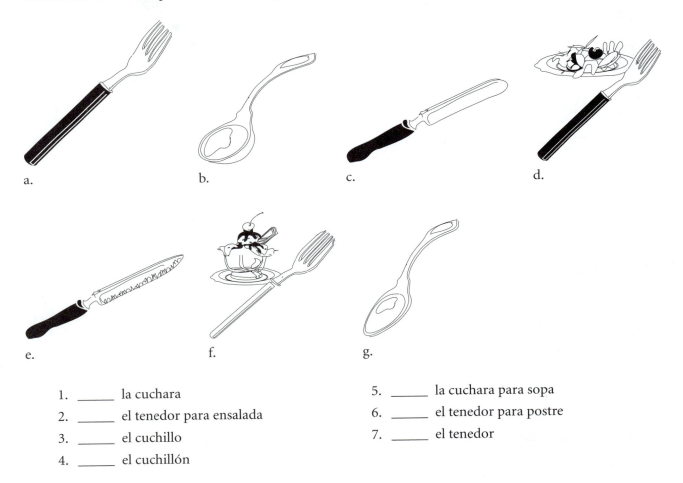

a.   b.   c.   d.

e.   f.   g.

1. _____ la cuchara

2. _____ el tenedor para ensalada

3. _____ el cuchillo

4. _____ el cuchillón

5. _____ la cuchara para sopa

6. _____ el tenedor para postre

7. _____ el tenedor

VOCABULARY EXERCISE

Write the Spanish word for each picture in the space provided.

1. _____

2. _____

3. _____

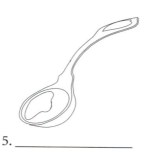

4. _____

5. _____

6. _____

7. _____

MATCHING EXERCISE

Write the letter of the Spanish word next to the English word it matches on the left.

1. _____ la cuchara para sopa   a. knife

2. _____ el tenedor para ensalada   b. steak knife

3. _____ el cuchillo   c. fork

4. _____ el cuchillón   d. salad fork

5. _____ la cuchara   e. dessert fork

6. _____ el tenedor para postre   f. spoon

7. _____ el tenedor   g. soup spoon

TRANSLATION EXERCISE

Translate the following to English:

1. la cuchara _____
2. el tenedor para ensalada _____
3. el cuchillón _____
4. el cuchillo _____
5. el tenedor _____
6. el tenedor para postre _____
7. la cuchara para sopa _____

Translate the following to Spanish:

1. soup spoon _____
2. dessert fork _____
3. steak knife _____
4. fork _____
5. spoon _____
6. dessert fork _____
7. knife _____

MULTIPLE CHOICE

Circle the letter of the correct answer.

1. fork
a. el tenedor
b. el cuchillón
c. la cuchara
d. el cuchillo

2. wine glass
a. la taza
b. el tazón
c. el vaso
d. la copa

3. saucer
a. el plato
b. el platillo
c. la copa
d. la cuchara

4. coffee cup
a. la taza
b. el tazón
c. el vaso
d. la copa

5. spoon
a. el tenedor
b. el cuchillón
c. la cuchara
d. el cuchillo

6. dinner plate
a. el plato
b. el platillo
c. la copa
d. la cuchara

7. bowl
a. la taza
b. el tazón
c. el vaso
d. la copa

8. knife
a. el tenedor
b. el cuchillón
c. la cuchara
d. el cuchillo

9. glass
a. la taza
b. el tazón
c. el vaso
d. la copa

CROSSWORD PUZZLES

Across

2. tazón
3. copa
5. cuchillón
9. tenedor para ensalada
10. cuchara para sopa
12. plato

Down

1. plato para ensalada
2. plato para pan
4. tenedor para postre
6. tenedor
7. taza
8. cuchillo
10. platillo
11. cuchara

Across

2. fork
3. plate
5. cup
6. spoon
8. glass
9. bread plate

Down

1. soup spoon
2. bowl
3. saucer
4. steak knife
6. knife
7. wine glass

ROLE PLAY

I need another. . . It's a graduation celebration and there are lots of guests at the table. As the guests are being seated, many table items drop to the floor. Working with a partner, ask the guest what he/she needs (*¿Qué necesita?*) then tell the guest you will bring it (*Traigo*). Follow the model.

ESTUDIANTE A:	¿Qué necesita?
ESTUDIANTE B:	Necesito_____.
ESTUDIANTE A:	Muy bien. Traigo_____.

1.

2.

3.

4.

5.

6.

7.

8.

9.

10.

11.

12.

13.

PART I—ACTIONS TO USE WITH CHINA AND FLATWARE

stock	surte	polish	pule
wash	lava	use	usa
bring	trae		

MATCHING EXERCISE

Write the letter of the Spanish word next to the English word it matches on the left.

1. _____ bring   a. lava

2. _____ polish   b. usa

3. _____ wash   c. surte

4. _____ stock   d. trae

5. _____ use   e. pule

TRANSLATION EXERCISE

Translate the following to English:

1. lava _____

2. pule _____

3. trae _____

4. usa _____

5. surte _____

Translate the following to Spanish:

1. stock _____

2. polish _____

3. wash _____

4. use _____

5. bring _____

MULTIPLE CHOICE

Circle the letter of the correct answer.

1. stock
  a. pule
  b. surte
  c. trae
  d. lava

2. polish
  a. usa
  b. trae
  c. lava
  d. pule

3. wash
  a. lava
  b. usa
  c. trae
  d. surte

4. use
  a. lava
  b. trae
  c. usa
  d. pule

5. bring
  a. trae
  b. usa
  c. lava
  d. pule

Translate the following to English:

1. Surte las cucharas para sopa. _____

2. Trae los tazones. _____

3. Lava los platos para ensalada. _____

4. Usa los platos. _____

5. Pule los tenedores para postre. _____

6. Surte los platillos. _____

7. Trae las tazas. _____

8. Lava los cuchillones. _____

9. Usa el cuchillo. _____

10. Pule las cucharas. _____

11. Lava los tenedores. _____

12. Trae los platos para el pan. _____

13. Surte los tazones. _____

14. Usa los cuchillones. _____

15. Pule los tenedores para ensalada. _____

Translate the following to Spanish:

1. Wash the dinner plates. _____

2. Bring the wine glass. _____

3. Stock the glasses. _____

4. Polish the forks. _____

5. Wash the knives. _____

6. Use the steak knife. _____

7. Stock the coffee cups. _____

8. Bring the saucer. _____

9. Use the salad plate. _____

10. Wash the spoons. _____

11. Polish the salad forks. _____

12. Use the bread plate. _____

13. Bring the bowls. _____

14. Stock the soup spoons. _____

15. Bring the dinner plates. _____

PART II—LOCATIONS

left
izquierda

right
derecha

in, on
en

on top
encima

up, above
arriba

down, below
abajo

in front
delante

behind
detrás

between
entre

around
alrededor

inside
dentro

outside
fuera

over
sobre

left	izquierda	behind	detrás
right	derecha	between	entre
in, on	en	around	alrededor
on top	encima	inside	dentro
up, above	arriba	outside	fuera
down, below	abajo	over	sobre
in front	delante		

MATCHING EXERCISE

Write the letter of each picture next to the Spanish word it matches below.

a.

b.

c.

d.

e.

f.

g.

h.

i.

j.

1. _____ encima

2. _____ arriba

3. _____ delante

4. _____ alrededor

5. _____ derecha

6. _____ dentro

7. _____ entre

8. _____ detrás

9. _____ fuera

10. _____ abajo

VOCABULARY EXERCISE

Write the Spanish word for each picture in the space provided.

1. _____

2. _____

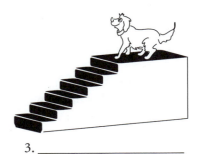

3. _____

4. _____

5. _____

6. _____

7. _____

8. _____

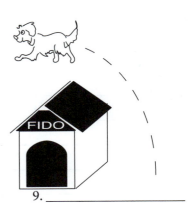

9. _____

10. _____

MATCHING EXERCISE

Write the letter of the Spanish word next to the English word it matches on the left.

1. _____ between   a. abajo
2. _____ over   b. alrededor
3. _____ on top   c. dentro
4. _____ up, above   d. detrás
5. _____ left   e. derecha
6. _____ outside   f. sobre
7. _____ down, below   g. encima
8. _____ around   h. arriba
9. _____ inside   i. delante
10. _____ behind   j. fuera
11. _____ in front   k. entre
12. _____ right   l. izquierda

TRANSLATION EXERCISE

Translate the following to English:

1. derecha _____
2. arriba _____
3. sobre _____
4. fuera _____
5. alrededor _____
6. izquierda _____
7. delante _____
8. entre _____
9. abajo _____
10. encima _____
11. detrás _____
12. dentro _____

Translate the following to Spanish:

1. between _____
2. right _____
3. on top _____
4. up, above _____
5. in front _____
6. left _____
7. down, below _____
8. around _____
9. inside _____
10. behind _____
11. over _____
12. outside _____

MULTIPLE CHOICE

Circle the letter of the correct answer.

1. outside
 a. dentro
 b. derecha
 c. sobre
 d. fuera

2. in front
 a. alrededor
 b. detrás
 c. delante
 d. entre

3. down, below
 a. abajo
 b. encima
 c. detrás
 d. delante

4. up, above
 a. dentro
 b. alrededor
 c. sobre
 d. arriba

5. behind
 a. detrás
 b. delante
 c. fuera
 d. entre

6. around
 a. abajo
 b. en
 c. alrededor
 d. izquierda

7. in, on
 a. encima
 b. en
 c. entre
 d. abajo

8. between
 a. entre
 b. en
 c. encima
 d. izquierda

9. outside
 a. dentro
 b. delante
 c. fuera
 d. arriba

10. over
 a. arriba
 b. sobre
 c. delante
 d. detrás

11. right
 a. dentro
 b. derecha
 c. sobre
 d. fuera

12. left
 a. entre
 b. en
 c. encima
 d. izquierda

CROSSWORD PUZZLES

Across

 2. down, below
 5. in, on
 6. behind
 8. around
 10. on top

Down

 1. outside
 2. up, above
 3. inside
 4. between
 7. over
 9. in front

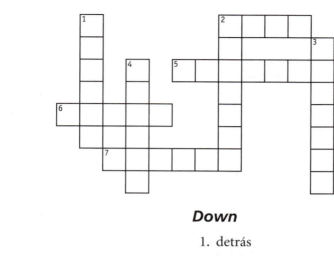

Across

2. sobre
5. entre
6. encima
7. dentro

Down

1. detrás
2. fuera
3. delante
4. alrededor

ROLE PLAY

Setting the Table. It's Tomás' first day working as a busboy in the restaurant. Choose an item that is on the table below. Begin to tell him where it should be placed. Tomás (your partner) finishes your sentence by expressing where it is located in relation to another item on the table. Follow the model.

ESTUDIANTE A:	Pon la cuchara . . .
ESTUDIANTE B:	¿A la derecha del cuchillo?
ESTUDIANTE A:	Sí. Muy bien, Tomás.

REVIEW

Dialogue

Read the dialogue aloud in Spanish. Then translate it to English.

Guillermo:	Buenos días.
John:	Buenos días.
Guillermo:	¿Cómo estás?
John:	Estoy cansado. Es temprano, ¿no?
Guillermo:	Sí, son las seis y media.
John:	Por favor. . . lava los vasos, las copas, cuarenta tazas y platillos.
Guillermo:	Está bien. ¿Cuántos vasos y copas?

Read the dialogue aloud in English. Then translate it to Spanish.

Guillermo:	Good morning.
John:	Good morning.
Guillermo:	How are you?
John:	I'm tired. It's early, right?
Guillermo:	Yes, it's six thirty.
John:	Please . . . wash the glasses, wine glasses, forty cups and saucers.
Guillermo:	Okay. How many glasses and wine glasses?

John:	Cincuenta, Guillermo. Lava los platos . . .		**John:**	Fifty, Guillermo. Wash the plates . . .
Guillermo:	¿Los platos para pan o para ensalada?		**Guillermo:**	Bread or salad plates?
John:	Los dos.		**John:**	Both.
Guillermo:	¿Cincuenta vasos y copas?		**Guillermo:**	Fifty glasses and wine glasses?
John:	Sí, correcto.		**John:**	Yes, correct.
Guillermo:	Muy bien. Hasta luego, John.		**Guillermo:**	Very good. See you later, John.
John:	Gracias. Buen trabajo, Guillermo.		**John:**	Thank you. Good work, Guillermo.
John:	¿Cómo estás, Lupe?		**John:**	How are you, Lupe?
Lupe:	¡Fantástica! Gracias.		**Lupe:**	Fantastic! Thanks.
John:	¿Fantástica? ¿Por qué?		**John:**	Fantastic? Why?
Lupe:	Hoy es mi cumpleaños. . . el 6 de enero.		**Lupe:**	Today is my birthday . . . January 6th.
John:	¡Feliz cumpleaños!		**John:**	Happy Birthday!
Lupe:	Gracias. ¿Cuándo es tu cumpleaños?		**Lupe:**	When is your birthday?
John:	El 30 de junio.		**John:**	June 30th.
Lupe:	En el verano, ¿no?		**Lupe:**	In the summer, right?
John:	Sí. Lupe, por favor, surte los cuchillos . . .		**John:**	Yes. Lupe, please stock the knives . . .
Lupe:	¿Y las cucharas y los tenedores?		**Lupe:**	And the spoons and forks?
John:	Sí, y pule la cubertería.		**John:**	Yes, and polish the silverware.
Lupe:	Está bien. ¿Doblo veinte y cuatro servilletas?		**Lupe:**	Okay. Fold twenty-four napkins?
John:	Sí. ¡Y por la tarde un examen!		**John:**	Yes. And this afternoon, an exam!
Lupe:	¿Sobre la posición de la cubertería?		**Lupe:**	About the position of the silverware?
John:	Sí. . . a la derecha, izquierda, entre . . .		**John:**	Yes . . . to the right, left, between . . .
Lupe:	¡Estoy nerviosa!		**Lupe:**	I'm nervous!
(El examen)			(The exam)	
John:	¿Dónde está el plato?		**John:**	Where is the plate?
Lupe:	Entre el tenedor y el cuchillo.		**Lupe:**	Between the fork and knife.
John:	Está bien. ¿Dónde está el tenedor de ensalada?		**John:**	Okay. Where is the salad fork?
Lupe:	A la derecha del tenedor.		**Lupe:**	To the right of the fork.
John:	No, no está correcto.		**John:**	No, it's not correct.
Lupe:	¿A la izquierda?		**Lupe:**	To the left?
John:	Sí, Lupe. ¿Y la cuchara para sopa?		**John:**	Yes, Lupe. And the soup spoon?
Lupe:	A la derecha de la cuchara.		**Lupe:**	To the right of the spoon.
John:	¿Y el platillo?		**John:**	And the saucer?
Lupe:	Debajo de la taza.		**Lupe:**	Under the coffee cup.
John:	Excelente. Eres muy inteligente, Lupe.		**John:**	Excellent. You are very intelligent, Lupe.

(En el restaurante)		(In the restaurant)	
Mujer:	Perdón. . .	**Woman:**	Pardon me . . .
Javier:	¿Qué necesita?	**Javier:**	What do you need?
Mujer:	Necesito un tenedor, por favor.	**Woman:**	I need a fork, please.
Javier:	¿Un tenedor para postre?	**Javier:**	A dessert fork?
Mujer:	No un tenedor para ensalada.	**Woman:**	No a salad fork.
Javier:	Está bien. Traigo otro.	**Javier:**	Okay. I'll bring another.
(en el estación de servicio)		(At the bus station)	
Javier:	Ay . . . ¡No hay tenedores!	**Javier:**	Ohhh . . . There are no forks!
Juan:	¿Qué necesitas, Javier?	**Juan:**	What do you need, Javier?
Javier:	Necesito un tenedor para la mujer.	**Javier:**	I need a fork for the woman.
Juan:	¿Para postre o para ensalada?	**Juan:**	For dessert or salad?
Javier:	Para ensalada. ¡Rápido . . . la mujer es impaciente!	**Javier:**	For salad. Fast! The woman is impatient!
(En la cocina)		(In the kitchen)	
Juan:	¿Dónde está el lavaplatos?	**Juan:**	Where is the dishwasher?
Paco:	Sí. . . Juan . . . ¿Qué necesitas?	**Paco:**	Yes . . . Juan. . . What do you need?
Juan:	¡Rápido! Lava los tenedores.	**Juan:**	Fast! Wash the forks.
Paco:	¿Tenedores para postre o para ensalada?	**Paco:**	Dessert or salad forks?

Translate the following to Spanish.

1. Hi, Hello. _____

2. How are you? _____

3. See you tomorrow. _____

4. Saturday, Sunday, Monday _____

5. What time is it? _____

6. I'll help you. _____

7. Watch me. _____

8. You are very patient. _____

9. It's good. It's bad. _____

10. Everything else is perfect. _____

11. When? Where? With whom? _____

12. I like to listen to music. _____

13. Do you like to play volleyball? _____

14. Wash the bathtub. _____

15. Dust the furniture. _____

16. Scrub the toilet. _____

17. Get the mop. _____

18. Empty the garbage can. _____

19. Use the polish. _____

20. Bring the cart. _____

CULTURE: HOW A COUNTRY'S HISTORY AFFECTS BEHAVIOR

There are so many differences between the United States and Latin American countries in their values, behavior, and lifestyles. These differences affect how business is conducted. A comparison of their histories will explain why the cultures are so different today.

Every high school student in the United States takes the class "United States History." To pass exams, they memorize the dates of battles *won*, territory *added* to the nation or some other *positive* accomplishment. During the middle 1800s, Mexico wouldn't sell its land to the United States, so the Mexicans fought for it. Popular historic sayings were "The West was won!" and "The Making of America!" To this day people educated in the United States give little thought to anything being lost.

As a result of this past, many United States citizens are positive, optimistic, self-confident, and able leaders. They usually don't fear a challenge. They are adventurers who are willing to take risks. They are forward thinkers. They want to change things and improve them so they are faster, stronger, and safer.

The Mexican story is different. They are a conquered people. In the 1500s, Cortez and his small band of soldiers completed the Conquest in less than two years and extended Spanish dominion south into Central America and as far north as Alaska. Spain ruled Mexico for the next three hundred years. In the 1800s, Maximilian and the French ruled Mexico. Then in 1846 the Mexican-American war took place and Mexico lost more than half of its territory to a self confident United States. It was a monumental event and a devastating loss of face to Mexico.

This continuous presence of a dominant group made some Latino cultures feel that if you were white, you were superior. It created a sense of inferiority. Some Latinos feel that the Spanish conquerors deliberately created an oppressed underclass with a mentality rooted in passivity and underachievement. The concept of authority has become the norm.

In the United States, "All men are created equal." The United States now uses "Ms." as equal with "Mr." In Latin American countries, differences make a difference. They are very hierarchical societies. Age, sex, role, and rank are extremely important in Latino culture, whereas in the United States, they are often downplayed because these things would threaten the U.S. value of equality.

RELATIONSHIP TIP

Don't forget the importance of putting a name to a face. Introduce your crews to everyone in your hotel. Take them around and have them shake hands with your accountant and the rest of the office staff. Start a small conversation asking them if they have ever been to Mexico, for example, and if Juan is from a small village outside of Puerta Vallarta or Acapulco. Make sure to have your Latino employees understand the importance of smiling when they see the guests and diners.

Health, Hygiene, Safety and Sanitation Concepts

PART I—HEALTH AND HYGIENE

la cabeza
head

el ojo
eye

el oído
ear

el cuello
neck

el hombro
shoulder

el pecho
chest

el estómago
stomach

la pierna
leg

la rodilla
knee

el tobillo
ankle

los pies
feet

la espalda
back

la sangre
blood

el brazo
arm

el codo
elbow

la mano
hand

los dedos
fingers

GRAMMAR

In Spanish we use the definite article "the" (*el, la, los, las*) when referring to parts of the body. The verb *doler* means to hurt, to ache.

MATCHING EXERCISE

Write the letter of the picture next to the Spanish word it matches.

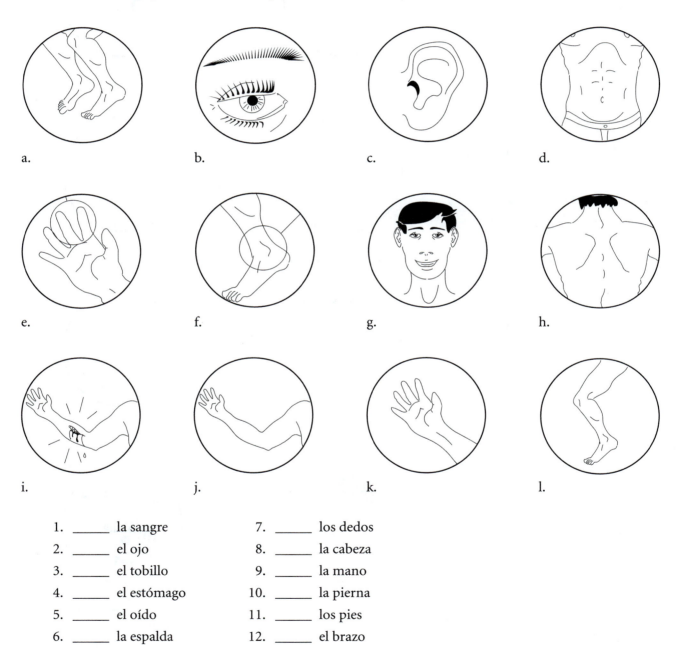

a. b. c. d.

e. f. g. h.

i. j. k. l.

1. _____ la sangre   7. _____ los dedos
2. _____ el ojo   8. _____ la cabeza
3. _____ el tobillo   9. _____ la mano
4. _____ el estómago   10. _____ la pierna
5. _____ el oído   11. _____ los pies
6. _____ la espalda   12. _____ el brazo

VOCABULARY EXERCISE

Write the Spanish word for each picture in the space provided.

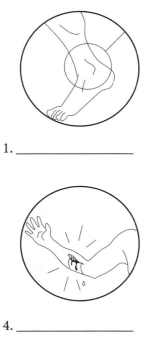

1. _____

2. _____

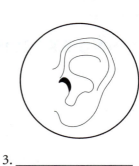

3. _____

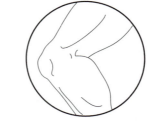

4. _____

5. _____

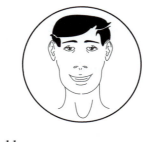

6. _____

7. _____

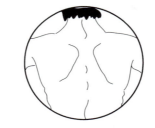

8. _____

9. _____

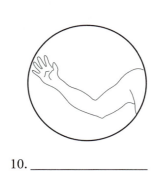

10. _____

11. _____

12. _____

MATCHING EXERCISE

Write the letter of the Spanish word next to the English word it matches on the left.

1. _____ feet
2. _____ knee
3. _____ eye
4. _____ ear
5. _____ hand
6. _____ elbow
7. _____ ankle
8. _____ leg

9. _____ stomach
10. _____ arm
11. _____ head
12. _____ chest
13. _____ fingers
14. _____ back
15. _____ shoulder
16. _____ neck

a. la cabeza
b. el brazo
c. el estómago
d. la pierna
e. el tobillo
f. los pies
g. la rodilla
h. la mano

i. el codo
j. el hombro
k. el cuello
l. el pecho
m. el oído
n. el ojo
o. los dedos
p. la espalda

CROSSWORD PUZZLES

Across

1. blood
4. hand
5. leg
8. knee
9. elbow
10. head
12. shoulder
15. ankle
16. eye

Down

2. back
3. fingers
5. chest
6. arm
7. feet
10. neck
11. stomach
13. hand
14. ear

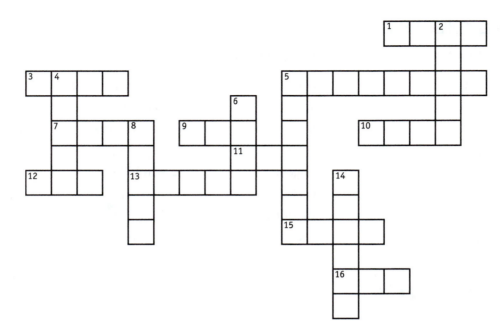

Across

1. cuello
3. espalda
5. hombro
7. rodilla
9. ojo
10. pies
11. brazo
12. pierna
13. sangre
15. mano
16. oído

Down

2. pecho
4. tobillo
5. estómago
6. cabeza
8. codo
14. dedo

TRANSLATION EXERCISE

Translate the following to English:

1. los pies_____
2. la mano _____
3. la rodilla _____
4. los dedos _____
5. la cabeza _____
6. la sangre_____
7. el oído _____

Translate the following to Spanish:

1. feet_____
2. hand _____
3. fingers _____
4. blood _____
5. head_____
6. eye _____
7. arm _____

8. el hombro _____

9. la espalda _____

10. el pecho _____

11. el brazo _____

12. el codo _____

13. la pierna _____

14. el tobillo _____

15. el ojo _____

8. ear _____

9. shoulder _____

10. chest _____

11. back _____

12. ankle _____

13. knee _____

14. stomach _____

15. leg _____

MULTIPLE CHOICE

Circle the letter of the correct answer.

1. fingers
a. los dedos
b. los pies
c. los brazos
d. la pierna

2. ankle
a. la rodilla
b. la pierna
c. el tobillo
d. el brazo

3. eye
a. la sangre
b. la mano
c. el oído
d. el ojo

4. head
a. la cabeza
b. la espalda
c. la pierna
d. el hombro

5. ear
a. el ojo
b. el oído
c. la rodilla
d. el pecho

6. back
a. la cabeza
b. el pecho
c. el estómago
d. la espalda

7. blood
a. el pulgar
b. el cuello
c. el codo
d. la sangre

8. feet
a. los pies
b. los dedos
c. la cabeza
d. la pierna

9. hand
a. la mano
b. el codo
c. el pecho
d. el tobillo

10. knee
a. el brazo
b. el tobillo
c. la rodilla
d. el cuello

ROLE PLAY

Imagine that your co-worker has been hurt on the job. Ask what hurts the person. Follow the model.

ESTUDIANTE A: ¿Qué te duele?
ESTUDIANTE B: Me duele el tobillo.

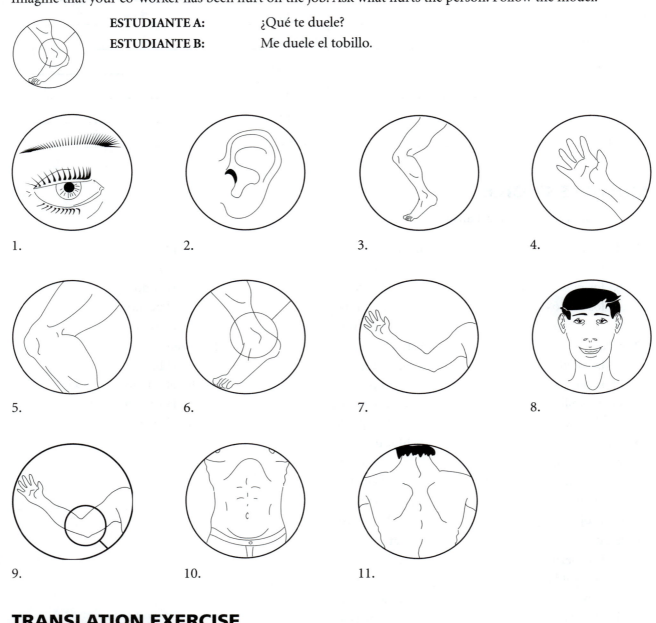

1.

2.

3.

4.

5.

6.

7.

8.

9.

10.

11.

TRANSLATION EXERCISE

Translate the following to Spanish:

1. What hurts? _____

2. My head hurts. _____

3. My eye hurts._____

4. My elbow hurts._____

5. My ankle hurts. _____

6. My knee hurts._____

7. What hurts?_____

8. My stomach hurts._____

9. My back hurts._____

10. My leg hurts. _____

PART II—SANITATION AND SAFETY

Wash your hands. Your clothes.
Lava las manos. Tu ropa.

Cut your hair. Your nails.
Cortate el pelo. Las uñas.

Shave your moustache. Your beard.
Razúrate el bigote. La barba.

Wear your hat.
Usa la gorra.

Don't come to work.
No vengas a trabajar.

If you are sick, don't work.
Si estás enfermo, no trabajes.

If you cough or sneeze much, let me know.
Si toces o estornudas mucho, dímelo.

If you have cuts or sores, let me know.
Si tienes cortadas o heridas, dímelo.

Sanitation and Safety
Sanidad y seguridad

Clean the table with iodine.
Limpia la mesa con el yodo.

Disinfect the table.
Desinfecta la mesa.

Use the red liquid. Blue. White.
Usa el líquido rojo. Azul. Blanco.

Wrap the food well.
Envuelve la comida bien.

Wrap the food in plastic.
Envuelve la comida en plástico.

Store the chicken (meat, fish) separately.
Guarda el pollo (la carne, el pescado) separado.

Store the milk quickly.
Guarda la leche rápido.

Close the containers well.
Cierra bien los recipientes.

Consequences

Or else they drip.	Si no, gotean.
Or else they absorb the smell.	Si no, se apestan.
Or else it gets contaminated.	Si no, se contamina.
Or else we get sick.	Si no, nos enfermamos.
Or else the customers get sick.	Si no, se enferman los clientes.

FIFO

First in, first out
Primera que entra, primera que sale.

Put the label on the container with the incoming label.
Pon la etiqueta en el recipiente con la fecha de entrada.

Put the new food all the way to the back.
Pon la comida nueva hasta atrás.

Put the oldest date to the front.
Pon la fecha más vieja en frente.

Take out the food with the oldest date first.
Saca la comida con la fecha mas vieja primero.

If not, it spoils.
Si no, se echa a perder.

If not, it's not good anymore.
Si no, ya no sirve.

Check the temperature.
Checa la temperatura.

Safety

Be careful with. . .
Cuidado con. . .

It's hazardous/dangerous.
Es peligroso.

It's heavy.
Está pesado.

It's hot.
Está caliente.

It's contaminated.
Está contaminado.

It's dirty.
Está sucio.

Wear black leather shoes with rubber soles.
Lleva zapatos negros de piel con suelas de hule.

If it is heavy, ask for help.
Si está pesado pide ayuda.

Use the ladder to bring things down.
Usa la escalera para bajar las cosas.

CULTURE: DIRECTING AND SUPERVISING

One of the most significant and troublesome work related issues involves how people treat one another and how supervisors and subordinates interact with one another. Cultures differ in how they view a person's age, sex, role and rank. In the United States there is a tendency to downplay such factors, but in Latin American cultures these differences are important and very meaningful.

Latinos highly respect authority. Traditionally, young employees never doubt or even comment on a decision their superior has made, even if they completely disagree with it. Nor do supervisors ordinarily accept such questioning from subordinates. In Latin American countries, delegation of authority is rare; the idea is foreign to many people. The supervisor keeps the power and makes all the decisions. Subordinates are not proactive but wait for specific instructions. Most subordinates like this approach better, since it frees them from making mistakes. Many times subordinates feel insecure and fear making errors. It is important, though, to point out that a new generation of supervisors is emerging, which, as a result of university training, firmly supports the idea of the delegation of responsibility.

In the United States, people are raised to be independent and like to make their own decisions. And so young employees are normally reluctant to ask for advice. They want as much responsibility and authority as possible. Having authority being exercised over them is distasteful and they don't like having to ask for approval for every decision and action they take. They feel capable and want to be allowed to make the majority of decisions by themselves.

They thrive on tackling new problems by themselves. They feel secure in their judgements and are aware that a small mistake will not lose them the support and respect of their supervisors, because making a minor mistake at the start is regarded as normal in the learning process.

It is important to be aware that sometimes when a Latino employee agrees and answers yes to his/her boss that it may not always mean yes. They do not want to disagree with their supervisor. Once a trust is established between the two of them, this behavior, of course changes.

RELATIONSHIP TIP

In Chapter 4 you learned about the supreme importance of the Latino family. Posting a picture of your Latino workers' families was suggested. To improve safety in the workplace, now post a large sign near the photos of their children that reads, "They love you! Work Safely!"

Meat and Seafood

PART I—MEAT

chicken
el pollo

turkey
el pavo

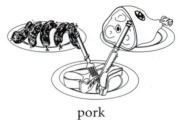

pork
el cerdo

bacon
el tocino

ham
el jamón

pork chop
la chuleta

sausage
la salchicha

meatball
la albóndiga

veal
la ternera

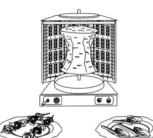

lamb
el cordero

hamburger
la hamburguesa

beef
la carne

roast
la carne asada

ground beef
la carne molida

steak
el bistec

GROUP I

chicken	el pollo		**ham**	el jamón
turkey	el pavo		**pork chop**	la chuleta
pork	el cerdo		**sausage**	la salchicha
bacon	el tocino		**meatball**	la albóndiga

GROUP II

beef	la carne	steak	el bistec
roast	la carne asada	lamb	el cordero
ground beef	la carne molida	veal	la ternera
hamburger	la hamburguesa		

GROUP I

MATCHING EXERCISE

Write the letter of each picture next to the Spanish word it matches below.

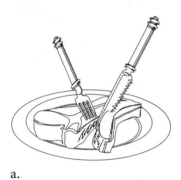

a.

b.

c.

d.

e.

f.

g.

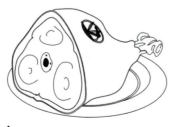

h.

1. _____ el jamón

2. _____ el cerdo

3. _____ el pollo

4. _____ el tocino

5. _____ el pavo

6. _____ la salchicha

7. _____ la albóndiga

8. _____ la chuleta

VOCABULARY EXERCISE

Write the Spanish word for each picture in the space provided.

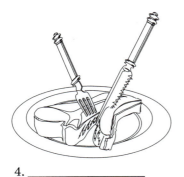

1. _____

2. _____

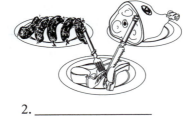

3. _____

4. _____

5. _____

6. _____

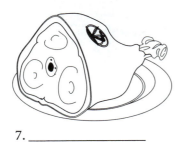

7. _____

8. _____

MATCHING EXERCISE

Write the letter of the Spanish word next to the English word it matches on the left.

1. _____ meatball
2. _____ sausage
3. _____ pork chop
4. _____ ham
5. _____ chicken
6. _____ turkey
7. _____ bacon
8. _____ pork

a. la salchicha
b. el jamón
c. la albóndiga
d. el pollo
e. el cerdo
f. la chuleta
g. el pavo
h. el tocino

TRANSLATION EXERCISE

Translate the following to English:

1. el cerdo _____
2. el pavo _____
3. el pollo _____
4. la albóndiga _____
5. la salchicha _____
6. la chuleta _____
7. el jamón _____
8. el tocino _____

Translate the following to Spanish:

1. ham _____
2. pork _____
3. pork chop _____
4. bacon _____
5. chicken _____
6. turkey _____
7. sausage _____
8. meatball _____

GROUP II
MATCHING EXERCISE

Write the letter of each picture next to the Spanish word it matches below.

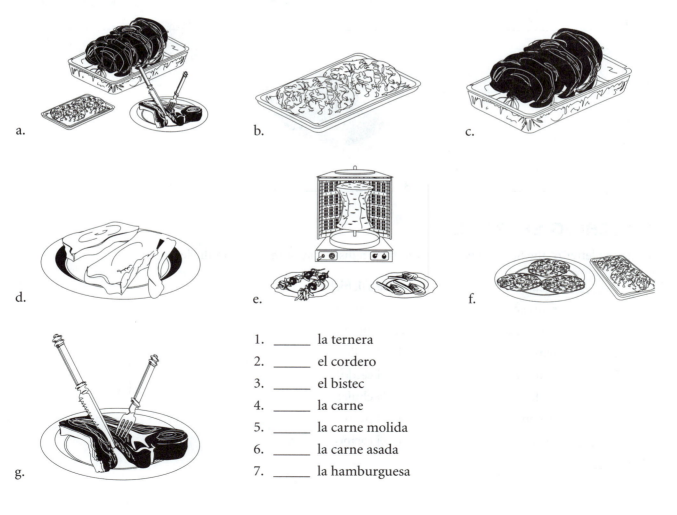

a.   b.   c.

d.   e.   f.

g.

1. _____ la ternera
2. _____ el cordero
3. _____ el bistec
4. _____ la carne
5. _____ la carne molida
6. _____ la carne asada
7. _____ la hamburguesa

VOCABULARY EXERCISE

Write the Spanish word for each picture in the space provided.

1. _____

2. _____

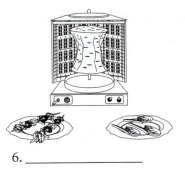

3. _____

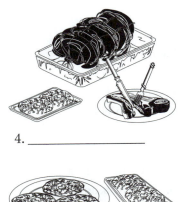

4. _____

5. _____

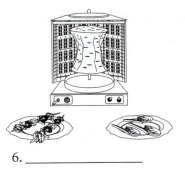

6. _____

7. _____

MATCHING EXERCISE

Write the letter of the Spanish word next to the English word it matches on the left.

1. _____ veal   a. la carne
2. _____ lamb   b. la ternera
3. _____ beef   c. el cordero
4. _____ roast   d. la carne asada
5. _____ steak   e. el bistec
6. _____ hamburger   f. la hamburguesa
7. _____ ground beef   g. la carne molida

TRANSLATION EXERCISE

Translate the following to English:

1. la carne _____

2. la carne asada _____

3. la carne molida _____

4. el bistec _____

5. el cordero _____

6. la ternera _____

7. la hamburguesa _____

Translate the following to Spanish:

1. ground beef _____

2. veal _____

3. beef _____

4. lamb _____

5. roast _____

6. hamburger _____

7. steak _____

MULTIPLE CHOICE

Circle the letter of the correct answer.

1. ham
   a. el jamón
   b. el tocino
   c. la salchicha
   d. la ternera

2. pork chop
   a. la carne
   b. el cerdo
   c. el cordero
   d. la chuleta

3. turkey
   a. el pollo
   b. el pavo
   c. la carne
   d. la chuleta

4. sausage
   a. la salchicha
   b. el jamón
   c. el pavo
   d. el tocino

5. beef
   a. la carne
   b. el cerdo
   c. el cordero
   d. la chuleta

6. pork
   a. la carne
   b. el cerdo
   c. el cordero
   d. la chuleta

7. lamb
   a. la carne
   b. el cerdo
   c. el cordero
   d. la chuleta

8. veal
   a. la ternera
   b. el tocino
   c. el pavo
   d. el cordero

9. bacon
   a. la ternera
   b. el jamón
   c. la salchicha
   d. el tocino

10. roast
   a. la carne molida
   b. la carne asada
   c. la salchicha
   d. el jamón

11. chicken
   a. el pollo
   b. el pavo
   c. el bistec
   d. la hamburguesa

12. ground beef
   a. el bistec
   b. la carne asada
   c. la carne molida
   d. la hamburguesa

CROSSWORD PUZZLES

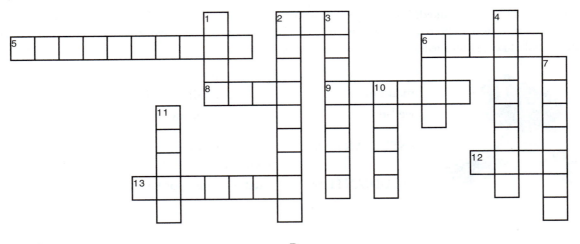

Across

2. jamón
5. carne molida
6. tocino
8. cordero
9. pavo
12. cerdo
13. salchicha

Down

1. ternera
2. hamburguesa
3. albóndiga
4. chuleta
6. carne
7. pollo
10. carne asada
11. bistec

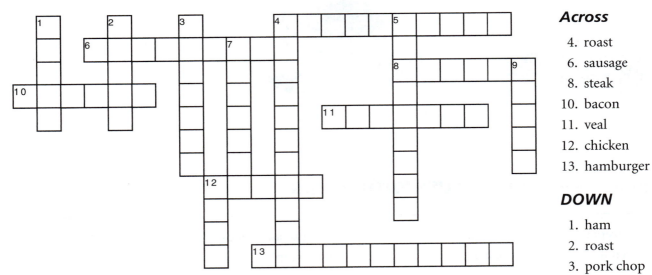

Across

4. roast
6. sausage
8. steak
10. bacon
11. veal
12. chicken
13. hamburger

DOWN

1. ham
2. roast
3. pork chop
4. ground beef
5. meatball
7. lamb
9. pork
12. turkey

ROLE PLAY

How would you like that cooked? You just got a new job as a waiter at the new steak house downtown! Since the chef needs to know how to prepare the dinners, don't forget to ask the diners. Working with a partner, ask how the guest would like his/her meat cooked by asking *¿Cómo le gustaría . . . ?*

rare	**poco cocido**
medium	**medio cocido**
well-done	**bien cocido**

ESTUDIANTE A: ¿Cómo le gustaría la carne. . . poco, medio o bien cocido?

ESTUDIANTE B: Medio cocido, por favor.

1.

2.

3.

4.

PART I—ACTIONS TO USE WITH MEATS

prepare	prepara		**put away (store)**	guarda
cook	cocina		**wrap**	envuelve
take out	saca			

MATCHING EXERCISE

Write the letter of the Spanish word next to the English word it matches on the left.

1. _____ wrap
2. _____ take out
3. _____ put away
4. _____ prepare
5. _____ cook

a. cocina
b. guarda
c. prepara
d. saca
e. envuelve

TRANSLATION EXERCISE

Translate the following to English:

1. prepara _____
2. guarda _____
3. cocina _____
4. envuelve _____
5. saca _____

Translate the following to Spanish:

1. cook _____
2. take out _____
3. wrap _____
4. put away _____
5. prepare _____

MULTIPLE CHOICE

Circle the letter of the correct answer.

1. cook
   a. guarda
   b. cocina
   c. saca
   d. envuelve

2. take out
   a. saca
   b. cocina
   c. prepara
   d. guarda

3. wrap
   a. guarda
   b. cocina
   c. saca
   d. envuelve

4. put away
   a. saca
   b. cocina
   c. prepara
   d. guarda

5. prepare
   a. prepara
   b. cocina
   c. saca
   d. envuelve

Translate the following to English:

1. Prepara el pollo. _____
2. Saca la salchicha. _____
3. Cocina la carne. _____
4. Envuelve el cordero. _____
5. Guarda el jamón. _____
6. Cocina el cerdo. _____

Translate the following to Spanish:

1. Wrap the pork. _____
2. Prepare the bacon. _____
3. Take out the ham. _____
4. Cook the roast. _____
5. Put away the ground beef. _____
6. Cook the sausage. _____

7. Saca las hamburguesas. _____

8. Envuelve el pavo. _____

9. Prepara el tocino. _____

10. Guarda las chuletas. _____

11. Saca la carne asada. _____

12. Cocina la carne molida. _____

13. Guarda la ternera. _____

14. Prepara las albóndigas. _____

15. Envuelve el bistec. _____

7. Wrap the veal. _____

8. Prepare the lamb. _____

9. Take out the steak. _____

10. Cook the turkey. _____

11. Prepare the chicken. _____

12. Put away the pork. _____

13. Wrap the pork chops. _____

14. Take out the beef. _____

15. Prepare the roast. _____

GRAMMAR: FOLLOWING UP ON JOB ASSIGNMENTS

In the last several chapters you have learned how to assign tasks. If you want to follow up with an employee later that afternoon to see if he/she has completed the assignment, you use the past tense.

The –a ending changes to the –aste ending and you raise your voice in a questioning tone. Spanish does not have the words "Did you." They are implied in the –aste ending. Read the Spanish words aloud and practice raising your voice.

Wash . . .	Lava . . .
Did you wash . . .	¿Lavaste . . . ?
Cut . . .	Corta . . .
Did you cut . . . ?	¿Cortaste . . . ?
Prepare . . .	Prepara . . .
Did you prepare . . . ?	¿Preparaste . . . ?

The –e ending changes to the –iste ending.

Sweep	Barre . . .
Did you sweep . . . ?	¿Barriste . . . ?
Wrap . . .	Envuelve . . .
Did you wrap . . .	¿Envolviste* . . . ?

* This form is irregular

Translate the following to English:

1. ¿Preparaste . . . ? _____

2. ¿Guardaste . . . ? _____

3. ¿Cocinaste . . . ? _____

4. ¿Sacaste . . . ? _____

5. ¿Envolviste . . . ? _____

Translate the following to Spanish:

1. Did you take out the turkey? _____

2. Did you put away the pork? _____

3. Did you prepare the chicken? _____

4. Did you wrap the bacon? _____

5. Did you cook the ground beef? _____

ROLE PLAY

Did you. . . ? You had asked Miguel to do several things after breakfast. It's noon and you are now having lunch with him. Working with a partner, ask and answer if he has done the tasks. Follow the model.

ESTUDIANTE A:	¿Guardaste el tocino?
ESTUDIANTE B:	Sí.
	No, todavia, no. (*No, not yet.*)

1. prepare

2. cook

3. wrap

4. take out

5. put away

6. prepare

7. cook

8. take out

9. wrap

10. prepare

PART II—SEAFOOD

lobster
la langosta

crab
el cangrejo

oysters
las ostras

clams
las almejas

shrimp
los camarones

seafood
los mariscos

tuna
el atún

fish
el pescado

skin
el cuero

salmon
el salmón

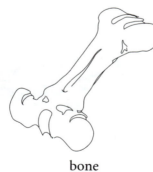

bone
el hueso

fat
la grasa

GROUP I

seafood (shellfish)	los mariscos	**shrimp**	los camarones
clams	las almejas	**crab**	el cangrejo
oysters	las ostras	**lobster**	la langosta

GROUP II

fish	el pescado	**bone**	el hueso
tuna	el atún	**skin**	el cuero
salmon	el salmón	**fat**	la grasa

GROUP I

MATCHING EXERCISE

Write the letter of each picture next to the Spanish word it matches below.

a.

b.

c.

d.

e.

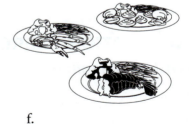

f.

1. _____ los camarones

2. _____ el cangrejo

3. _____ los mariscos

4. _____ la langosta

5. _____ las ostras

6. _____ las almejas

VOCABULARY EXERCISE

Write the Spanish word for each picture in the space provided.

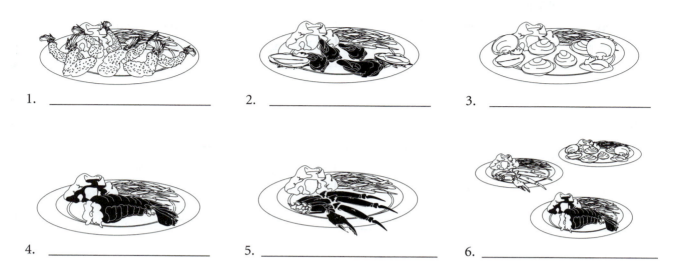

1. _____

2. _____

3. _____

4. _____

5. _____

6. _____

MATCHING EXERCISE

Write the letter of the Spanish word next to the English word it matches on the left.

1. _____ lobster   a. el cangrejo

2. _____ shrimp   b. los mariscos

3. _____ seafood   c. las almejas

4. _____ clams   d. la langosta

5. _____ oysters   e. las ostras

6. _____ crab   f. los camarones

TRANSLATION EXERCISE

Translate the following to English:

1. los ostras _____

2. los camarones _____

3. los mariscos_____

4. las almejas _____

5. el congrejo_____

6. la langosta _____

Translate the following to Spanish:

1. seafood _____

2. oysters _____

3. clams _____

4. lobster _____

5. crab _____

6. shrimp _____

GROUP II

MATCHING EXERCISE

Write the letter of each picture next to the Spanish word it matches below.

a.

b.

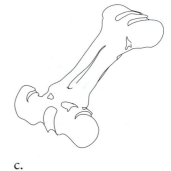

c.

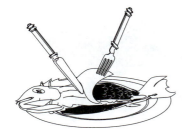

d.

e.

f.

1. _____ el cuero

2. _____ el pescado

3. _____ la grasa

4. _____ el salmón

5. _____ el atún

6. _____ el hueso

VOCABULARY EXERCISE

Write the Spanish word for each picture in the space provided.

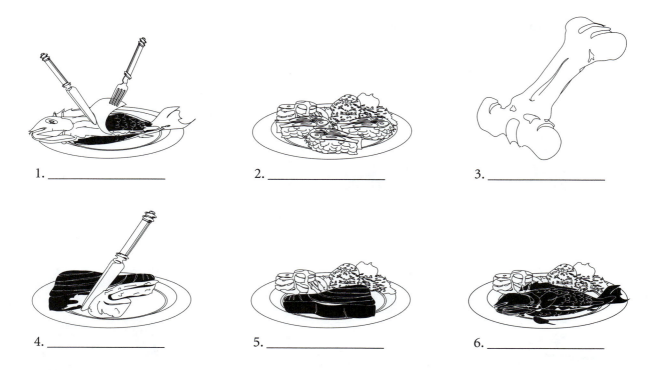

1. _____

2. _____

3. _____

4. _____

5. _____

6. _____

MATCHING EXERCISE

Write the letter of the Spanish word next to the English word it matches on the left.

1. _____ fat   a. el atún

2. _____ bone   b. el hueso

3. _____ skin   c. el pescado

4. _____ tuna   d. el salmón

5. _____ fish   e. el cuero

6. _____ salmon   f. la grasa

TRANSLATION EXERCISE

Translate the following to English:

1. el salmón _____

2. la grasa _____

3. el cuero _____

4. el pescado _____

5. el atún _____

6. el hueso _____

Translate the following to Spanish:

1. skin _____

2. fat _____

3. bone _____

4. fish _____

5. salmon _____

6. tuna _____

MULTIPLE CHOICE

Circle the letter of the correct answer.

1. shrimp
   a. los camarones
   b. las ostras
   c. la langosta
   d. los mariscos

2. crab
   a. el cuero
   b. el cangrejo
   c. el pescado
   d. la grasa

3. fish
   a. el cuero
   b. el pescado
   c. el cangrejo
   d. el hueso

4. lobster
   a. la langosta
   b. las ostras
   c. los mariscos
   d. los camarones

5. skin
   a. el cuero
   b. el hueso
   c. el pescado
   d. el cangrejo

6. seafood
   a. las ostras
   b. los mariscos
   c. la langosta
   d. los camarones

7. fat
   a. la grasa
   b. el hueso
   c. la langosta
   d. el cuero

8. bone
   a. el hueso
   b. el cangrejo
   c. el pescado
   d. el cuero

9. oysters
   a. los mariscos
   b. los camarones
   c. la langosta
   d. las ostras

CROSSWORD PUZZLES

Across

1. bone
5. seafood
7. clams
9. tuna
10. fish
11. fat

Down

2. salmon
3. shrimp
4. oysters
6. lobster
8. skin

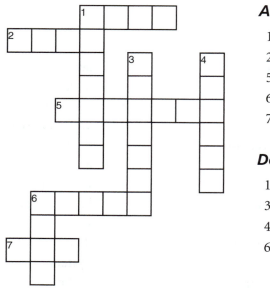

Across

1. cuero
2. hueso
5. langosta
6. almejas
7. grasa

Down

1. mariscos
3. ostras
4. camarones
6. cangrejo

ROLE PLAY: FRESH OR FROZEN?

You have just gotten a new job as a waiter in a new restaurant near the ocean that specializes in seafood. The clients want to know if the seafood is fresh (*fresco*) or frozen (*congelado*). Working with a partner, answer the clients with one of the words. Follow the model.

ESTUDIANTE A: ¿Está fresco o congelado el salmon?

ESTUDIANTE B: El salmon está fresco.

El salmon está congelado.

1.

2.

3.

4.

5.

6.

PART II—ACTIONS TO USE WITH SEAFOOD

clean	limpiar
remove	quita
broil	asa a la parilla
sauté	saltea
boil	hierve

MATCHING EXERCISE

Write the letter of the Spanish word next to the English word it matches on the left.

1. _____ broil   a. saltea
2. _____ remove   b. limpia
3. _____ sauté   c. quita
4. _____ clean   d. hierve
5. _____ boil   e. asa a la parilla

TRANSLATION EXERCISE

Translate the following to English:

1. asa a la parilla _____
2. quita _____
3. saltea _____
4. hierve _____
5. limpia _____

Translate the following to Spanish:

1. remove _____
2. broil _____
3. boil _____
4. sauté _____
5. clean _____

MULTIPLE CHOICE

Circle the letter of the correct answer.

1. **sauté**
   a. asa a la parilla
   b. limpia
   c. saltea
   d. quita

2. **boil**
   a. hierve
   b. quita
   c. limpia
   d. asa a la parilla

3. **clean**
   a. asa a la parilla
   b. limpia
   c. saltea
   d. quita

4. **broil**
   a. quita
   b. hierve
   c. saltea
   d. asa a la parilla

5. **remove**
   a. asa a la parilla
   b. limpia
   c. saltea
   d. quita

Translate the following to English:

1. Hierve la langosta. _____
2. Saltea los camarones. _____
3. ¿Quitaste la grasa? _____
4. Limpia los mariscos. _____
5. Asa a la parilla el salmón. _____
6. Hierve las almejas. _____
7. Quita los huesos. _____
8. ¿Limpiaste el pescado? _____
9. Saltea el cangrejo. _____
10. Asa a la parilla el atún. _____
11. Quita el cuero. _____
12. Limpia los camarones. _____

Translate the following to Spanish:

1. Clean the fish. _____
2. Boil the shrimp. _____
3. Did you remove the bones? _____
4. Sauté the seafood. _____
5. Broil the salmon. _____
6. Did you clean the oysters? _____
7. Boil the seafood. _____
8. Remove the fat. _____
9. Sauté the shrimp. _____
10. Broil the tuna. _____
11. Remove the skin. _____
12. Boil the lobster. _____

DIALOGUE

Read the dialogue aloud in Spanish. Then translate it to English.

Chef: Hola, buenos días.
Ernesto: Hola, señor.
Chef: ¿Lavaste tu uniforme?
Ernesto: Sí, señor.
Chef: Muy bien. Lava las manos, por favor.
Ernesto: Está bien.
Chef: Saca el tocino.
(Lo busca pero no lo encuentra)
Chef: ¿Hay un problema?
Ernesto: Sí, no hay tocino.
Chef: Sí, hay.
Ernesto: ¿Dónde está?
Chef: Detrás de la salchicha. . . entre el cordero y la ternera.
Ernesto: Eres muy organizado, Chef.
Chef: Prepara el tocino para ochenta personas.
Ernesto: ¿Y el jamón?
Chef: Sí. Y cocina la salchicha.

Read the dialogue aloud in English. Then translate it to Spanish.

Chef: Hello, good morning.
Ernesto: Hello, sir.
Chef: Did you wash your uniform?
Ernesto: Yes, sir.
Chef: Very good. Wash your hands, please.
Ernesto: Okay.
Chef: Take out the bacon.
(He looks for it but does not find it.)
Chef: Is there a problem?
Ernesto: Yes, there is no bacon.
Chef: Yes, there is.
Ernesto: Where is it?
Chef: Behind the sausage. . . between the lamb and the veal.
Ernesto: You are very organized, Chef.
Chef: Prepare the bacon for 80 people.
Ernesto: And the ham?
Chef: Yes. And cook the sausage.

(más tarde)

Chef:	¿Preparaste el tocino y el jamón?
Ernesto:	Sí, señor. Soy muy responsable.
Chef:	¿Concinaste la salchicha?
Ernesto:	No, todavia, no.
Chef:	Soy paciente.

(Durante el almuerzo)

Doris:	Hay muchas actividades en la cocina.
Chef:	Hola Ernesto.
Ernesto:	Chef, quiero presentarte a una estudiante.
Doris:	Hola. Me llamo Doris. Soy estudiante a la universidad.
Chef:	Mucho gusto, Doris. ¿De dónde eres?
Doris:	Soy de Boston.
Chef:	Bienvenida a la cocina.
Doris:	Hay muchas actividades aquí, ¿no?
Chef:	Sí. . . Roberto saca y guarda la carne.
Ernesto:	Y Jóse Miguel limpia el pescado.
Chef:	Victor quita la grasa y el cuero.
Doris:	Me gusta comer el atún y el salmón.
Chef:	Lava los manos, Doris.
Doris:	Está bien.
Chef:	Mírame.

(Chef limpia el pescado)

Chef:	Trátalo.
Doris:	¿Está correcto?
Chef:	Continua tratando.
Doris:	Eres muy paciente, Chef. ¿Está correcto?
Chef:	Está perfecto. Buen trabajo.
Doris:	¿Quito la grasa y los huesos?
Chef:	Házlo como yo.
Doris:	Está bien.
Chef:	Ernesto. . . limpia los mariscos.
Ernesto:	¿Y las almejas y las ostras?
Chef:	Sí, e hierve los camarones.
Ernesto:	¿Y las langostas?

(later)

Chef:	Did you prepare the bacon and the ham?
Ernesto:	Yes, sir. I am very responsible.
Chef:	Did you cook the sausage?
Ernesto:	No, not yet.
Chef:	I am patient.

(During lunch)

Doris:	There are many activities in the kitchen.
Chef:	Hi, Ernesto.
Ernesto:	Chef, I'd like to introduce you to a student.
Doris:	Hi, my name is Doris. I am a student at the university.
Chef:	Nice to meet you, Doris. Where are you from?
Doris:	I'm from Boston.
Chef:	Welcome to the kitchen.
Doris:	There are many activities here, right?
Chef:	Yes. . . Roberto takes out and puts away the meat.
Ernesto:	And Jóse Miguel cleans the fish.
Chef:	Victor removes the fat and skin.
Doris:	I like to eat tuna and salmon.
Chef:	Wash your hands, Doris.
Doris:	Okay.
Chef:	Watch me.

(Chef cleans the fish.)

Chef:	Try it.
Doris:	Is this correct?
Chef:	Keep trying.
Doris:	You are very patient, Chef.
Chef:	It's perfect. Good work.
Doris:	Remove the fat and bones?
Chef:	Do it like me.
Doris:	Okay.
Chef:	Ernesto. . . clean the seafood.
Ernesto:	The clams and the oysters?
Chef:	Yes, and boil the shrimp.
Ernesto:	And the lobster?

Chef:	Sí, gracias. Eres muy trabajador.		**Chef:**	Yes, thank you. You are a hard worker.
Doris:	Chef, gracias y hasta luego.		**Doris:**	Chef. . . thanks and see you later.
Chef:	Adiós. Hasta mañana.		**Chef:**	Goodbye. See you tomorrow.
(En el comedor)			(In the dining room)	
Jane:	Hola, buenas noches.		**Jane:**	Hello. Good evening.
Una familia:	Buenas noches.		**A family:**	Good evening.
Jane:	Soy Jane, su mesera esta noche.		**Jane:**	I'm Jane, your server tonight.
Una familia:	Mucho gusto.		**A family:**	Nice to meet you.
Jane:	Hay muchas especialidades esta noche.		**Jane:**	There are many specialties tonight.
Todd:	¿Hay pescado?		**Todd:**	Is there fish?
Jane:	Sí, hay atún y salmón.		**Jane:**	Yes, tuna and salmon.
Tyler:	¿Hay mariscos?		**Tyler:**	Is there seafood?
Jane:	Sí, hay almejas, langosta, ostras. . .		**Jane:**	Yes, there are clams, lobster, oysters. . .
Tyler:	¿Y camarones?		**Tyler:**	And shrimp?
Jane:	Sí, y hay chuletas, hamburguesas. . .		**Jane:**	Yes, and there are pork chops, hamburgers. . .
Tyler:	Una hamburguesa, por favor.		**Tyler:**	A hamburger, please.
Jane:	¿Cómo le gustaría su hamburguesa. . . poco, medio o bien cocida?		**Jane:**	How would you like your hamburger. . . rare, medium or well done?
Tyler:	Medio cocida.		**Tyler:**	Medium.
Todd:	Un bistec, por favor.		**Todd:**	A steak, please.
Jane:	¿Cómo le gustaría su bistec. . . poco, medio o bien cocido?		**Jane:**	How would you like your steak. . . rare, medium or well done?
Todd:	Poco cocido.		**Todd:**	Rare.
Jane:	¿Una ensalada o sopa?		**Jane:**	A salad or soup?
Todd:	Una ensalada, por favor.		**Todd:**	A salad, please.
Sarah:	Solo una ensalada para mí. Gracias.		**Sarah:**	Only a salad for me. Thank you.
Jane:	Está bien.		**Jane:**	Okay.

REVIEW

Translate the following to Spanish.

1. Goodbye. _____

2. What's your name? _____

3. Tuesday, Thursday, Saturday _____

4. At what time? _____

5. Man, woman, child _____

6. Vacuum the dining room. _____

7. Mop the floor. _____

8. The bartender is in the bathroom. _____

9. The cook is in the kitchen. _____

10. Dust the furniture. _____

11. Replenish the toilet paper. _____

12. When? Where? With whom? _____

13. To the right, to the left _____

14. Under, over _____

15. Fold the sheets. _____

16. Dry the linens. _____

17. Get the bucket. _____

18. Replenish the plates and glasses. _____

19. Does your hand hurt? _____

20. My stomach hurts. _____

CULTURE: LEADERSHIP TIPS FOR LATINOS

As Anglo businesses grow, they are looking to Latino employees to take on positions of leadership. But what Anglos don't understand is that many Latinos tend to *like* the comfortable job that they have. Many Latinos will sacrifice riches for security.

Working at Anglo businesses, Latinos are at a crossroads. They can either struggle on with a secure, yet low-paying job and muddle through *poco a poquito* or they can recognize and seize a great opportunity. To be a successful Latino leader in the United States, in addition to learning about the two cultures, you need to:

1.   Learn English.

Good business depends on effective communication, and so it is important for Latinos dealing with Anglo businesses to speak the same language. Most Anglos speak only English. Even though they are hiring Spanish-speaking employees, they feel they shouldn't have to learn Spanish. If a Latino wants to be successful working in the United States, it is essential to learn English. It is the most fundamental business skill.

2.   Trust others.

This is the most controversial characteristic with Latinos. Before trusting others, many Latinos feel that you should first study people, check them out thoroughly. They feel it is better to be safe than sorry. At first, this seems reasonable but ultimately it is not. Lack of trust and overcaution breeds more of the same to the point that everyone is distrustful. If a person feels he is honest and trustworthy, others will feel that way about him or her as well. Trust breeds trust and distrust breeds distrust. This is a positive attitude to live by.

3.   Change your "Don't make waves" attitude.

Latinos are hesitant to state their opinions. Anglos, on the other hand, can't wait to give their opinions. Opinions and ideas are the basis of business success. The Anglos value the Latinos' opinions very much, yet Latino employees remain silent. Since many Latinos are working in the trenches they know a lot—for example, what works and what doesn't work. Latinos must believe in themselves and give their valuable input. Learning to be more open and free with feelings, opinions and intimacies will also help build a trusting, long lasting relationship.

4.   Always do what you say you will do.

To be successful in business, as well as in life, remember the letters: DWYSYWD. Backwards or forwards it stands for "<u>D</u>o <u>w</u>hat <u>y</u>ou <u>s</u>ay <u>y</u>ou <u>w</u>ill <u>d</u>o." Or in Spanish, *Dicho y hecho:* "Once spoken, it's done." Make sure to keep every promise you make. Perhaps it is stereotypical, but to a large degree it is a Latino's nature to feel okay if they don't quite keep a commitment. Perhaps it is a Latino's reluctance to say "no". If you cannot do what you said you would or something goes wrong, tell your boss or client as soon as you know it yourself. It happens to everybody. Very often others they will help you with the problem.

Are Latin immigrants destined to become an entrenched underclass? Will they always be the "working poor"? Latinos must understand their mind set and once aware of it, they can change. Latinos are the bridge between the Americas. Companies would be crazy not to hire and promote Latinos—and they know it. They need you. They are making it easy for you. Now you must recognize certain factors within yourself that may be obstacles to your success. Once you are aware of them you can overcome them. Believe in yourself. You have a lot to offer. It's a great time to be a bilingual, bicultural Latino in the United States.

RELATIONSHIP TIP

During the holidays, give your Latino workers a phone card that they can use to call their families. The directions on how to use them are printed in English as well as in Spanish.

11

Fruits, Vegetables, and Colors

PART I—FRUITS

fruit
la fruta

grapes
las uvas

lime
la lima

orange
la naranja

strawberry
la fresa

watermelon
la sandía

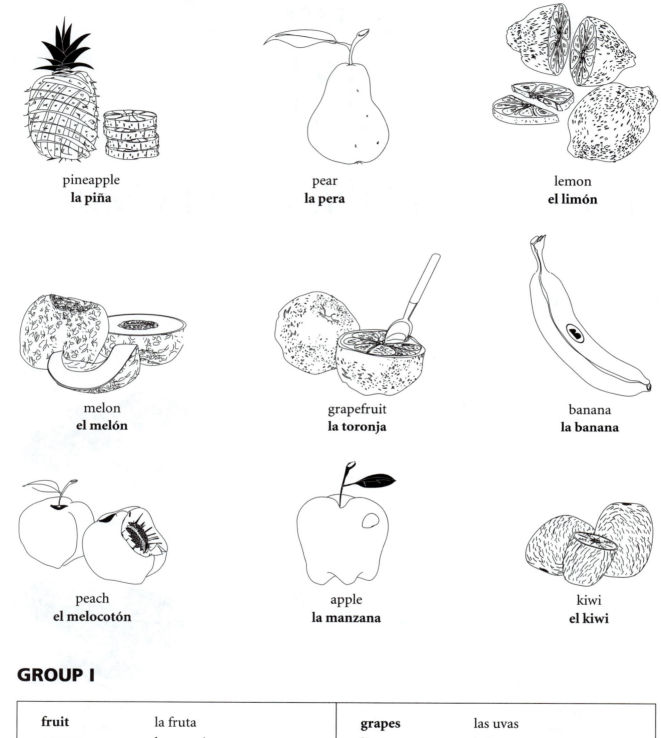

pineapple
la piña

pear
la pera

lemon
el limón

melon
el melón

grapefruit
la toronja

banana
la banana

peach
el melocotón

apple
la manzana

kiwi
el kiwi

GROUP I

fruit	la fruta		**grapes**	las uvas
orange	la naranja		**lime**	la lima
strawberry	la fresa		**pineapple**	la piña
banana	la banana		**watermelon**	la sandía

GROUP II

peach	el melocotón		**pear**	la pera
melon	el melón		**grapefruit**	la toronja
kiwi	el kiwi		**apple**	la manzana
lemon	el limón			

GROUP I

MATCHING EXERCISE

Write the letter of each picture next to the Spanish word it matches below.

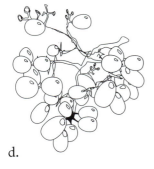

a.

b.

c.

d.

e.

f.

g.

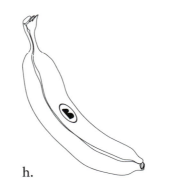

h.

1. _____ la fruta
2. _____ la naranja
3. _____ la sandía
4. _____ la piña
5. _____ la lima
6. _____ la fresa
7. _____ la banana
8. _____ las uvas

VOCABULARY EXERCISE

Write the Spanish word for each picture in the space provided.

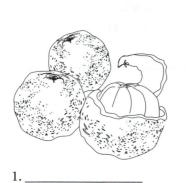

1. _____

2. _____

3. _____

4. _____

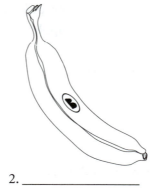

5. _____

6. _____

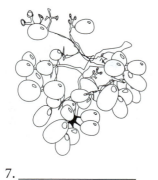

7. _____

8. _____

MATCHING EXERCISE

Write the letter of the Spanish word next to the English word it matches on the left.

1. _____ fruit
2. _____ orange
3. _____ strawberry
4. _____ watermelon
5. _____ lime
6. _____ pineapple
7. _____ grapes
8. _____ banana

a. la sandía
b. la lima
c. la fruta
d. la naranja
e. la fresa
f. las uvas
g. la piña
h. la banana

TRANSLATION EXERCISE

Translate the following to English:

1. la naranja_____
2. la fresa _____
3. la lima _____
4. la banana _____
5. la piña _____
6. la fruta_____
7. la sandía_____
8. las uvas _____

Translate the following to Spanish:

1. lime _____
2. orange _____
3. grapes _____
4. pineapple_____
5. watermelon _____
6. fruit _____
7. banana_____
8. strawberry _____

GROUP II

MATCHING EXERCISE

Write the letter of each picture next to the Spanish word it matches below.

a.

b.

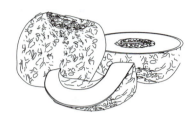

c.

d.

e.

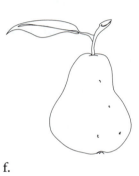

f.

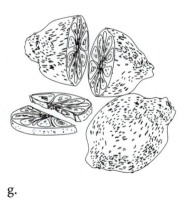

g.

1. _____ la manzana

2. _____ la toronja

3. _____ el melocotón

4. _____ la pera

5. _____ el kiwi

6. _____ el melón

7. _____ el limón

VOCABULARY EXERCISE

Write the Spanish word for each picture in the space provided.

1. _____

2. _____

3. _____

4. _____

5. _____

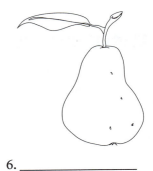

6. _____

7. _____

MATCHING EXERCISE

Write the letter of the Spanish word next to the English word it matches on the left.

1. _____ peach   a. la manzana

2. _____ melon   b. la pera

3. _____ kiwi   c. el limón

4. _____ lemon   d. el kiwi

5. _____ pear   e. el melón

6. _____ grapefruit   f. el melocotón

7. _____ apple   g. la toronja

TRANSLATION EXERCISE

Translate the following to English:

1. la toronja _____

2. el melón _____

3. la manzana _____

4. la pera _____

5. el limón _____

6. el kiwi _____

7. el melocotón _____

Translate the following to Spanish:

1. peach _____

2. apple _____

3. grapefruit _____

4. melón _____

5. kiwi _____

6. pear _____

7. lemon _____

MULTIPLE CHOICE

Circle the letter of the correct answer.

1. orange
a. la toronja
b. la naranja
c. la sandía
d. la fruta

2. strawberry
a. la fresa
b. la banana
c. las uvas
d. la lima

3. grapes
a. las uvas
b. la fresa
c. la lima
d. la fruta

4. pineapple
a. la piña
b. la pera
c. el kiwi
d. el melón

5. watermelon
a. la sandía
b. la naranja
c. la toronja
d. la manzana

6. peach
a. el melocotón
b. el melón
c. la toronja
d. la piña

7. pear
a. la pera
b. la piña
c. el kiwi
d. el melón

8. grapefruit
a. la toronja
b. la sandía
c. la naranja
d. la manzana

9. apple
a. la manzana
b. la fresa
c. la naranja
d. la sandía

CROSSWORD PUZZLES

Across

5. fresa
6. melón
9. manzana
11. fruta
12. naranja
13. uvas
14. kiwi
15. pera

Down

1. sandía
2. toronja
3. lima
4. banana
7. limón
8. piña
10. melocotón

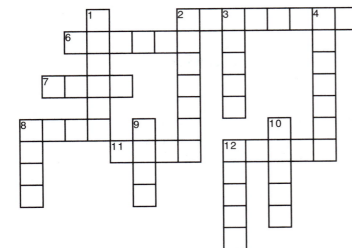

Across

2. peach
6. watermelon
7. grapes
8. pineapple
11. lime
12. strawberry

Down

1. banana
2. apple
3. lemon
4. grapefruit
5. orange
8. pear
9. kiwi
10. melon
12. fruit

PART I—ACTIONS TO USE WITH FRUITS

wash	lava		**prepare**	prepara
peel	pela		**slice**	rebana
cut	corta			

MATCHING EXERCISE

Write the letter of the Spanish word next to the English word it matches on the left.

1. _____ slice   a. pela
2. _____ prepare   b. corta
3. _____ peel   c. lava
4. _____ wash   d. rebana
5. _____ cut   e. prepara

TRANSLATION EXERCISE

Translate the following to English:

1. lava _____
2. pela _____
3. rebana _____
4. corta _____
5. prepara _____

Translate the following to Spanish:

1. slice _____
2. wash _____
3. prepare _____
4. peel _____
5. cut _____

MULTIPLE CHOICE

Circle the letter of the correct answer.

1. peel
   a. corta
   b. lava
   c. pela
   d. rebana

2. cut
   a. prepara
   b. lava
   c. corta
   d. rebana

3. slice
   a. corta
   b. lava
   c. pela
   d. rebana

4. wash
   a. prepara
   b. lava
   c. corta
   d. rebana

5. prepare
   a. prepara
   b. lava
   c. corta
   d. rebana

GRAMMAR DO NOT. . . DON'T. . .

To express the words "Do not" or "Don't" in Spanish simply say "No" before the action and change the "*a*" ending to "*es*" or the "*e*" ending to "*as*". Study the examples.

Cut	**Corta**
Don't cut	**No cortes**
Prepare	**Prepara**
Don't prepare	**No prepares**
Peel	**Pela**
Don't peel	**No peles**

If this is difficult for you to remember, simply say "*No*" before the action word that ends in "*a*". For example, *No corta. . . No prepara. . .* It is not grammatically correct but your Spanish-speaking co-workers will understand not to do the action.

ROLE PLAY

Do not. . . Don't Working with a partner translate the first sentence to English. Next, in Spanish, say not to do it. Follow the model.
Lava las manzanas.

ESTUDIANTE A:	Wash the apples.
ESTUDIANTE B:	No laves las manzanas.

1. Rebana el melón.
2. Pela la piña.
3. Lava la fruta.
4. Prepara la sandía.
5. Corta las manzanas.
6. Rebana los melocotónes.
7. Pela las peras.
8. Lava las uvas.
9. Prepara los limónes.
10. Corta las toronjas.
11. Rebana las bananas.
12. Pela las naranjas.
13. Prepara el kiwi.
14. Lava las fresas.
15. Corta las limas.

Translate the following to Spanish:

1. Prepare the watermelon. _____
2. Peel the pineapple._____
3. Wash the grapes. _____
4. Don't cut the fruit. _____
5. Slice the oranges._____
6. Prepare the melon. _____
7. Wash the fruit._____
8. Cut the grapefruit._____
9. Peel the lemons._____
10. Slice the kiwi._____
11. Wash the peaches. _____
12. Don't prepare the apples. _____
13. Slice the strawberries. _____
14. Cut the bananas. _____
15. Peel the limes. _____

PART II—VEGETABLES

vegetables
los vegetales

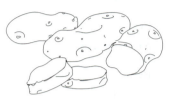

potatoes
las papas

carrots
las zanahorias

onions
las cebollas

tomatoes
los tomates

cucumbers
los pepinos

mushrooms
los champiñones

celery
el apio

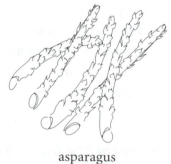

asparagus
el espárrago

lettuce
la lechuga

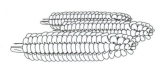

corn
el maíz

broccoli
el brocolí

spinach
la espinaca

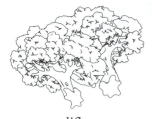

cauliflower
la coliflor

GROUP I

vegetables	los vegetales		**tomatoes**	los tomates
carrots	las zanahorias		**cucumbers**	los pepinos
onions	las cebollas		**peppers**	los pimientos
potatoes	las papas		**mushrooms**	los champiñones

GROUP II

lettuce	la lechuga		**asparagus**	el espárrago
spinach	la espinaca		**broccoli**	el brocolí
cauliflower	la coliflor		**corn**	el maíz
celery	el apio			

GROUP I

MATCHING EXERCISE

Write the letter of each picture next to the Spanish word it matches below.

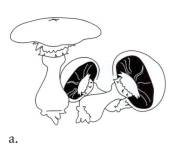

a.

b.

c.

d.

e.

f.

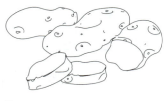

g.

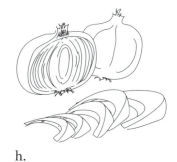

h.

1. _____ los vegetales
2. _____ las zanahorias
3. _____ los champiñones
4. _____ las cebollas
5. _____ las papas
6. _____ los pepinos
7. _____ los tomates
8. _____ los pimientos

VOCABULARY EXERCISE

Write the Spanish word for each picture in the space provided.

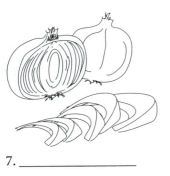

1. _____

2. _____

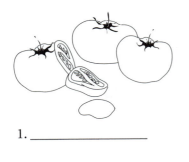

3. _____

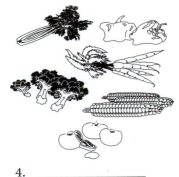

4. _____

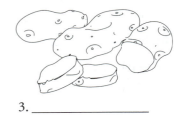

5. _____

6. _____

7. _____

8. _____

MATCHING EXERCISE

Write the letter of the Spanish word next to the English word it matches on the left.

1. _____ vegetables   a. los pimientos

2. _____ carrots   b. los champiñones

3. _____ onions   c. los pepinos

4. _____ potatoes   d. los vegetales

5. _____ tomatoes   e. las zanahorias

6. _____ cucumbers   f. las cebollas

7. _____ peppers   g. las papas

8. _____ mushrooms   h. los tomates

TRANSLATION EXERCISE

Translate the following to English:

1. los champiñones _____
2. las cebollas _____
3. los tomates _____
4. las papas _____
5. los pimientos _____
6. los pepinos _____
7. los vegetales _____
8. las zanahorias _____

Translate the following to Spanish:

1. cucumbers _____
2. potatoes _____
3. mushrooms _____
4. tomatoes _____
5. carrots _____
6. vegetables _____
7. peppers _____
8. onions _____

GROUP II

MATCHING EXERCISE

Write the letter of each picture next to the Spanish word it matches below.

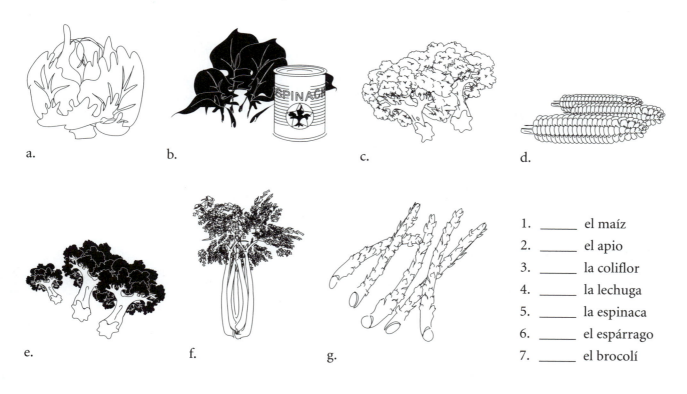

a.
b.
c.
d.

e.
f.
g.

1. _____ el maíz
2. _____ el apio
3. _____ la coliflor
4. _____ la lechuga
5. _____ la espinaca
6. _____ el espárrago
7. _____ el brocolí

VOCABULARY EXERCISE

Write the Spanish word for each picture in the space provided.

1. _____

2. _____

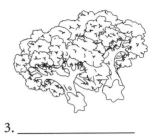

3. _____

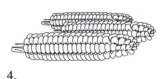

4. _____

5. _____

6. _____

7. _____

MATCHING EXERCISE

Write the letter of the Spanish word next to the English word it matches on the left.

1. _____ corn

2. _____ broccoli

3. _____ asparagus

4. _____ celery

5. _____ cauliflower

6. _____ spinach

7. _____ lettuce

a. la espinaca

b. el apio

c. el maíz

d. la lechuga

e. el brocolí

f. el espárrago

g. la coliflor

TRANSLATION EXERCISE

Translate the following to English:

1. la coliflor _____

2. el brocolí _____

3. el maíz _____

4. la espinaca _____

5. el espárrago _____

6. la lechuga _____

7. el apio _____

Translate the following to Spanish:

1. cauliflower _____

2. celery _____

3. lettuce _____

4. spinach _____

5. asparagus _____

6. corn _____

7. broccoli _____

MULTIPLE CHOICE

Circle the letter of the correct answer.

1. onion
   a. el apio
   b. la lechuga
   c. la cebolla
   d. la espinaca

2. lettuce
   a. el brocolí
   b. el cebolla
   c. el apio
   d. la lechuga

3. mushrooms
   a. el apio
   b. los champiñones
   c. la lechuga
   d. las cebollas

4. cucumber
   a. el pepino
   b. el pimiento
   c. el apio
   d. el champiñon

5. celery
   a. la zanahoria
   b. el espárrago
   c. la lechuga
   d. el apio

6. corn
   a. el maíz
   b. la lechuga
   c. la coliflor
   d. el apio

7. peppers
   a. las papas
   b. los pimientos
   c. los pepinos
   d. las zanahorias

8. carrot
   a. el pimiento
   b. el pepino
   c. la coliflor
   d. la zanahoria

9. vegetables
   a. los vegetales
   b. las zanahorias
   c. el apio
   d. las cebollas

CROSSWORD PUZZLES

Across

2. maíz
3. papas
8. brocolí
9. champiñones
10. tomates
13. apio
14. espárrago

Down

1. zanahorias
2. coliflor
4. cebollas
5. espinaca
6. lechuga
7. pepinos
11. vegetales
12. pimientos

Across

2. lettuce
8. onions
9. spinach
11. corn
13. carrots
14. broccoli

Down

1. celery
3. mushrooms
4. vegetables
5. tomatoes
6. potatoes
7. asparagus
10. cucumbers
12. cauliflower

PART II—ACTIONS TO USE WITH VEGETABLES

chop	pica		**refill**	rellena
cook	cocina		**make**	haz
bring	trae			

MATCHING EXERCISE

Write the letter of the Spanish word next to the English word it matches on the left.

1. _____ refill   a. cocina
2. _____ cook   b. trae
3. _____ make   c. pica
4. _____ bring   d. rellena
5. _____ chop   e. haz

TRANSLATION EXERCISE

Translate the following to English:

1. pica _____

2. rellena _____

3. haz _____

4. cocina _____

5. trae _____

Translate the following to Spanish:

1. chop _____

2. cook _____

3. make _____

4. bring _____

5. refill _____

MULTIPLE CHOICE

Circle the letter of the correct answer.

1. refill
   a. pica
   b. trae
   c. haz
   d. rellena

2. make
   a. pica
   b. cocina
   c. haz
   d. rellena

3. cook
   a. trae
   b. cocina
   c. haz
   d. rellena

4. chop
   a. pica
   b. cocina
   c. haz
   d. rellena

5. bring
   a. pica
   b. trae
   c. haz
   d. rellena

TRANSLATION EXERCISE

Translate the following to English:

1. Trae las papas. _____

2. Rellena los pepinos. _____

3. Cocina el maíz. _____

4. Pica las cebollas. _____

5. Haz el brocolí. _____

6. Trae la espinaca. _____

7. Cocina la coliflor. _____

8. Pica el apio. _____

9. Rellena los champiñones. _____

10. Trae la lechuga. _____

11. Cocina las papas. _____

Translate the following to Spanish:

1. Chop the onions. _____

2. Refill the peppers. _____

3. Make the cauliflower. _____

4. Bring the potatoes. _____

5. Cook the broccoli. _____

6. Chop the mushrooms. _____

7. Make the spinach. _____

8. Bring the corn. _____

9. Refill the tomatoes. _____

10. Cook the vegetables. _____

11. Bring the asparagus. _____

12. Haz el brocolí. _____   12. Refill the cucumbers._____

13. Pica los pimientos. _____   13. Chop the celery._____

14. Rellena el apio. _____   14. Make the spinach. _____

15. Trae el maíz. _____   15. Bring the lettuce._____

PART III—COLORS

red	rojo		**orange**	anaranjado
white	blanco		**pink**	rosado
blue	azul		**negro**	black
green	verde		**brown**	café
purple	morado		**gray**	gris
yellow	amarillo			

MATCHING EXERCISE

Write the letter of the Spanish word next to the English word it matches on the left.

1. _____ black   a. blanco
2. _____ brown   b. negro
3. _____ red   c. café
4. _____ white   d. anaranjado
5. _____ green   e. verde
6. _____ blue   f. gris
7. _____ gray   g. azul
8. _____ pink   h. rosado
9. _____ orange   i. rojo
10. _____ yellow   j. morado
11. _____ purple   k. amarillo

CROSSWORD PUZZLES

Across

3. yellow
4. brown
6. gray
8. black
9. white
10. purple

Down

1. green
2. pink
3. orange
5. blue
7. red

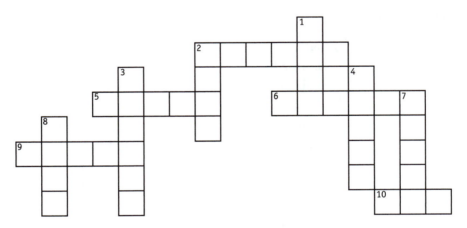

Across

2. morado
5. verde
6. amarillo
9. café
10. rojo

Down

1. azul
2. rosado
3. anaranjado
4. negro
7. blanco
8. gris

TRANSLATION EXERCISE

Translate the following to English:

1. verde _____

2. amarillo _____

3. rojo _____

4. blanco _____

5. azul _____

6. anaranjado _____

7. rosado _____

8. black _____

9. morado _____

10. café _____

11. gris _____

Translate the following to Spanish:

1. blue _____

2. green _____

3. red _____

4. white _____

5. purple _____

6. gray _____

7. yellow _____

8. orange _____

9. black _____

10. brown _____

11. pink _____

MULTIPLE CHOICE

Circle the letter of the correct answer.

1. pink
   a. anaranjado
   b. rosado
   c. rojo
   d. morado

2. green
   a. gris
   b. azul
   c. verde
   d. blanco

3. purple
   a. anaranjado
   b. morado
   c. azul
   d. amarillo

4. red
   a. rosado
   b. blanco
   c. café
   d. rojo

5. yellow
   a. rojo
   b. verde
   c. anaranjado
   d. amarillo

6. blue
   a. morado
   b. gris
   c. azul
   d. verde

7. white
   a. blanco
   b. azul
   c. morado
   d. negro

8. black
   a. blanco
   b. azul
   c. morado
   d. negro

9. orange
   a. anaranjado
   b. rosado
   c. rojo
   d. morado

ROLE PLAY

A. **Attractive and Colorful Foods.** Now Open! In the restaurant you have just opened, you pride yourself on serving not only good food, but attractive and colorful food. Working with a partner, ask and answer what color the following foods are. Follow the model.

ESTUDIANTE A: ¿De qué color es la espinaca?

ESTUDIANTE B: Verde.

1. la naranja
2. la fresa
3. la banana
4. la sandía
5. la piña
6. la uva
7. el melocotón
8. el melón

9. el limón
10. la pera
11. la toronja
12. la manzana
13. la zanahoria
14. la cebolla
15. la papa
16. el tomate

17. el pepino
18. los pimientos
19. la lechuga
20. la espinaca
21. la coliflor
22. el apio
23. el espárrago
24. el maíz

B. **Menu Planning.** To plan your menu for the day, you first must separate foods into colors. Using the fruits and vegetables in part A, write the food item under the appropriate color.

rojo
_____
_____
_____
_____
_____

verde
_____
_____
_____
_____
_____

anaranjado
_____
_____
_____
_____
_____

blanco
_____
_____
_____
_____

morado
_____
_____
_____
_____

rosado
_____
_____
_____
_____

azul
_____
_____
_____
_____
_____

amarillo
_____
_____
_____
_____
_____

DIALOGUE

Read the dialogue aloud in Spanish. Then translate it to English.	*Read the dialogue aloud in English. Then translate it to Spanish.*
George: Hola. . . ¿ Dónde está Steve?	**George:** Hi. . . Where is Steve?
Manuel: Steve está preparando la fruta.	**Manuel:** Steve is preparing the fruit.
George: ¿Dónde está Teresa?	**George:** Where is Teresa?
Manuel: Teresa está lavando la fruta.	**Manuel:** Teresa is washing the fruit.
George: ¿Puedes ayudarme, Manuel?	**George:** Can you help me, Manuel?
Manuel: No, Mark. Estoy muy ocupado.	**Manuel:** No, Mark. I am very busy.
George: Está bien. ¿Dónde está Luisa?	**George:** Okay. Where is Luisa?
Manuel: Luisa está ayudando a Teresa.	**Manuel:** Luisa is helping Teresa.
George: ¿Y Steve?	**George:** And Steve?
Manuel: Steve está preparando la sandía.	**Manuel:** Steve is preparing the watermelon.
George: ¿Y Jóse?	**George:** And Jóse?
Manuel: Jóse está rebanando las piñas.	**Manuel:** Jóse is slicing the pineapples.
George: Manuel. . . por favor. . . ¡ Ayúdame!	**George:** Manuel. . . please. . . Help me!
Manuel: Está bien.	**Manuel:** Okay.
George: Primero, pela las manzanas.	**George:** First, peel the apples.
Manuel: ¿Las rojas o las verdes?	**Manuel:** The red ones or the green ones?
George: No peles las rojas. Pela las verdes. Segundo, lava las uvas.	**George:** Do not peel the red ones. Peel the green ones. Second, wash the grapes.
Manuel: ¿Las moradas o las verdes?	**Manuel:** The purple ones or the green ones?
George: Las moradas.	**George:** The purple ones.
Manuel: Está bien.	**Manuel:** Okay.
George: ¿Rebanaste las bananas?	**George:** Did you slice the bananas?
Manuel: No, todavia, no.	**Manuel:** No, not yet.
George: ¿Por qué no?	**George:** Why not?
Manuel: ¿Las rojas, las verdes o las amarillas?	**Manuel:** The red, green, or yellow ones?
George: ¡Eres cómico, Manuel!	**George:** You are funny, Manuel.
Manuel: No. . . está correcto, George. En México hay bananas de muchos colores.	**Manuel:** No, that's correct, George. In Mexico there are bananas of many colors.
George: ¿Dónde está Jesús?	**George:** Where is Jesús?
Manuel: Jesús no está aquí. Está estudiando el inglés hoy.	**Manuel:** Jesús is not here. He is studying English today.
George: ¿Dónde?	**George:** Where?
Manuel: Hay clases en la universidad.	**Manuel:** In the university.
George: ¿Qué días de la semana?	**George:** What day are the classes?

Manuel:	El lunes, el miércoles, y el viernes.		**Manuel:**	On Mondays, Wednesdays, and Fridays.
George:	¿Por la mañana o por la noche?		**George:**	In the morning or at night?
Manuel:	Por la noche.		**Manuel:**	At night.
George:	¿Hablas inglés, Manuel?		**George:**	Do you speak English, Manuel?
Manuel:	Sí, señor. ¿Hablas español, George?		**Manuel:**	Yes, sir. Do you speak Spanish, George?
George:	Ahhh. . .		**George:**	Ahhh. . .
Manuel:	¿De qué color son las cebollas, las papas y la coliflor?		**Manuel:**	What color are onions, potatoes, and cauliflower?
George:	Blanco.		**George:**	White.
Manuel:	¿De qué color es la lechuga, el brocolí y la espinaca?		**Manuel:**	What color is lettuce, broccoli, and spinach?
George:	Verde.		**George:**	Green.
Manuel:	¿Y el maíz?		**Manuel:**	And corn?
George:	Rosado.		**George:**	Pink.
Manuel:	¿Rosado? No.		**Manuel:**	Pink?
George:	Morado.		**George:**	Purple.
Manuel:	¿Morado?		**Manuel:**	Purple?
George:	Amarillo.		**George:**	Yellow.
Manuel:	Sí. ¿Y de qué color es la zanahoria?		**Manuel:**	Yes. And what color is the carrot?
George:	¿A-na-na-ra-ra-hado?		**George:**	Orange.
Manuel:	No, anaranjado. A-na-ran-ja-do.		**Manuel:**	No, orange. Orange.
George:	A-na-ran-ja-do. Anaranjado.		**George:**	Orange. Orange.
Manuel:	Perfecto. Buena pronunciación.		**Manuel:**	Perfect. Good pronunciation.
George:	Gracias.		**George:**	Thanks.
Manuel:	Eres muy inteligente.		**Manuel:**	You are intelligent.
George:	Por favor. . . pica las cebollas y los pimientos.		**George:**	Please. . . chop the onions and the peppers.
Manuel:	¿Y las champiñones y el apio?		**Manuel:**	And the mushrooms and celery?
George:	Sí. Prepara los tomates.		**George:**	Yes. Prepare the tomatoes.
Manuel:	Está bien.		**Manuel:**	Okay.
George:	¿Cocinaste los vegetales?		**George:**	Did you cook the vegetables?
Manuel:	No, todavia, no.		**Manuel:**	No, not yet.
George:	Rápido. Haz la coliflor y el brocolí. Y trae una ensalada a la mujer.		**George:**	Quick. Make the cauliflower and the broccoli. And bring a salad to the woman.
Manuel:	¿Dónde?		**Manuel:**	Where?
George:	La mujer en el suéter a-na-ra-na-ha. . .		**George:**	The woman in the orange sweater.
Manuel:	¡ANARANJADO!		**Manuel:**	ORANGE!

REVIEW

Translate the following to Spanish:

1. You're a hard worker! _____
2. Come with me. _____
3. Who? Where? When? _____
4. The guest is angry. _____
5. Do you like to play billiards? _____
6. Wash the mirror. _____
7. Dust the furniture. _____
8. Get the mop. _____
9. Replenish the forks. _____
10. Fold the napkins. _____
11. Mop the floor. _____
12. The manager is in the office. _____
13. The supervisor is in the dining room. _____
14. Does your finger hurt? _____
15. Under, over _____
16. To the left, to the right _____
17. Red, green, yellow _____
18. Brown, black, white _____
19. Lettuce, tomatoes, onions _____
20. Orange, grapefruit, strawberry _____

CULTURE: NAMES AND NICKNAMES

The importance of the family in Latino culture is seen in the Spanish system of last names. The majority of Latinos have two last names. The system confuses many employees working in the personnel offices of organizations in the United States.

The father's name comes first, followed by the mother's name. Juan Martínez López has a father whose surname is Martínez and a mother whose maiden name is López. If Juan's sister Ana marries Javier Hernández Rodríguez she keeps her father's name, drops her mother's name and becomes Ana Martínez Hernández.

Nicknames are popular in both cultures. In English, the nickname for Robert is Bob, for William it's Bill and for Michael, Mike. In Spanish, common nicknames are Pepe for José, Paco for Francisco and Memo for Guillermo. In

English, young children often use the diminutive form of their name. In English the name ends in-*v* or–*ie* and in Spanish the names end in–*ito* or–*ita*.

Many terms of endearment in the Latin culture may surprise Anglos. *Gordo* (chubby), *Flaco* (skinny), *pelón* (bald) and *Cuatro ojos* (four eyes) are used often and affectionately with no intent to offend the person. In the United States it is the reverse. This type of nickname is often used to be cruel.

A person's name is important to a person. It is important to learn to pronounce and spell your co-workers' names correctly.

CHAPTER

12

Beverages

PART I—BEVERAGES

coffee
el café

decaf coffee
el café decaf

tea
el té

iced tea
el té helado

milk
la leche

lemonade
la limonada

water
el agua

juice
el jugo

champagne
la champaña

soft drink
el refresco

shake
el batido

beer
la cerveza

wine
el vino

red wine
el vino tinto

white wine
el vino blanco

GROUP I

water	el agua	**iced tea**	el té helado
coffee	el café	**juice**	el jugo
decaf coffee	el café decaf	**lemonade**	la limonada
tea	el té	**milk**	la leche

GROUP II

beer	la cerveza	**champagne**	la champaña
wine	el vino	**soft drink**	el refresco
red wine	el vino tinto	**shake**	el batido
white wine	el vino blanco		

GROUP I

MATCHING EXERCISE

Write the letter of each picture next to the Spanish word it matches below.

a.

b.

c.

d.

e.

f.

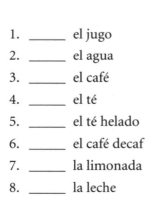

g.

h.

1. _____ el jugo

2. _____ el agua

3. _____ el café

4. _____ el té

5. _____ el té helado

6. _____ el café decaf

7. _____ la limonada

8. _____ la leche

VOCABULARY EXERCISE

Write the Spanish word for each picture in the space provided.

1. _____

2. _____

3. _____

4. _____

5. _____

6. _____

7. _____

8. _____

MATCHING EXERCISE

Write the letter of the Spanish word next to the English word it matches on the left.

1. _____ iced tea		a. la leche	
2. _____ milk		b. el té	
3. _____ juice		c. el té helado	
4. _____ tea		d. el café	
5. _____ lemonade		e. el café decaf	
6. _____ coffee		f. la limonada	
7. _____ water		g. el jugo	
8. _____ decaf coffee		h. el agua	

TRANSLATION EXERCISE

Translate the following to English:

1. el jugo _____

2. la leche _____

3. el agua _____

4. el café _____

5. el café decaf _____

6. el té _____

7. el té helado _____

8. la limonada _____

Translate the following to Spanish:

1. decaf coffee _____

2. iced tea _____

3. juice _____

4. coffee _____

5. tea _____

6. milk _____

7. lemonade _____

8. water _____

GROUP II

MATCHING EXERCISE

Write the letter of each picture next to the Spanish word it matches below.

a.

b.

c.

d.

e.

f.

g.

1. _____ el vino tinto

2. _____ la cerveza

3. _____ el refresco

4. _____ el vino blanco

5. _____ el batido

6. _____ el vino

7. _____ la champaña

VOCABULARY EXERCISE

Write the Spanish word for each picture in the space provided.

1. _____

2. _____

3. _____

4. _____

5. _____

6. _____

7. _____

MATCHING EXERCISE

Write the letter of the Spanish word next to the English word it matches on the left.

1. _____ wine   a. el batido

2. _____ soft drink   b. la cerveza

3. _____ champagne   c. el vino

4. _____ white wine   d. el vino tinto

5. _____ beer   e. el refresco

6. _____ shake   f. la champaña

7. _____ red wine   g. el vino blanco

TRANSLATION EXERCISE

Translate the following to English:

1. el vino blanco _____

2. el batido _____

3. el refresco _____

4. el vino tinto _____

5. la champaña _____

6. la cerveza _____

7. el vino _____

Translate the following to Spanish:

1. wine _____

2. red wine _____

3. white wine _____

4. soft drink _____

5. champagne _____

6. shake _____

7. beer _____

MULTIPLE CHOICE

Circle the letter of the correct answer.

1. juice
   a. el vino
   b. el jugo
   c. la leche
   d. el agua

2. milk
   a. la leche
   b. el vino
   c. el jugo
   d. el agua

3. wine
   a. la leche
   b. el vino
   c. el jugo
   d. el agua

4. water
   a. la leche
   b. el vino
   c. el jugo
   d. el agua

5. tea
   a. el batido
   b. el té
   c. la champaña
   d. el refresco

6. beer
   a. el refresco
   b. el jugo
   c. el batido
   d. la cerveza

7. soft drink
   a. el refresco
   b. el jugo
   c. el batido
   d. la cerveza

8. shake
   a. el jugo
   b. el batido
   c. la champaña
   d. el refresco

9. champagne
   a. la champaña
   b. el batido
   c. el té
   d. el refresco

CROSSWORD PUZZLES

Across

4. agua
7. te helado
8. jugo
11. refresco
12. batido
13. vino
14. café decaf

Down

1. leche
2. limonada
3. cerveza
5. té
6. vino tinto
9. café
10. vino blanco
15. champaña

Across

9. tea
10. iced tea
12. red wine
13. coffee
14. champagne
15. water

Down

1. juice
2. soft drink
3. beer
4. milk
5. decaf coffee
6. white wine
7. shake
8. wine
11. lemonade

GRAMMAR: EXPRESSING WANTS

To express wants and desires in Spanish, we use the verb *Querer*. Study the examples.

Would you like something to drink?	¿Quisieras algo para tomar?
What would you like?	¿Qué quisieras?
I would like . . .	Quisiera . . .
What do you want?	¿Qué quieres?
I want	Quiero
Do you want. . . ?	¿Quieres. . . ?

ROLE PLAY

A. Would you like something to drink? A Wedding Reception! Pretend it's a warm summer evening and you have been dining and dancing with your friends and family all night. And you are thirsty! The server wants to know what you would like to drink. Working with a partner ask *¿Qué quisieras tomar?* (*Un* and *una* mean a) Follow the model.

ESTUDIANTE A: ¿Quisieras algo para tomar?
ESTUDIANTE B: Quisiera una cerveza.

1.

2.

3.

4.

5.

6.

7.

8.

9.

10.

11.

12.

13.   14.   15.

B. May I suggest. . . ? Using the same word from Part A. Suggest a drink to the diners. Follow the model.

ESTUDIANTE A: Recomendaría. . .
ESTUDIANTE B: ¡Buen idea! Gracias.

PART I—ACTIONS TO USE WITH BEVERAGES

make	haz		**serve**	sirve
fill	llena		**bring**	trae
refill	rellena			

MATCHING EXERCISE

Write the letter of the Spanish word next to the English word it matches on the left.

1. _____ serve   a. haz
2. _____ refill   b. trae
3. _____ make   c. llena
4. _____ fill   d. sirve
5. _____ bring   e. rellena

TRANSLATION EXERCISE

Translate the following to English: *Translate the following to Spanish:*

1. rellena _____   1. make _____

2. haz _____   2. serve _____

3. sirve _____   3. fill _____

4. trae _____   4. refill _____

5. llena _____   5. bring _____

MULTIPLE CHOICE

Circle the letter of the correct answer.

1. serve
  a. haz
  b. llena
  c. rellena
  d. sirve

2. bring
  a. sirve
  b. trae
  c. haz
  d. llena

3. make
  a. haz
  b. llena
  c. rellena
  d. sirve

4. fill
  a. sirve
  b. trae
  c. haz
  d. llena

5. refill
  a. haz
  b. llena
  c. rellena
  d. sirve

TRANSLATION EXERCISE

Translate the following to English:

1. Llena el té helado. _____

2. Rellena el agua. _____

3. Sirve el batido._____

4. Haz el café. _____

5. Trae la leche. _____

6. Llena la limonada._____

7. Rellena el café decaf. _____

8. Trae el vino tinto. _____

9. Sirve la champaña. _____

10. Haz el té. _____

11. Trae el refresco. _____

12. Haz el batido. _____

13. Llena el vino tinto. _____

14. Sirve la cerveza._____

15. Rellena el café._____

Translate the following to Spanish:

1. Make the coffee. _____

2. Fill the juice. _____

3. Refill the iced tea. _____

4. Serve the lemonade. _____

5. Bring the milk. _____

6. Make the iced tea. _____

7. Serve the champagne. _____

8. Fill the water. _____

9. Refill the decaf coffee. _____

10. Bring the wine. _____

11. Serve the soft drink. _____

12. Make the shake._____

13. Fill the tea. _____

14. Bring the beer._____

15. Refill the white wine._____

PART II—THE SERVICE STATION

plates
los platos

glasses
los vasos

silverware
los cubiertos

pitcher
la jarra

ice
el hielo

bread basket
la cesta para el pan

pepper shaker
el pimentero

tray
la charola

tray jack
las tijeras

condiments
los condimentos

containers
los recipientes

ash tray
el cenicero

matches
los cerillos

ice bucket
la hielera

napkins
las servilletas

GROUP I

ice	el hielo	**silverware**	los cubiertos
ice bucket	la hielera	**glasses**	los vasos
pitcher	la jarra	**tray**	la charola
plates	los platos	**tray jack**	las tijeras

GROUP II

condiments	los condimentos	**bread basket**	la cesta para el pan
containers	los recipientes	**ash tray**	el cenicero
napkins	las servilletas	**matches**	los cerillos
pepper shaker	el pimentero		

GROUP I

MATCHING EXERCISE

Write the letter of each picture next to the Spanish word it matches below.

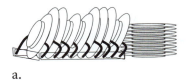

a.

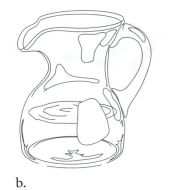

b.

c.

d.

e.

f.

g.

h.

1. _____ las tijeras
2. _____ los vasos
3. _____ el hielo
4. _____ la jarra
5. _____ la hielera
6. _____ la charola
7. _____ los cubiertos
8. _____ los platos

VOCABULARY EXERCISE

Write the Spanish word for each picture in the space provided.

1. _____

2. _____

3. _____

4. _____

5. _____

6. _____

7. _____

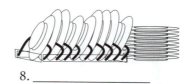

8. _____

MATCHING EXERCISE

Write the letter of the Spanish word next to the English word it matches on the left.

1.	_____	silverware	a.	los cubiertos
2.	_____	plates	b.	los platos
3.	_____	pitcher	c.	la jarra
4.	_____	tray	d.	la charola
5.	_____	ice	e.	las tijeras
6.	_____	glasses	f.	la hielera
7.	_____	ice bucket	g.	el hielo
8.	_____	tray jack	h.	los vasos

TRANSLATION EXERCISE

Translate the following to English:

1. la jarra _____

2. los vasos _____

3. la hielera _____

4. los cubiertos _____

5. los platos _____

6. la jarra _____

7. la charola _____

8. las tijeras _____

Translate the following to Spanish:

1. tray jack _____

2. tray _____

3. ice _____

4. ice bucket _____

5. glasses _____

6. silverware _____

7. plates _____

8. pitcher _____

GROUP II

MATCHING EXERCISE

Write the letter of each picture next to the Spanish word it matches below.

a.

b.

c.

d.

e.

f.

g.

1. _____ los cerillos

2. _____ el cenicero

3. _____ la cesta para el pan

4. _____ las servilletas

5. _____ los recipientes

6. _____ los condimentos

7. _____ el pimentero

VOCABULARY EXERCISE

Write the Spanish word for each picture in the space provided.

1. _____

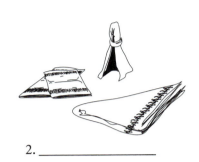

2. _____

3. _____

4. _____

5. _____

6. _____

7. _____

MATCHING EXERCISE

Write the letter of the Spanish word next to the English word it matches on the left.

1. _____ ash tray
2. _____ bread basket
3. _____ napkins
4. _____ pepper shaker
5. _____ matches
6. _____ containers
7. _____ condiments

a. el pimentero
b. los cerillos
c. la cesta para el pan
d. los recipientes
e. el cenicero
f. los condimentos
g. las servilletas

TRANSLATION EXERCISE

Translate the following to English:

1. los condimentos _____

2. los recipientes _____

3. los cerillos _____

4. el cenicero _____

5. las servilletas _____

6. la cesta para el pan_____

7. el pimentero _____

Translate the following to Spanish:

1. matches _____

2. pepper shaker _____

3. condiments _____

4. ash tray _____

5. containers _____

6. napkins _____

7. bread basket _____

MULTIPLE CHOICE

Circle the letter of the correct answer.

1. ash tray
   a. la charola
   b. el cenicero
   c. los cerillos
   d. los cubiertos

2. containers
   a. los recipientes
   b. las tijeras
   c. el hielo
   d. la hielera

3. silverware
   a. la charola
   b. el cenicero
   c. los cubiertos
   d. los cerillos

4. ice bucket
   a. la jarra
   b. las tijeras
   c. el hielo
   d. la hielera

5. matches
   a. la charola
   b. el cenicero
   c. los cubiertos
   d. los cerillos

6. tray jack
   a. la jarra
   b. las tijeras
   c. el hielo
   d. la hielera

7. tray
   a. la charola
   b. el cenicero
   c. los cubiertos
   d. los cerillos

8. ice
   a. la jarra
   b. las tijeras
   c. el hielo
   d. la hielera

9. pitcher
   a. la hielera
   b. las tijeras
   c. los recipientes
   d. la jarra

CROSSWORD PUZZLES

Across

5. hielera
7. charola
10. condimentos
11. tijeras
13. vasos
15. hielo

Down

1. cesta para el pan
2. cubiertos
3. pimentero
4. cerillos
6. recipientes
8. servilletas
9. cenicero
12. platos
14. jarra

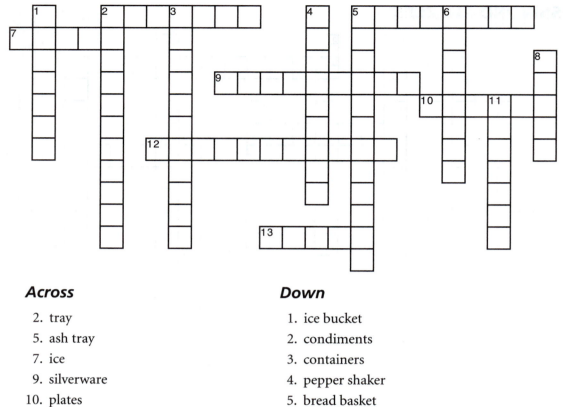

Across

2. tray
5. ash tray
7. ice
9. silverware
10. plates
12. napkins
13. pitcher

Down

1. ice bucket
2. condiments
3. containers
4. pepper shaker
5. bread basket
6. matches
8. glasses
11. tray jack

PART II—ACTIONS TO USE WITH THE SERVICE STATION

bring   trae
fill   llena
fold   dobla
polish   pule
clear   quita

MATCHING EXERCISE

Write the letter of the Spanish word next to the English word it matches on the left.

1. _____ fold   a. trae
2. _____ clear   b. llena
3. _____ polish   c. dobla
4. _____ fill   d. pule
5. _____ bring   e. quita

TRANSLATION EXERCISE

Translate the following to English:

1. quita _____

2. dobla _____

3. trae _____

4. llena _____

5. pule _____

Translate the following to Spanish:

1. fold _____

2. bring _____

3. clear _____

4. polish _____

5. fill _____

MULTIPLE CHOICE

Circle the letter of the correct answer.

1. polish
   a. dobla
   b. llena
   c. quita
   d. pule

2. fold
   a. trae
   b. dobla
   c. quita
   d. llena

3. clear
   a. dobla
   b. llena
   c. quita
   d. pule

4. fill
   a. trae
   b. dobla
   c. quita
   d. llena

5. bring
   a. trae
   b. dobla
   c. quita
   d. llena

Translate the following to English:

1. Llena los vasos. _____

2. Quita las tijeras. _____

3. Trae el pimentero. _____

4. Dobla las servilletas. _____

5. Llena la jarra. _____

6. Quita el cenicero. _____

7. Trae la cesta para el pan. _____

8. Pule los cubiertos. _____

9. Dobla ocho servilletas. _____

10. Quita los platos. _____

11. Llena los condimentos. _____

12. Trae los cerillos. _____

13. Pule la hielera. _____

14. Trae la charola. _____

15. Quita las tijeras. _____

Translate the following to Spanish:

1. Clear the plates. _____

2. Polish the silverware. _____

3. Fold the napkins. _____

4. Bring the pepper shaker. _____

5. Fill the bread basket. _____

6. Clear the tray jack. _____

7. Fold ten napkins. _____

8. Bring the matches. _____

9. Polish the ice bucket. _____

10. Fill the condiments. _____

11. Bring the ice. _____

12. Clear the glasses. _____

13. Bring the pitcher. _____

14. Fill the containers. _____

15. Clear the ash tray. _____

DIALOGUE

Read the dialogue aloud in Spanish. Then translate it to English.	*Read the dialogue aloud in English. Then translate it to Spanish.*
Margarita: Buenas noches, Jennifer.	**Margarita:** Good evening, Jennifer.
Jennifer: Hola. ¿Qué tal? ¿Hay problemas?	**Jennifer:** Hello. How's it going? Any problems?
Margarita: No, todo está perfecto. Soy muy organizada.	**Margarita:** No everything is perfect. I am very organized.
Jennifer: Gracias. Por favor, haz el cáfe.	**Jennifer:** Thank you. Please, make the coffee.
Jennifer: ¿Y el té helado?	**Jennifer:** And the iced tea?
Margarita: Sí. Y Geraldo, llena los vasos de agua.	**Margarita:** Yes. And Geraldo, fill the water glasses.
Geraldo: Está bien.	**Geraldo:** Okay.
(a la mesa)	(at the table)
Margarita: Hola. Buenas noches.	**Margarita:** Hello. Good evening.
Peter: Hola.	**Peter:** Hello.
Margarita: Soy Margarita, su mesera.	**Margarita:** I'm Margarita, your server.
Peter: Mucho gusto. ¿Hay una lista de vinos?	**Peter:** Nice to meet you. Is there a wine list?
Margarita: Sí, y aquí está una lista de cervezas.	**Margarita:** Yes, and here is a list of beers.
Peter: Ahhh.	**Peter:** Hmmm.
Margarita: ¿Qué quisieras tomar, señor?	**Margarita:** What would you like, sir?
Peter: Emily. . . ¿Quisieras una copa de vino o una botella?	**Peter:** Emily. . . Would you like a glass of wine or a bottle?
Emily: Solo quiero una copa.	**Emily:** I only want a glass.
Margarita: ¿El vino tinto o blanco?	**Margarita:** Red wine or white?
Emily: Blanco, por favor.	**Emily:** White, please.
Margarita: ¿Qué quisiera tomar, señor?	**Margarita:** What would you like, sir?
Peter: Emily. . . ¿Está bien una botella de vino?	**Peter:** Emily. . . Is a bottle of wine okay?
Emily: Está bien. Eres muy romántico, Peter.	**Emily:** Okay. You are very romantic, Peter.
Margarita: ¿Y para sus hijos?	**Margarita:** And for your children?
Emily: ¿Qué hay?	**Emily:** What is there?
Margarita: Hay limonada, jugo, leche o refrescos.	**Margarita:** There is lemonade, juice, milk or soft drinks.
Danny: Un jugo, por favor.	**Danny:** Juice, please.
Margarita: ¿De naranja, de toronja, de tomate, de piña, o de manzana?	**Margarita:** Orange, grapefruit, tomato, pineapple or apple?
Danny: Un jugo de naranja.	**Danny:** Orange juice.
Emily: Jacky. . . ¿Qué quieres tomar?	**Emily:** Jacky, what do you want to drink?
Jacky: Un batido. ¿Está bien?	**Jacky:** A shake. Is that okay?
Margarita: ¿De fresa, de vainilla, o de chocolate?	**Margarita:** Strawberry, vanilla, or chocolate?

Jacky:	De fresa.
Margarita:	Está bien.
(en la estación de servicio)	
Margarita:	¡Qué noche! ¿Puedes ayudarme, Armando?
Armando:	¿Qué necesitas, Margarita?
Margarita:	No estoy muy organizada.
Armando:	Sí, estás organizada. ¿Qué necesitas?
Margarita:	Trae la hielera a la mesa número diez y ocho.
Armando:	Está bien. ¿Qué más?
Margarita:	Estoy muy ocupada. . . el pimentero a veinte y cinco.
Armando:	¿Y la cesta para el pan?
Margarita:	Sí, y llena las jarras.
Armando:	¿Sí. . . sí, señor? ¿Qué necesitas?
Hombre:	Un cenicero, por favor.
Armando:	¿Y cerillos?
Hombre:	Sí, gracias.
Margarita:	Armando, quita los platos en las mesas.
Armando:	¿Y los vasos y los cubiertos?
Margarita:	Sí. . . trae una charola.
Armando:	¿Qué mesas?
Margarita:	Cinco, quince y veinte. Trae los recipientes.
Armando:	Muy bien. ¡Qué noche!

Jacky:	Strawberry.
Margarita:	Okay.
(at the service station)	
Margarita:	What a night! Can you help me, Armando?
Armando:	What do you need, Margarita?
Margarita:	I'm not very organized.
Armando:	Yes, you are organized. What do you need?
Margarita:	Bring the ice bucket to table number eighteen.
Armando:	Okay. What else?
Margarita:	I am very busy. . . the pepper shaker to twenty five.
Armando:	And the bread basket?
Margarita:	Yes, and fill the pitchers.
Armando:	Yes. . . yes, sir? What do you need?
Hombre:	An ashtray, please.
Armando:	And matches?
Hombre:	Yes, thank you.
Margarita:	Armando, clear the plates on the tables.
Armando:	And the glasses and silverware?
Margarita:	Yes. . . bring a tray.
Armando:	What tables?
Margarita:	Five, fifteen, and twenty. Bring containers.
Armando:	Very good. What a night!

REVIEW

Translate the following to Spanish:

1. What's your name? _____

2. Where are you from? _____

3. I'm from Florida. _____

4. What time is it? _____

5. It's five o'clock. _____

6. It's good. It's bad. _____

7. Everything else is perfect. _____

8. Come with me. _____

9. Where is the bellhop? _____

10. The cook is in the kitchen. _____

11. Do you like to watch television? _____

12. Where, When, With whom _____

13. There is no toilet paper. _____

14. Replenish the paper towels. _____

15. Wash the shower. _____

16. Dust the mirror. _____

17. Clean the sink. _____

18. Peel the pineapples. _____

19. Chop the onions. _____

20. Refill the peppers. _____

CULTURE: INDEPENDENCE DAYS

Country	*Independence Day*
United States	July 4
Argentina	July 9
Bolivia	August 6
Chile	September 18
Colombia	July 20
Costa Rica	September 15
Cuba	May 20
Dominican Republic	February 22
Ecuador	October 3
El Salvador	September 15
Guatemala	September 15
Honduras	September 15
Mexico	September 16
Nicaragua	September 15
Panama	November 28 (from Spain)
	November 3 (from Colombia)
Paraguay	May 14
Peru	July 28
Uruguay	August 25
Venezuela	July 5

RELATIONSHIP TIP

Call the country's consulate office in your city and ask them to send you several travel posters of your employees' countries. Hang them in the employee lounge. The beautiful posters are free!

Tack in a piece of string into a map of their country and into the exact city they come from. Attach your employee's photo and name to it.

HOLIDAYS

January 6: Feast of the Epiphany is the day the Three Kings bring gifts to Latino children.

March–April: *Semana Santa* (Holy Week), the week leading to Easter Sunday, is observed with parades and passion plays.

May 1: Labor Day is a day for workers to parade through the streets.

May 5: *Cinco de Mayo* marks, with great fanfare throughout Mexico, the anniversary of the French defeat by Mexican troops in Puebla in 1862.

June 24: Saint John the Baptist Day, a popular national holiday, sees many Mexicans observing a tradition of tossing a "blessing" of water on most anyone within reach!

August 15: Feast of the Assumption of the Blessed Virgin Mary is celebrated nationwide with religious processions.

October 31–November 2: On *el Día de los Muertos,* families welcome back the spirits of departed relatives to elaborate altars and refurbished gravesites.

December 12: On the Feast Day of the Virgin of Guadalupe, Mexico's patron saint is honored with processions and native folk dances.

13

The Table, Condiments, and Additional Food Items

PART I—THE TABLE

las galletas
crackers

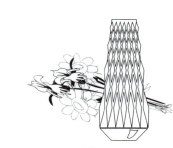

el pan
bread

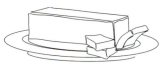

la mantequilla
butter

el azúcar
sugar

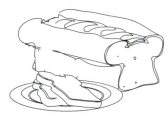

la vela
candle

el florero
vase

el agua
water

sal y pimienta
salt and pepper

el dinero
money

la cuenta
check

la tarjeta de crédito
credit card

la propina
tip

el cambio
change

la mesa
table

la silla
chair

GROUP I

water	el agua	**candle**	la vela
bread	el pan	**vase**	el florero
butter	la mantequilla	**salt and pepper**	sal y pimienta
crackers	las galletas	**sugar**	el azúcar

GROUP II

table	la mesa	credit card	la tarjeta de crédito
chair	la silla	change	el cambio
money	el dinero	tip	la propina
check, bill	la cuenta		

GROUP I

MATCHING EXERCISE

Write the letter of each picture next to the Spanish word it matches below.

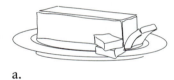

a.

b.

c.

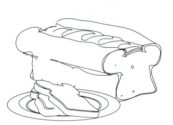

d.

e.

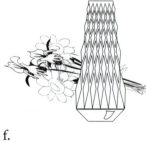

f.

g.

h.

1. _____ el florero
2. _____ la vela
3. _____ el agua
4. _____ el pan

5. _____ las galletas
6. _____ la mantequilla
7. _____ la sal y pimienta
8. _____ el azúcar

VOCABULARY EXERCISE

Write the Spanish word for each picture in the space provided.

1. _____

2. _____

3. _____

4. _____

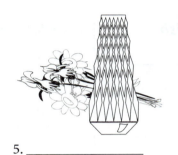

5. _____

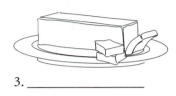

6. _____

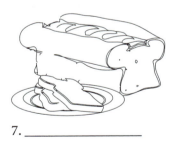

7. _____

8. _____

MATCHING EXERCISE

Write the letter of the Spanish word next to the English word it matches on the left.

1. _____ vase   a. el azúcar
2. _____ butter   b. la vela
3. _____ crackers   c. el agua
4. _____ bread   d. el pan
5. _____ candle   e. la mantequilla
6. _____ sugar   f. las galletas
7. _____ salt and pepper   g. el florero
8. _____ water   h. la sal y pimienta

TRANSLATION EXERCISE

Translate the following to English:

1. las galletas _____
2. el pan _____
3. el azúcar _____
4. la sal y pimienta _____
5. el agua _____
6. el florero _____
7. la vela _____
8. la mantequilla _____

Translate the following to Spanish:

1. bread _____
2. crackers _____
3. sugar _____
4. salt and pepper _____
5. vase _____
6. candle _____
7. butter _____
8. water _____

GROUP II

MATCHING EXERCISE

Write the letter of each picture next to the Spanish word it matches below.

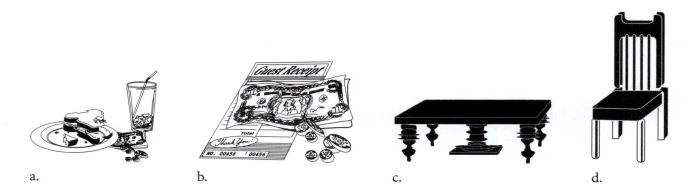

a.   b.   c.   d.

e.

f.

g.

1. _____ la tarjeta de crédito

2. _____ el dinero

3. _____ el cambio

4. _____ la propina

5. _____ la mesa

6. _____ la cuenta

7. _____ la silla

VOCABULARY EXERCISE

Write the Spanish word for each picture in the space provided.

1. _____

2. _____

3. _____

4. _____

5. _____

6. _____

7. _____

MATCHING EXERCISE

Write the letter of the Spanish word next to the English word it matches on the left.

1. _____ tip
2. _____ money
3. _____ chair
4. _____ credit card
5. _____ change
6. _____ table
7. _____ check, bill

a. la mesa
b. la cuenta
c. el dinero
d. el cambio
e. la tarjeta de crédito
f. la propina
g. la silla

TRANSLATION EXERCISE

Translate the following to English:

1. la mesa _____
2. la tarjeta de crédito _____
3. la silla _____
4. la cuenta _____
5. el cambio _____
6. la propina _____
7. el dinero _____

Translate the following to Spanish:

1. check _____
2. change _____
3. chair _____
4. credit card _____
5. money _____
6. table _____
7. tip _____

MULTIPLE CHOICE

Circle the letter of the correct answer.

1. butter
   a. la mantequilla
   b. el azúcar
   c. la vela
   d. la silla

2. tip
   a. el dinero
   b. la propina
   c. el cambio
   d. la cuenta

3. crackers
   a. la cuenta
   b. las galletas
   c. la mantequilla
   d. la vela

4. candle
   a. la silla
   b. el azúcar
   c. la vela
   d. la mantequilla

5. check, bill
   a. la propina
   b. la cuenta
   c. el cambio
   d. el dinero

6. sugar
   a. la mantequilla
   b. el azúcar
   c. la vela
   d. la silla

7. chair
   a. la mantequilla
   b. la silla
   c. el azúcar
   d. la vela

8. money
   a. la cuenta
   b. la propina
   c. el cambio
   d. el dinero

9. change
   a. la cuenta
   b. la propina
   c. el cambio
   d. el dinero

CROSSWORD PUZZLES

Across

7. cambio
8. la sal y pimienta
10. pan
11. silla
12. mesa
13. galletas
14. florero

Down

1. dinero
2. tarjeta de crédito
3. cuenta
4. propina
5. vela
6. agua
7. tarjeta de crédito
9. azúcar
10. mantequilla

Across

6. crackers
8. chair
9. bread
11. credit card
13. sugar
14. water

Down

1. salt and pepper
2. table
3. butter
4. money
5. vase
7. check, bill
9. tip
10. change
12. candle

PART I—ACTIONS TO USE WITH THE TABLE

set	pon		**check**	checa
clear	quita		**sign**	firma
bring	trae			

MATCHING EXERCISE

Write the letter of the Spanish word next to the English word it matches on the left.

1. _____ check
2. _____ sign
3. _____ clear
4. _____ bring
5. _____ set

a. quita
b. pon
c. checa
d. trae
e. firma

TRANSLATION EXERCISE

Translate the following to English:

1. checa _____
2. pon _____
3. firma _____
4. trae _____
5. quita _____

Translate the following to Spanish:

1. sign _____
2. set _____
3. clear _____
4. bring _____
5. check _____

MULTIPLE CHOICE

Circle the letter of the correct answer.

1. set
   a. firma
   b. checa
   c. pon
   d. quita

2. clear
   a. firma
   b. checa
   c. trae
   d. quita

3. sign
   a. firma
   b. checa
   c. trae
   d. quita

4. check
   a. firma
   b. checa
   c. pon
   d. quita

5. bring
   a. trae
   b. pon
   c. quita
   d. firma

TRANSLATION EXERCISE

Translate the following to English:

1. Quita la mesa. _____
2. Trae el pan. _____
3. Checa el agua. _____
4. Firma la tarjeta de crédito. _____
5. Pon la mesa. _____
6. Trae el azúcar. _____
7. Quita las galletas. _____
8. Checa el dinero. _____
9. Trae la silla. _____
10. Quita la vela. _____
11. Quita la mesa. _____
12. Trae la sal y pimienta. _____
13. Pon la mesa. _____
14. Firma la cuenta. _____
15. Checa la mantequilla. _____

Translate the following to Spanish:

1. Clear the table. _____
2. Bring the chair. _____
3. Sign the credit card. _____
4. Check the bread. _____
5. Bring the candle. _____
6. Clear the crackers. _____
7. Set the table. _____
8. Check the change. _____
9. Bring the tip. _____
10. Sign the check. _____
11. Clear the bread. _____
12. Check the sugar. _____
13. Bring the salt and pepper. _____
14. Set the table. _____
15. Check the water. _____

PART II—CONDIMENTS AND ADDITIONAL FOOD ITEMS

la ensalada
salad

la sopa
soup

el sandwich
sandwich

la salsa de tomate
ketchup

la mostaza
mustard

la salsa para la ensalada
salad dressing

el aceite
oil

el vinagre
vinegar

la mayonesa
mayonnaise

el ajo
garlic

el queso
cheese

el pan tostado
toast

las huevos
eggs

las papas fritas
french fries

el encurtido
pickle

GROUP I

ketchup	la salsa de tomate	**oil**	el aceite
mustard	la mostaza	**vinegar**	el vinagre
mayonnaise	la mayonesa	**garlic**	el ajo
salad dressing	la salsa para la ensalada	**cheese**	el queso

GROUP II

soup	la sopa	**pickle**	el encurtido
salad	la ensalada	**toast**	el pan tostado
sandwich	el sandwich	**eggs**	los huevos
french fries	las papas fritas		

GROUP I

MATCHING EXERCISE

Write the letter of each picture next to the Spanish word it matches below.

a.

b.

c.

d.

e.

f.

g.

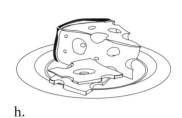

h.

1. _____ el queso
2. _____ el ajo
3. _____ el aceite
4. _____ el vinagre
5. _____ la salsa de tomate
6. _____ la mostaza
7. _____ la mayonesa
8. _____ la salsa para la ensalada

VOCABULARY EXERCISE

Write the Spanish word for each picture in the space provided.

1. _____

2. _____

3. _____

4. _____

5. _____

6. _____

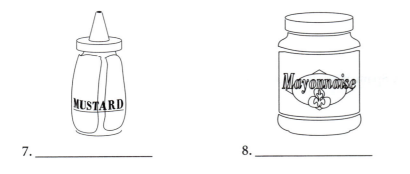

7. _____   8. _____

MATCHING EXERCISE

Write the letter of the Spanish word next to the English word it matches on the left.

1. _____ mustard   a. el ajo

2. _____ oil   b. la mayonesa

3. _____ vinegar   c. el vinagre

4. _____ garlic   d. la salsa de tomate

5. _____ cheese   e. la mostaza

6. _____ salad dressing   f. el queso

7. _____ mayonnaise   g. el aceite

8. _____ ketchup   h. la salsa para la ensalada

TRANSLATION EXERCISE

Translate the following to English:

1. el queso _____

2. el ajo _____

3. el aceite _____

4. la salsa para la ensalada _____

5. el vinagre _____

6. la mostaza _____

7. la salsa de tomate _____

8. la mayonesa _____

Translate the following to Spanish:

1. salad dressing _____

2. garlic _____

3. cheese _____

4. ketchup _____

5. mustard _____

6. mayonnaise _____

7. oil _____

8. vinegar _____

GROUP II

MATCHING EXERCISE

Write the letter of each picture next to the Spanish word it matches below.

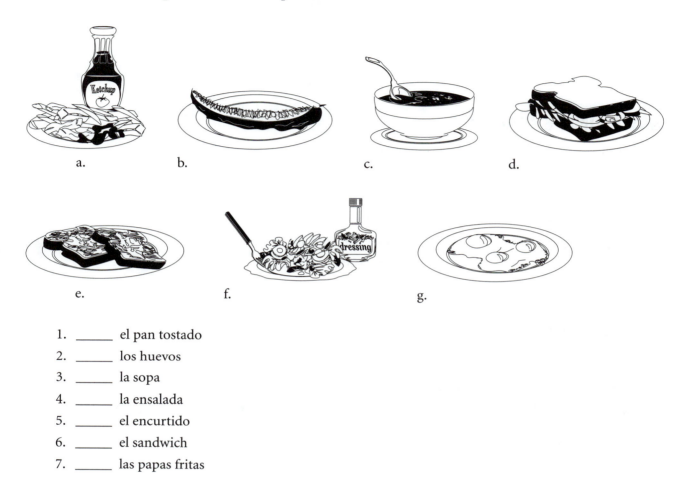

a.

b.

c.

d.

e.

f.

g.

1. _____ el pan tostado
2. _____ los huevos
3. _____ la sopa
4. _____ la ensalada
5. _____ el encurtido
6. _____ el sandwich
7. _____ las papas fritas

VOCABULARY EXERCISE

Write the Spanish word for each picture in the space provided.

1. _____

2. _____

3. _____

4. _____

5. _____

6. _____

7. _____

MATCHING EXERCISE

Write the letter of the Spanish word next to the English word it matches on the left.

1. _____ french fries
2. _____ pickle
3. _____ soup
4. _____ sandwich
5. _____ salad
6. _____ eggs
7. _____ toast

a. los huevos
b. el pan tostado
c. el encurtido
d. la ensalada
e. las papas fritas
f. el sandwich
g. la sopa

TRANSLATION EXERCISE

Translate the following to English:

1. el pan tostado _____

2. los huevos _____

3. el encurtido _____

4. el sandwich _____

5. la ensalada _____

6. la sopa _____

7. las papas fritas _____

Translate the following to Spanish:

1. salad _____

2. eggs _____

3. french fries _____

4. soup _____

5. sandwich _____

6. pickle _____

7. toast _____

MULTIPLE CHOICE

Circle the letter of the correct answer.

1. oil
a. el aceite
b. el vinagre
c. el ajo
d. el queso

2. soup
a. el encurtido
b. la sopa
c. las papas fritas
d. los huevos

3. vinegar
a. el aceite
b. el vinagre
c. el ajo
d. el queso

4. pickle
a. la mostaza
b. el queso
c. la sopa
d. el encurtido

5. garlic
a. el aceite
b. la ensalada
c. el ajo
d. el queso

6. mustard
a. la mostaza
b. los huevos
c. el aceite
d. el ajo

7. cheese
a. el aceite
b. el vinagre
c. el ajo
d. el queso

8. toast
a. el pan tostado
b. la salsa de tomate
c. el ajo
d. el queso

9. eggs
a. el pan tostado
b. los huevos
c. el aceite
d. la mayonesa

CROSSWORD PUZZLES

Across

1. huevos
6. mayonesa
10. vinagre
11. ensalada
12. pan tostado
13. salsa de tomate

Down

2. salsa para la ensalada
3. papas fritas
4. queso
5. ajo
6. mostaza
7. aceite
8. sandwich
9. encurtido
11. sopa

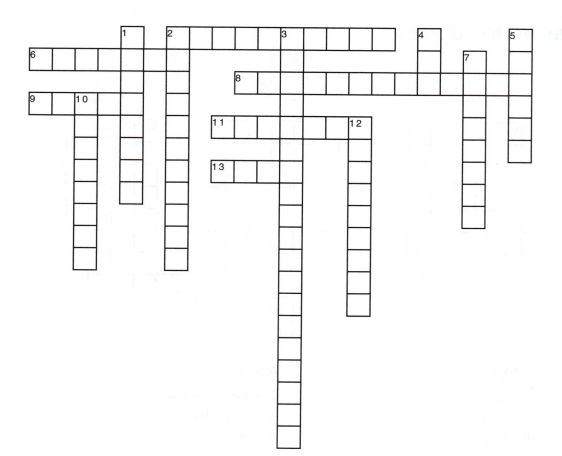

Across

2. toast
6. mustard
8. ketchup
9. cheese
11. vinegar
13. soup

Down

1. mayonnaise
2. french fries
3. salad dressing
4. garlic
5. oil
7. sandwich
10. salad
12. pickle

THE TABLE, CONDIMENTS, AND ADDITIONAL FOOD ITEMS

291

ROLE PLAY

Would you prefer . . . ? Pretend that you are setting up the dining room for your restaurant's weekly Sunday buffet. While setting up the salad bar and buffet tables, you are reminded of what foods you prefer and which ones you don't. Ask your co-worker what he/she prefers.

ESTUDIANTE A: ¿Prefieres la ensalada o la sopa?
ESTUDIANTE B: Prefiero la sopa.

1.

2.

3.

4.

5.

6.

7.

8.

9.

10.

11.

PART II—ACTIONS TO USE WITH CONDIMENTS AND ADDITIONAL FOOD ITEMS

marry	combina	**add**	añade
finish	termina	**serve**	sirve
refill	rellena		

MATCHING EXERCISE

Write the letter of the Spanish word next to the English word it matches on the left.

1. _____ finish
2. _____ marry
3. _____ add
4. _____ serve
5. _____ refill

a. sirve
b. termina
c. rellena
d. combina
e. añade

TRANSLATION EXERCISE

Translate the following to English:

1. combina _____
2. termina _____
3. sirve _____
4. añade _____
5. rellena _____

Translate the following to Spanish:

1. serve _____
2. marry _____
3. finish _____
4. add _____
5. clear _____

MULTIPLE CHOICE

Circle the letter of the correct answer.

1. clear
  a. termina
  b. sirve
  c. quita
  d. añade

2. finish
  a. combina
  b. añade
  c. termina
  d. rellena

3. serve
  a. termina
  b. sirve
  c. combina
  d. añade

4. marry
  a. añade
  b. rellena
  c. combina
  d. termina

5. add
  a. termina
  b. sirve
  c. combina
  d. añade

GRAMMAR: DID THEY FINISH . . . ?

You have learned how to follow up on actions by using the words "Did you . . . ?" By adding *–aste* to the end of the action word.

  The following is a review of speaking to *one person.*

Did you wash the plates?	¿Lav**aste** los platos?
Did you prepare the sandwiches ?	¿Prepar**aste** los sandwiches?

To ask *about a group of diners,* add the *–aron* ending to the action word.

Did they finish their salads?	¿Termin**aron** sus ensaladas?
Did they finish their soups?	¿Termin**aron** sus sopas?
No, not yet.	No, todavia, no.

TRANSLATION EXERCISE

Translate the following to English.

1. ¿Terminaron sus sandwiches? _____

2. ¿Terminaron sus ensaladas? _____

3. ¿Terminaron sus sopas? _____

4. ¿Terminaron sus papas fritas? _____

Translate the following to Spanish:

1. Did they finish their salads? _____

2. Did they finish their french fries? _____

3. Did they finish their sandwiches? _____

4. Did they finish their soups? _____

ROLE PLAY

Did they finish their salads? Pretend that you are working at a busy restaurant. The server wants to know if the diners have finished their food so that he can bring their next course. Working with a partner ask and answer if the diners have finished the food by asking ¿*Terminaron sus . . .*? And answering *Sí* or *No, todavia, no.* Follow the model.

ESTUDIANTE A:	¿Terminaron sus sopas?
ESTUDIANTE B:	No, todavia, no.

1.

2.

3.

4.

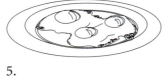

5.

6.

Translate the following to English:

1. Sirve las ensaladas. _____

2. Combina la salsa de tomate. _____

3. Rellena las papas fritas. _____

4. Añade un encurtido. _____

5. ¿Terminaron sus ensaladas? _____

6. Combina la mostaza. _____

7. Rellena la salsa para la ensalada. _____

8. Añade el queso. _____

9. Sirve las sopas. _____

10. ¿Terminaron sus sopas? _____

Translate the following to Spanish:

1. Refill the salad dressing. _____

2. Marry the mustards. _____

3. Add french fries. _____

4. Refill the oil and vinegar. _____

5. Did they finish their salads? _____

6. Marry the ketchup. _____

7. Add the garlic. _____

8. Refill the cheese. _____

9. Serve the eggs and toast. _____

10. Did they finish their soups? _____

11. Combina la salsa para la ensalada. _____

12. Añade el pan tostado. _____

13. Rellena la mayonesa. _____

14. ¿Terminaron sus sandwiches? _____

15. Sirve los huevos y el pan tostado. _____

11. Marry the mayonnaise. _____

12. Add a pickle. _____

13. Serve the salads. _____

14. Refill the eggs. _____

15. Did they finish their sandwiches? _____

PART III—THE MENU

breakfast	el desayuno	**hors d'oeuvres**	los entremeses
lunch	el almuerzo	**specials**	las especialidades
dinner	la cena	**ice cream**	el helado
dessert	el postre	**cake**	el pastel
appetizers	los entremeses		

MATCHING EXERCISE

Write the letter of the Spanish word next to the English word it matches on the left.

1. _____ specials   a. los entremeses

2. _____ lunch   b. la cena

3. _____ cake   c. el almuerzo

4. _____ dinner   d. el helado

5. _____ dessert   e. el desayuno

6. _____ appetizers   f. las especialidades

7. _____ breakfast   g. el pastel

8. _____ ice cream   h. el postre

TRANSLATION EXERCISE

Translate the following to English:

1. las especialidades_____

2. el helado _____

3. el pastel _____

4. el desayuno _____

5. la cena _____

6. el postre_____

7. los entremeses _____

8. el almuerzo _____

Translate the following to Spanish:

1. appetizers _____

2. ice cream _____

3. dinner _____

4. dessert _____

5. specials _____

6. breakfast _____

7. cake _____

8. lunch _____

MULTIPLE CHOICE

Circle the letter of the correct answer.

1. dessert
   a. el pastel
   b. el postre
   c. el helado
   d. la cena

2. appetizers
   a. el almuerzo
   b. el desayuno
   c. los entremeses
   d. las especialidades

3. cake
   a. el pastel
   b. el postre
   c. el helado
   d. la cena

4. breakfast
   a. el almuerzo
   b. el desayuno
   c. los entremeses
   d. las especialidades

5. dinner
   a. el pastel
   b. el postre
   c. el helado
   d. la cena

6. lunch
   a. el almuerzo
   b. el desayuno
   c. los entremeses
   d. las especialidades

7. ice cream
   a. el pastel
   b. el postre
   c. el helado
   d. la cena

8. specials
   a. el almuerzo
   b. el desayuno
   c. los entremeses
   d. las especialidades

ACTIVITY

Bed and Breakfast. Pretend that you are opening your own restaurant. Think of a name for it and then plan the menu. Include two or three soups, several salads, sandwiches, meat and fish dishes, fruits and vegetables, as well as beverages. Be sure to include prices. Bring it to class, read other students' menus, and practice your Spanish!

DIALOGUE

Read the dialogue aloud in Spanish. Then translate it to English.	*Read the dialogue aloud in English. Then translate it to Spanish.*
Lisa: Hola. Buenas tardes.	**Lisa:** Hello. Good afternoon.
Juan: Buenas tardes.	**Juan:** Good afternoon.
Lisa: ¡Hay muchas personas aquí hoy!	**Lisa:** There are many people here today!
Juan: ¿Estás muy ocupada?	**Juan:** Are you very busy?
Lisa: Sí, ayúdame, por favor.	**Lisa:** Yes, help me, please.
Juan: Está bien. ¿Qué necesitas?	**Juan:** Okay. What do you need?
Lisa: Llena los vasos con agua.	**Lisa:** Fill the glasses with water.
Juan: ¿Y las jarras?	**Juan:** And the pitchers?
Lisa: Sí, y haz el té helado y el café.	**Lisa:** Yes, and make the iced tea and coffee.
Juan: Está bien.	**Juan:** Okay.
Lisa: Trae el sal y pimienta a las mesas.	**Lisa:** Bring the salt and pepper to the tables.
Juan: ¿Y el azúcar?	**Juan:** And the sugar?
Lisa: Sí. Dobla veinte servilletas y rellena los tenedores.	**Lisa:** Yes. Fold twenty napkins and replace the forks.
Juan: ¿Y los cuchillos y las cucharas?	**Juan:** And the knives and spoons?

Lisa:	Sí. Trae las velas y las floreros a las mesas.		**Lisa:**	Yes. Bring the candles and vases to the tables.
Juan:	¿Y las galletas y la mantequilla?		**Juan:**	And the crackers and butter?
Lisa:	Sí. Y trae dos sillas a la mesa número trece, por favor.		**Lisa:**	Yes. And bring two chairs to table number thirteen, please.
Juan:	Está bien.		**Juan:**	Okay.
Lisa:	Muchas gracias. Eres muy trabajador, Juanito.		**Lisa:**	Thank you very much. You're a hard worker, Juanito.
(a la mesa)			(at the table)	
Lisa:	Buenas tardes.		**Lisa:**	Good afternoon.
Jeff and Cherie:	Buenas tardes.		**Jeff and Cherie:**	Good afternoon.
Lisa:	¿Qué quisiera tomar, señor?		**Lisa:**	What would you like to drink, sir?
Jeff:	Una botella de cerveza.		**Jeff:**	A bottle of beer, please.
Lisa:	¿Y para su esposa?		**Lisa:**	And for your wife?
Cherie:	Una cerveza, por favor.		**Cherie:**	Una cerveza, por favor.
Lisa:	¿Habla español?		**Lisa:**	Do you speak Spanish?
Cherie:	Sí, soy profesora.		**Cherie:**	Yes, I am a professor.
Lisa:	¿Y para comer?		**Lisa:**	Very good. And to eat?
Cherie:	¿Hay especialidades?		**Cherie:**	Are there specials?
Lisa:	Sí . . . hay camarones, atún, salmón . . .		**Lisa:**	Yes . . . there is shrimp, tuna, salmon. . .
Jeff:	Solo quiero un sandwich.		**Jeff:**	I only want a sandwich.
Lisa:	¿Un sandwich de queso, jamón, pavo o pollo?		**Lisa:**	A cheese, ham, turkey or chicken sandwich?
Jeff:	Un sandwich de jamón y queso.		**Jeff:**	A ham and cheese sandwich.
Lisa:	¿Quisiera papas fritas?		**Lisa:**	Would you like french fries?
Jeff:	Sí, gracias.		**Jeff:**	Yes, thank you.
Lisa:	¿Una ensalada o sopa?		**Lisa:**	A salad or soup?
Jeff:	Los dos.		**Jeff:**	Both.
Lisa:	¿Qué salsa para la ensalada?		**Lisa:**	What salad dressing?
Jeff:	Aceite y vinagre.		**Jeff:**	Oil and vinegar.
Cherie:	Quisiera una hamburguesa.		**Cherie:**	I would like a hamburger.
Lisa:	¿Con queso?		**Lisa:**	With cheese?
Cherie:	No, gracias.		**Cherie:**	No, thanks.
Lisa:	¿Cómo te gustaría su hamburguesa?		**Lisa:**	How would you like your hamburger?
Cherie:	Medio cocida.		**Cherie:**	Medium.
Lisa:	¿Sopa o ensalada?		**Lisa:**	¿Soup or salad?
Cherie:	Una ensalada con tomates, cebolla, pepinos, pimientos, apio y champiñones.		**Cherie:**	A salad with tomatoes, onion, cucumbers, peppers, celery and mushrooms.

Lisa:	¿Qué salsa para la ensalada?		**Lisa:**	What salad dressing?
Cherie:	El aceite y vinagre.		**Cherie:**	Oil and vinegar.
Lisa:	Muy bien.		**Lisa:**	Okay.
(en la estación de servicio)			(at the service station)	
Lisa:	Juan . . . ¿ Terminaron sus sopas?		**Lisa:**	Juan. . . Did they finish their soups?
Juan:	Sí.		**Juan:**	Yes.
Lisa:	Quita los tazones y las botellas de cerveza.		**Lisa:**	Clear the bowls and beer bottles.
Juan:	Está bien.		**Juan:**	Okay.
Lisa:	Ayúdame, Juan.		**Lisa:**	Help me, Juan.
Juan:	¿Qué necesitas?		**Juan:**	What do you need?
Lisa:	Sirve las ensaladas y trae. . .		**Lisa:**	Serve the salads and bring . . .
Juan:	¿El aceite y vinagre?		**Juan:**	The oil and vinegar?
Lisa:	Sí. Y la mostaza y la salsa de tomate.		**Lisa:**	Yes, and the mustard and ketchup.
Juan:	Está bien.		**Juan:**	Okay.
(un poco más tarde)			(a little later)	
Lisa:	Juan. . . ¿ Terminaron las ensaladas?		**Lisa:**	Juan. . . Did they finish their salads?
Juan:	Sí.		**Juan:**	Yes.
Lisa:	Muy bien. Quita los platos para la ensalada.		**Lisa:**	Very good. Clear the salad plates.
Juan:	Sí. ¿Qué más?		**Juan:**	Yes. What else?
Lisa:	Trae agua, pan y mantequilla a la mesa número diez y ocho.		**Lisa:**	Bring water, bread and butter to table number eighteen.
Juan:	¿Ocho o diez y ocho?		**Juan:**	Eight or eighteen?
Lisa:	Ocho. ¡Rápido, Juan!		**Lisa:**	Eighteen. Fast, Juan!
Lisa:	¿Cómo está su hamburguesa?		**Lisa:**	How is your hamburger?
Cherie:	Excelente. Tráeme un poco de mayonesa, por favor.		**Cherie:**	Excellent. Bring me a little mayonnaise, please.
Lisa:	¿Como está su sandwich?		**Lisa:**	How is your sandwich?
Jeff:	Perfecto. Una servilleta y dos más cervezas, por favor.		**Jeff:**	Perfect. A napkin and two more beers, please.
Lisa:	Está bien.		**Lisa:**	Okay.
Lisa:	Juan. . . ¿ Terminaron sus sandwiches?		**Lisa:**	Juan. . . Did they finish their sandwiches?
Juan:	Sí y el hombre quiere la cuenta.		**Juan:**	Yes and the man wants the check.
Lisa:	Está bien. . . señor, aquí está la cuenta.		**Lisa:**	Okay. . . Sir, here is the check.
Jeff:	¿Está bien una tarjeta de crédito?		**Jeff:**	Is a credit card okay?
Lisa:	Sí, señor.		**Lisa:**	Yes, sir.
Jeff:	Lisa. . . hablo español un poco.		**Jeff:**	Lisa. . . I speak Spanish a little.
Lisa:	¿Sí?		**Lisa:**	Oh?
Jeff:	Sí. ¡*Yo-ocho-dos-mucho!*		**Jeff:**	Yes. *I-eight-two-much!*

REVIEW

Translate the following to Spanish:

1. Hello. How are you? _____

2. Fine, and you? _____

3. Nice to meet you. _____

4. See you tomorrow. _____

5. Monday, Wednesday, Friday _____

6. Saturday, Sunday, Tuesday _____

7. The bartender is in the kitchen. _____

8. The server is in the dining room. _____

9. Vacuum the hallway. _____

10. Mop the stairs. _____

11. Wash the sheets. _____

12. Fold the towels. _____

13. Use the polish. _____

14. Replace the glasses and plates. _____

15. Make the iced tea and coffee. _____

16. Fill the water. _____

17. Polish the silverware. _____

18. Fold the napkins. _____

19. Slice the lemons and limes. _____

20. Chop the onions. _____

CULTURE: IMMIGRANT LABOR

During times of low unemployment, labor is difficult to find. Many organizations hire foreign-born employees. If an employer is unsure of the steps to take in hiring this type of worker, the U. S. Immigration and Naturalization Service (INS) will send you a handbook that explains hiring guidelines. The INS can be contacted at: www.usdoj.gov/ins/.

Penalties for "knowingly" hiring illegal workers and being audited by the INS can be severe, so many organizations are hiring employees from Mexico through the United States government's H-2B program. The program is specifically intended for seasonal, temporary employment. Getting employees from Mexico is a bit time consuming and expensive, yet it is worth the effort in the long run.

The process takes approximately 120 days and involves two major steps: (1) finding and recruiting the workers, and (2) completing the paperwork to allow them to come to the United States and work for your organization.

RELATIONSHIP TIP

Latinos are very patriotic. Hang their country's flag next to the U.S. flag. Be sure and hang it high or secure it tightly. They are so popular they often disappear. Post a colorful map of Mexico or of your employee's country. Show genuine interest in their town or village.

14

The Catering/Banquet Department

PART I—ROOM SETUP

theater style
el estilo teatro

classroom style
el estilo salón de clase

head table
la mesa principal

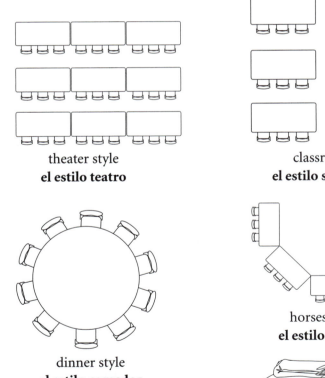

dinner style
el estilo comedor

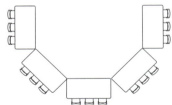

horseshoe style
el estilo herradura

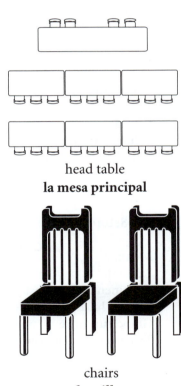

chairs
las sillas

table
la mesa

linen
la ropa

301

theater style	el estilo teatro
horseshoe style	el estilo herradura
dinner style	el estilo comedor
classroom style	el estilo salón de clase
table	la mesa
head table	la mesa principal
chairs	las sillas
linens	la ropa

CATERING/BANQUET EVENT ORDER

The Great Hotel
2233 Maple Avenue
White Lake, MN 45678
(773) 847-1300
(773) 847-1311

Post As: Golf Course Superintendents Breakfast
Function: Annual Meeting
Organization: Golf Course Superintendents Association
Address: 6434 Fairway Lane
Orlando, Florida 20215
Telephone: (344) 251-7700
Fax: (344) 251-7708
Contact: Steve Smith
#Guaranteed 150
#Expected

Day	Date	Time		Function	Room
Saturday	May 24	7:30AM-12:00PM		Meeting	Grey Rock

Bar Setup: N/A

Wine:
Floral:
Music:

Menu:
7:30 AM
Continental Breakfast
Orange Juice
Grapefruit Juice
Tomato Juice
Fruit
Rolls
Coffee, Tea, Decaf Coffee

Audio Visual:

Linen: White

Set up:
Classroom Style seating
Head table for two
Coffee Break Set Up
(1) 6′ table for registration
at entrance with 2 chairs

Signature _____

Date _____

MATCHING EXERCISE

Write the letter of each picture next to the Spanish word it matches below.

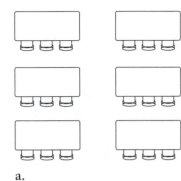

a.

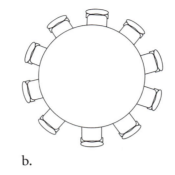

b.

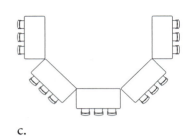

c.

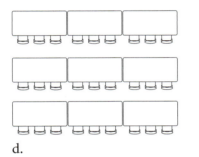

d.

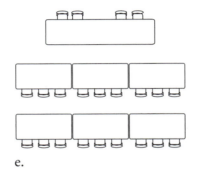

e.

f.

g.

h.

1. _____ la mesa principal
2. _____ el estilo salón de clase
3. _____ la mesa
4. _____ el estilo comedor
5. _____ las sillas
6. _____ el estilo herradura
7. _____ la ropa
8. _____ el estilo teatro

VOCABULARY EXERCISE

Write the Spanish word for each picture in the space provided.

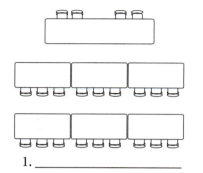

1. _____

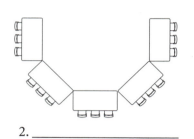

2. _____

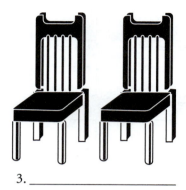

3. _____

4. _____

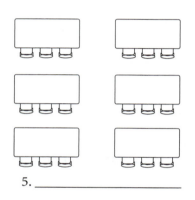

5. _____

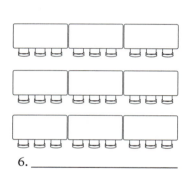

6. _____

7. _____

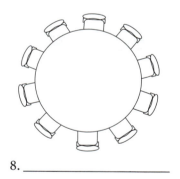

8. _____

MATCHING EXERCISE

Write the letter of the Spanish word next to the English word it matches on the left.

1. _____ theater style
2. _____ dinner style
3. _____ table
4. _____ chairs
5. _____ linen
6. _____ head table
7. _____ classroom style
8. _____ horseshoe style

a. la mesa
b. las sillas
c. la ropa
d. la mesa principal
e. el estilo teatro
f. el estilo herradura
g. el estilo comedor
h. el estilo salón de clase

TRANSLATION EXERCISE

Translate the following to English:

1. la ropa _____
2. el estilo herradura _____
3. la mesa _____
4. el estilo salón de clase _____
5. el estilo comedor _____
6. las sillas _____
7. la mesa principal _____
8. el estilo teatro _____

Translate the following to Spanish:

1. classroom style _____
2. linen _____
3. theater style _____
4. chairs _____
5. dinner style _____
6. table _____
7. head table _____
8. horseshoe style _____

CROSSWORDS

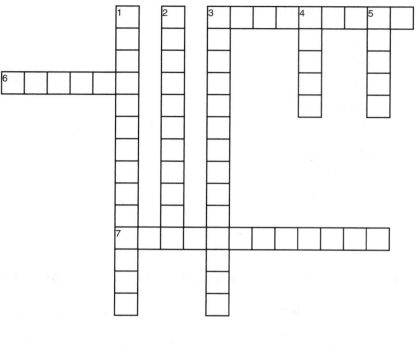

Across

3. mesa principal
6. sillas
7. estilo teatro

Down

1. estilo salón de clase
2. estilo comedor
3. estilo herradura
4. mesa
5. ropa

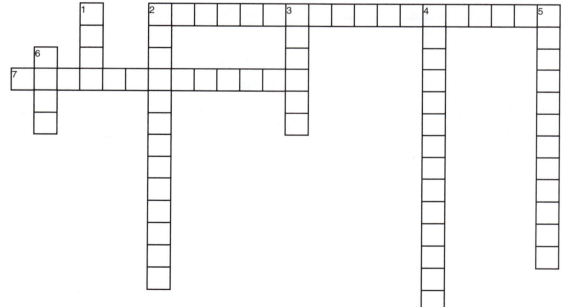

Across

2. classroom style
7. head table

Down

1. linen
2. dinner style
3. chairs
4. horseshoe style
5. theater style
6. table

PART II—TAKING FOOD ORDERS

guests
los huéspedes

orders
los órdenes

beverages
las bebidas

appetizers
los aperitivos

entrees
los platos principales

desserts
los postres

after dinner drinks
las bebidas después de la cena

coffee
el café

guests	los huéspedes
orders	los órdenes
beverages	las bebidas
appetizers	los aperativos
entres	los platos principales
desserts	los postres
after dinner drinks	las bebidas después de cena
coffee	el café

MATCHING EXERCISE

Write the letter of each picture next to the Spanish word it matches below.

a.

c.

d.

e.

f.

g.

h.

1. _____ las bebidas

2. _____ los órdenes

3. _____ los aperitivos

4. _____ los postres

5. _____ los huéspedes

6. _____ el café

7. _____ los platos principales

8. _____ las bebidas después de cena

VOCABULARY EXERCISE

Write the Spanish word for each picture in the space provided.

1. _____

2. _____

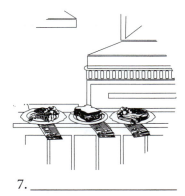

3. _____

4. _____

5. _____

6. _____

7. _____

8. _____

MATCHING EXERCISE

Write the letter of the Spanish word next to the English word it matches on the left.

1. _____ beverages
2. _____ entrees
3. _____ guests
4. _____ coffee
5. _____ desserts
6. _____ after dinner drinks
7. _____ appetizers
8. _____ orders

a. los huéspedes
b. los órdenes
c. bebidas después de la cena
d. el café
e. las bebidas
f. los aperitivos
g. los platos principales
h. los postres

TRANSLATION EXERCISE

Translate the following to English:

1. las bebidas _____
2. los postres _____
3. los huéspedes _____
4. los aperitivos _____
5. el café _____
6. los platos principales _____
7. los órdenes _____
8. las bebidas después de la cena _____

Translate the following to Spanish:

1. appetizers _____
2. desserts _____
3. orders _____
4. entrees _____
5. beverages _____
6. coffee _____
7. guests _____
8. after dinner drinks _____

CROSSWORDS

Across

2. órdenes
4. bebidas
6. aperitivos
7. platos principales
8. huéspedes

Down

1. café
3. postres
5. bebidas después de la cena

Across

3. orders
5. coffee
6. after dinner drinks
7. entrees

Down

1. guests
2. appetizers
4. beverages

PART I—ACTIONS TO USE WITH TAKING FOOD ORDERS

greet	saluda
take	toma
check	checa
recommend (suggest)	recomienda
bring	trae

MATCHING EXERCISE

Write the letter of the Spanish word next to the English word it matches on the left.

1. _____ recommend   a. checa
2. _____ take   b. saluda
3. _____ bring   c. toma
4. _____ greet   d. recomienda
5. _____ check   e. trae

RELATIONSHIP TIP

Music motivates, just ask Chicago Cubs big hitter, Sammy Sosa. Before charging onto the baseball field he has salsa music blaring in the locker room! It excites people. It boosts energy. It's great to pass the time.

Try playing music while your employees are setting up for a large occasion. A job that takes four hours will take only two! While working in the laundry room or kitchen, change the radio station to Latin music once in awhile. For prizes, buy them gift certificates for CDs and play them in your restaurant or hotel while they are setting up. You'll score a home run with your workers!

TRANSLATION EXERCISE

Translate the following to English:

1. trae _____

2. checa _____

3. saluda _____

4. toma _____

5. recomienda _____

Translate the following to Spanish:

1. greet _____

2. recommend _____

3. take _____

4. bring _____

5. check _____

MULTIPLE CHOICE

Circle the letter of the correct answer.

1. recommend
   a. saluda
   b. toma
   c. checa
   d. recomienda

2. greet
   a. saluda
   b. recomienda
   c. checa
   d. toma

3. take
   a. recomienda
   b. trae
   c. saluda
   d. toma

4. check
   a. saluda
   b. toma
   c. checa
   d. recomienda

5. bring
   a. recomienda
   b. trae
   c. saluda
   d. toma

ROLE PLAY

A. **Taking food orders.** Pretend that you and your business associates have finished an important meeting and are now having dinner. In groups of three or four, gather around a table. Have each person practice being the server and taking the food and beverage orders. Try not to read the script too much!

Good evening! (afternoon, morning)	¡Buenas noches! (buenos días, buenas noches)
Would you like something to drink?	¿Quisieran algo para tomar?
And for you?	¿Y para usted?
Would you like to order now?	¿Quisieran ordenar ahora?
May I recommend . . .	Recomendaría . . .
Is everything okay?	¿Todo está bien?
Do you need anything more?	¿Necesitan algo más?
Have you finished?	¿Ha terminado usted?
May I take your plate?	¿Está bien si tomo su plato?

Translate the following to English:

1. Saluda los huéspedes. _____
2. Checa el café. _____
3. Recomienda los aperitivos. _____
4. Toma los ordenes. _____
5. Recomienda los postres. _____
6. Trae el café. _____
7. Trae los postres. _____
8. Recomienda las bebidas. _____
9. Recomienda el café. _____
10. Checa las bebidas. _____

Translate the following to Spanish:

1. Greet the guests. _____
2. Take the orders. _____
3. Check the coffee. _____
4. Recommend the appetizers. _____
5. Bring the coffee. _____
6. Greet the guests. _____
7. Recommend the desserts. _____
8. Bring the beverages. _____
9. Check the beverages. _____
10. Recommend the coffee. _____

REVIEW

Translate the following to Spanish.

1. Welcome! _____
2. Where is the elevator? _____
3. Tuesday, Thursday, Saturday _____
4. At what time? _____
5. Where is the ice machine? _____
6. Vacuum the dining room. _____
7. Mop the floor. _____
8. Where is the server? _____
9. The cook is in the kitchen. _____
10. Dust the furniture. _____
11. Replace the toilet paper. _____
12. Where is the vending machine? _____
13. to the right, to the left _____
14. under, over _____
15. Fold the sheets. _____
16. Dry the linens. _____
17. Recommend the desserts. _____
18. Replace the plates and glasses. _____
19. Does your hand hurt? _____
20. My stomach hurts. _____

DIALOGUE

Read the dialogue aloud in English. Then translate it to Spanish.

Ruben:	Good evening.
The guests:	Good evening!
Ruben:	How are you?
The guests:	Fine, and you?
Ruben:	Very well, thanks.
Mr. Wagner:	What's your name?
Ruben:	My name is Ruben.
Mr. Wagner:	We are from Los Angeles.
Ruben:	Welcome to Boston! Would you like something to drink?
Mrs. Wagner:	I would like a glass of white wine.
Ruben:	And for you?
Mrs. Fleming:	I would like a glass of white wine, also.
Ruben:	May I recommend a bottle?
Mr. Wagner:	The wine menu, please.
Ruben:	Would you like something to drink, sir?
Mr. Fleming:	A bottle of beer for me.
Mr. Wagner:	Ruben . . . a bottle of white wine and three glasses, please.
Ruben:	Okay. Very good.
(While Ruben opens and pours the wine . . .)	
Ruben:	May I recommend an appetizer?
All the guests:	What do you have?
Ruben:	The oysters are excellent and the brochetta . . .
Mrs. Fleming:	I love brochetta!
Ruben:	Very good. Brochetta . . . anything more?
All the guests:	That's all, thank you.
(a little later . . .)	
Ruben:	Would you like another beer, sir?
Mr. Fleming:	Yes, thank you. Matches and an ashtray, too.

Read the dialogue aloud in Spanish. Then translate it to English

Ruben:	¡Buenas noches!
The guests:	¡Buenas noches!
Ruben:	¿Cómo están ustedes?
The guests:	Bien. ¿Y tú?
Ruben:	Muy bien, gracias.
Mr. Wagner:	¿Cómo te llamas?
Ruben:	Me llamo Ruben.
Mr. Wagner:	Somos de Los Angeles.
Ruben:	Bienvenidos a Boston! ¿Quisieran algo para tomar?
Mrs. Wagner:	Quisiera un vaso de vino blanco.
Ruben:	¿Y para usted?
Mrs. Fleming:	Quisiera un vaso de vino blanco, también.
Ruben:	¿Les recomiendo una botella?
Mr. Wagner:	El menú de vinos, por favor.
Ruben:	¿Quisiera algo para tomar, señor?
Mr. Fleming:	Una botella de cerveza para mí.
Mr. Wagner:	Ruben . . . una botella de vino blanco y tres vasos, por favor.
Ruben:	Okay. Está bien.
(Mientras Ruben abre y sirve el vino . . .)	
Ruben:	¿Les recomiendo un aperitivo?
All the guests:	¿Qué hay?
Ruben:	Las ostras son exellentes y la brochetta . . .
Mrs. Fleming:	¡Me encanta la brochetta!
Ruben:	Muy bien, la brochetta. ¿Algo más?
All the guests:	Es todo, gracias.
(un poco más tarde . . .)	
Ruben:	¿Quisiera otra botella de cerveza, Señor Fleming?
Mr. Fleming:	Sí, gracias. Cerillos y un cenicero, también.

Ruben:	Okay. Would you like to order now?		**Ruben:**	Okay. ¿Quisieran ordenar ahora?
Mrs. Wagner:	Yes . . . I would like the salmon.		**Mrs. Wagner:**	Sí . . . Quissiera el salmon.
Ruben:	And for you?		**Ruben:**	¿Y para usted?
Mrs. Fleming:	I would like the shrimp.		**Mrs. Fleming:**	Quisiera los camarones.
Mr. Fleming:	I would like the New York strip steak.		**Mr. Fleming:**	Quisiera el bistec Nueva York.
Ruben:	How would you like your steak . . . rare, medium or well done?		**Ruben:**	¿Cómo le gustaría?
Mr. Fleming:	Rare.		**Mr. Fleming:**	Poco cocido.
Ruben:	Another bottle of beer, Mr. Fleming?		**Ruben:**	¿Otra botella de cerveza, Mr. Fleming?
Mr. Fleming:	Yes.		**Mr. Fleming:**	Sí.
Ruben:	And for you, Mr. Wagner?		**Ruben:**	¿Y para usted, Señor Wagner?
Mr. Wagner:	I would like the lobster.		**Mr. Wagner:**	Quisiera la langosta.
Ruben:	Another bottle of wine, sir?		**Ruben:**	¿Otra botella de vino, señor?
Mr. Wagner:	Oh yes! Thank you! Good idea!		**Mr. Wagner:**	¡Oh, sí! ¡Gracias! ¡Buen idea!
(Ruben returns and places the plates on the table. He returns three or four minutes later . . .)			(Ruben regresa y pone los platos sobre la mesa. Regresa tres o cuatro minutos más tarde . . .)
Ruben:	Is everything okay? Do you need anything more?		**Ruben:**	¿Todo está bien? ¿Necesitan algo más?
The guests:	No. Thank you, Ruben.		**The guests:**	No, gracias Ruben.
Ruben:	Enjoy your meal.		**Ruben:**	¡Buen provecho!

CULTURE: ¡BUEN PROVECHO! BON APETIT! ENJOY YOUR MEAL!

In restaurants meals are served and eaten at a more leisurely pace than in the United States. The servers assume that the guests have come for a relaxed meal and not to gulp down the food as fast as they can. There is no pressure for the diners to hurry off to make sure the tables are turned often during the evening. Servers who are well trained in Latin countries hold the check until the diners request it. People in the United States often tend to be casual with the restaurant servers. In Latin countries this friendliness is not customary.

Desayuno (Breakfast)   Breakfast is eaten at a convenient time in the morning for the individual. It is a light meal similar to what people in the U.S. refer to as a continental breakfast. It consists of rolls, bread, butter, marmalade and coffee. Lots of cream and sugar are popular.

Almuerzo (Lunch)   This is similar to the light lunch in the United States.

Comida (Dinner, the main meal of the day)   This midday meal is usually eaten between two and three o'clock. It is the main meal of the day and consists of several courses. Traditionally, the entire family would return home for this meal. One and a half to two hours was reserved for this time to eat and rest. The family members then return to school and work.

Merienda (Snack)   A small snack of sandwiches and pastries is often eaten around five or six o'clock. It is very informal.

Cena (Supper, dinner)   This evening meal is eaten around nine or ten at night. It is a light meal of eggs, sandwiches, or salad.

The Engineering Department

PART I—GROUNDS AND POOL MAINTENANCE

trees
los árboles

shrubs
los arbustos

flowers
las flores

plants
las plantas

leaves
las hojas

branches
las ramas

weeds
las hierbas

grass
el zacate

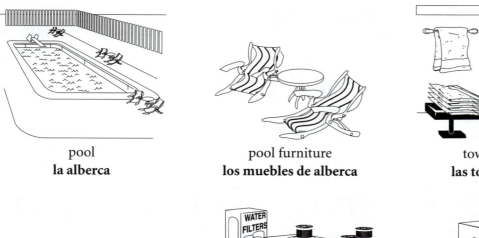

pool
la alberca

pool furniture
los muebles de alberca

towels
las toallas

locker room
el vestuario

filters
los filtros

chlorine
el cloro

chemicals
las químicas

GROUP I

trees	**los árboles**		leaves	**las hojas**
shrubs	**los arbustos**		branches	**las ramas**
flowers	**las flores**		weeds	**las hierbas**
plants	**las plantas**		grass	**el zacate**

GROUP II

pool	**la alberca**	filters	**los filtros**
pool furniture	**los muebles de alberca**	chlorine	**el cloro**
towels	**las toallas**	chemicals	**las químicas**
locker room	**el vestuario**		

GROUP I

MATCHING EXERCISE

Write the letter of each picture next to the Spanish word it matches below.

a.

b.

c.

d.

e.

f.

g.

h.

1. _____ las hierbas

2. _____ el zacate

3. _____ las flores

4. _____ las hojas

5. _____ las plantas

6. _____ los arbustos

7. _____ las ramas

8. _____ los árboles

VOCABULARY EXERCISE

Write the Spanish word for each picture in the space provided.

1. _____

2. _____

3. _____

4. _____

5. _____

6. _____

7. _____

8. _____

MATCHING EXERCISE

Write the letter of the Spanish word next to the English word it matches on the left.

1. _____ weeds   a. los arbustos

2. _____ plants   b. las plantas

3. _____ grass   c. las flores

4. _____ trees   d. las hojas

5. _____ shrubs   e. las hierbas

6. _____ flowers   f. los árboles

7. _____ branches   g. las ramas

8. _____ leaves   h. el zacate

TRANSLATION EXERCISE

Translate the following to English:

1. el zacate _____

2. las hojas _____

3. los arbustos _____

4. las ramas _____

5. los árboles _____

6. las plantas _____

7. las flores _____

8. las hierbas _____

Translate the following to Spanish:

1. shrubs _____

2. weeds _____

3. flowers _____

4. trees _____

5. grass _____

6. plants _____

7. branches _____

8. leaves _____

MULTIPLE CHOICE

Circle the letter of the correct answer.

1. leaves
   a. las plantas
   b. las hojas
   c. las ramas
   d. el zacate

2. shrubs
   a. los arbustos
   b. los árboles
   c. las hierbas
   d. las plantas

3. flowers
   a. las ramas
   b. las flores
   c. las hojas
   d. las plantas

4. plants
   a. las plantas
   b. el zacate
   c. las hierbas
   d. los flores

5. branches
   a. las flores
   b. las hojas
   c. las plantas
   d. las ramas

6. trees
   a. los arbustos
   b. los árboles
   c. las hierbas
   d. las plantas

7. weeds
   a. las hojas
   b. los arbustos
   c. las hierbas
   d. el zacate

8. grass
   a. las hojas
   b. los arbustos
   c. las hierbas
   d. el zacate

PART I—ACTIONS TO USE WITH GROUNDS MAINTENANCE

water	**riega**	rake	**rastrilla**
prune	**poda**	plant	**planta**
cut	**corta**	edge	(see below)

'TO EDGE' (ORILLAR)

The word and action, "to edge" is very common in the United States. There is no exact translation for it in the Spanish language. Latinos have come up with many ways to express it. Ask one of your employees what word you should use.

MATCHING EXERCISE

Write the letter of the Spanish word next to the English word it matches on the left.

1. _____ prune   a. corta

2. _____ water   b. poda

3. _____ plant   c. rastrilla

4. _____ rake   d. planta

5. _____ cut   e. riega

TRANSLATION EXERCISE

Translate the following to English:

1. rastrilla _____

2. corta _____

3. poda _____

4. riega _____

5. planta _____

Translate the following to Spanish:

1. prune _____

2. cut _____

3. water _____

4. plant _____

5. rake _____

MULTIPLE CHOICE

Circle the letter of the correct answer.

1. water
a. poda
b. rastrilla
c. corta
d. riega

2. prune
a. planta
b. poda
c. rastrilla
d. riega

3. cut
a. poda
b. rastrilla
c. corta
d. riega

4. rake
a. poda
b. riega
c. corta
d. rastrilla

5. plant
a. poda
b. rastrilla
c. corta
d. planta

Translate the following to English:

1. Riega los árboles. _____
2. Corta el zacate. _____
3. Rastrilla las hojas. _____
4. Poda las ramas. _____
5. Planta los arbustos. _____
6. Riega las flores. _____
7. Poda los árboles. _____
8. Planta las plantas. _____

Translate the following to Spanish:

1. Prune the branches. _____
2. Rake the leaves. _____
3. Cut the grass. _____
4. Water the trees. _____
5. Plant the flowers. _____
6. Prune the shrubs. _____
7. Water the plants. _____
8. Plant the shrubs. _____

ROLE PLAY

A. **Did you . . . ?** It's the end of the day and you and your co-worker are walking back to the maintenance facility. Ask and answer if certain tasks that you assigned him have been done. Earlier you learned to ask 'Did you . . .' by changing the 'a' ending of the word to *aste*. Follow the model.

prune

ESTUDIANTE A: ¿Podaste los arbustos?
ESTUDIANTE B: Sí.
No, todavia, no. (*No, not yet.*)

1. plant 2. cut 3. water 4. prune

5. rake 6. cut 7. plant

8. prune 9. plant 10. cut

GROUP II

MATCHING EXERCISE

Write the letter of each picture next to the Spanish word it matches below.

a.

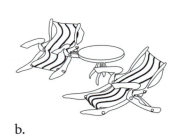

b.

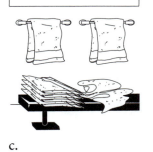

c.

d.

e.

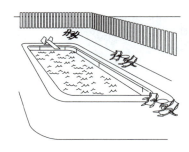

f.

g.

1. _____ las toallas

2. _____ la alberca

3. _____ el vestuario

4. _____ las químicas

5. _____ los muebles de alberca

6. _____ el cloro

7. _____ los filtros

VOCABULARY EXERCISE

Write the Spanish word for each picture in the space provided.

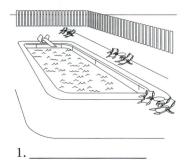

1. _____

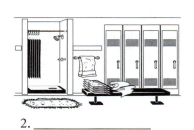

2. _____

3. _____

4. _____

5. _____

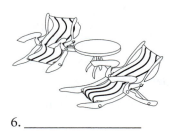

6. _____

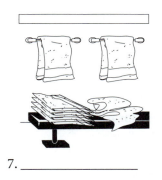

7. _____

MATCHING EXERCISE

Write the letter of the Spanish word next to the English word it matches on the left.

1. _____ pool   a. el vestuario
2. _____ chlorine   b. los muebles de alberca
3. _____ chemicals   c. los filtros
4. _____ locker room   d. las toallas
5. _____ pool furniture   e. la alberca
6. _____ towels   f. el cloro
7. _____ filters   g. las químicas

TRANSLATION EXERCISE

Translate the following to English:

1. las toallas _____
2. el cloro _____
3. la alberca _____
4. los filtros _____
5. las químicas _____
6. los muebles de alberca _____
7. el vestuario _____

Translate the following to Spanish:

1. pool furniture _____
2. chlorine _____
3. chemicals _____
4. pool _____
5. filters _____
6. locker room _____
7. towels _____

MULTIPLE CHOICE

Circle the letter of the correct answer.

1. filters
 a. el cloro
 b. los filtros
 c. las químicas
 d. las toallas

2. chlorine
 a. el cloro
 b. la alberca
 c. las químicas
 d. el vestuario

3. towels
 a. el cloro
 b. la alberca
 c. las químicas
 d. las toallas

4. pool
 a. el cloro
 b. la alberca
 c. las químicas
 d. las toallas

5. locker room
 a. el cloro
 b. la alberca
 c. las químicas
 d. el vestuario

6. chemicals
 a. el cloro
 b. la alberca
 c. las químicas
 d. las toallas

PART I—ACTIONS TO USE WITH POOL MAINTENANCE

change	**cambia**	add	**añade**
clean	**limpia**	pick up	**recoge**
test	**examina**		

MATCHING EXERCISE

Write the letter of the Spanish word next to the English word it matches on the left.

1. _____ test   a. limpia
2. _____ add   b. examina
3. _____ clean   c. recoge
4. _____ pick up   d. añade
5. _____ change   e. cambia

TRANSLATION EXERCISE

Translate the following to English:

1. recoge _____
2. añade _____
3. cambia _____
4. examina _____
5. limpia _____

Translate the following to Spanish:

1. add _____
2. clean _____
3. pick up _____
4. change _____
5. test _____

MULTIPLE CHOICE

Circle the letter of the correct answer.

1. test
   a. recoge
   b. añade
   c. examina
   d. limpia

2. change
   a. limpia
   b. recoge
   c. cambia
   d. añade

3. add
   a. recoge
   b. añade
   c. examina
   d. limpia

4. clean
   a. limpia
   b. recoge
   c. examina
   d. añade

5. pick up
   a. limpia
   b. añade
   c. examina
   d. recoge

TRANSLATION EXERCISE

Translate the following to English:

1. Limpia la alberca. _____

2. Examina el cloro. _____

3. Añade las químicas. _____

4. Recoge las toallas. _____

5. Limpia los muebles de alberca. _____

6. Limpia el vestuario. _____

7. Añade el cloro. _____

8. Cambia los filtros. _____

Translate the following to Spanish:

1. Pick up the towels. _____

2. Change the filters. _____

3. Clean the pool furniture. _____

4. Test the chlorine. _____

5. Add the chemicals. _____

6. Clean the locker room. _____

7. Clean the pool. _____

8. Add the chlorine. _____

CROSSWORD PUZZLES

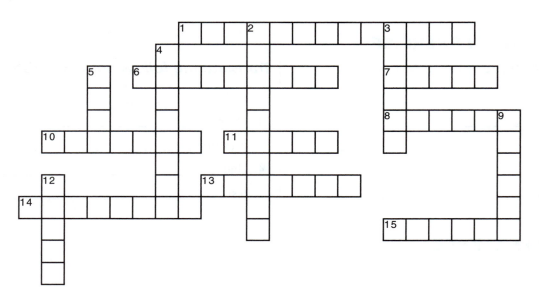

Across

1. muebles de alberca
6. químicas
7. hierbas
8. hojas
10. filtros
11. zacate
13. flores
14. ramas
15. plantas

Down

2. vestuario
3. toallas
4. cloro
5. alberca
9. arbustos
12. árboles

Across

3. flowers
5. filters
14. pool furniture
15. weeds

Down

1. plants
2. trees
4. chemicals
6. locker room
7. towels
8. pool
9. grass
10. chlorine
11. branches
12. shrubs
13. leaves

ROLE PLAY

Did you . . . ? Pretend it's summer vacation and the pool area must be ready for all the children. Ask your co-worker if he has completed the tasks you had assigned him that morning. Working with a partner ask and answer *'Did you . . . '* (Remember to change the 'a' ending of the word to 'aste' or the 'e' ending to 'iste'. Follow the model.

clean

ESTUDIANTE A:	¿Limpiaste la alberca?
ESTUDIANTE B:	Sí.
	No, todavia, no. (No, not yet.)

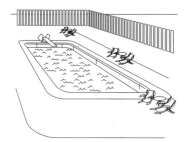

1. clean

2. change

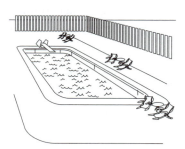

3. pick up

4. test

5. clean

6. add

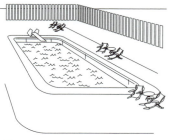

7. test

8. clean

PART II—BUILDING MAINTENANCE

work orders
los órdenes

lights
las luces

light bulb
el foco

smoke detector
el detector de humo

batteries
las pilas

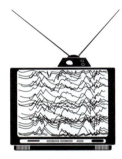

television
la televisión

lock
la cerradura

air conditioner
el aire acondicionado

heater
la calefacción

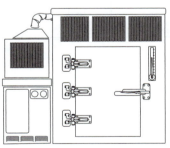

refrigeration system
el sistema de refrigeración

cord, wire
el cable

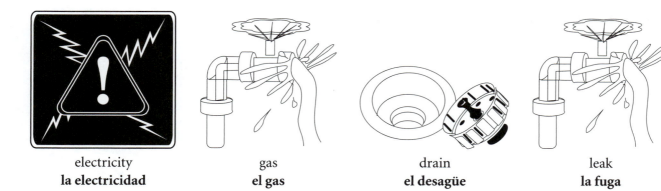

electricity	gas	drain	leak
la electricidad	**el gas**	**el desagüe**	**la fuga**

GROUP I

work orders	**los órdenes**	batteries	**las pilas**
lights	**las luces**	television	**la televisión**
light bulb	**el foco**	lock	**la cerradura**
smoke detector	**el detector de humo**		

GROUP II

air conditioner	**el aire acondicionado**	electricity	**la electricidad**
heater	**la calefacción**	gas	**el gas**
refrigeration system	**el sistema de refrigeración**	drain	**el desagüe**
cord, wire	**el cable**	leak	**la fuga**

GROUP I

MATCHING EXERCISE

Write the letter of each picture next to the Spanish word it matches below.

a.

b.

c.

d.

e.

f.

g.

1. _____ las pilas

2. _____ la cerradura

3. _____ los órdenes

4. _____ las luces

5. _____ el detector de humo

6. _____ la televisión

7. _____ el foco

VOCABULARY EXERCISE

Write the Spanish word for each picture in the space provided.

1. _____

2. _____

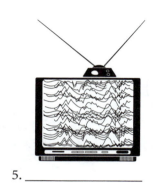

3. _____

4. _____

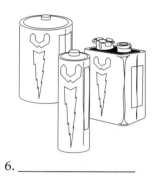

5. _____

6. _____

7. _____

MATCHING EXERCISE

Write the letter of the Spanish word next to the English word it matches on the left.

1. _____ work orders   a. el foco
2. _____ lock   b. la cerradura
3. _____ smoke detector   c. las pilas
4. _____ light bulb   d. los órdenes
5. _____ television   e. las luces
6. _____ batteries   f. el detector de humo
7. _____ lights   g. la televisión

TRANSLATION EXERCISE

Translate the following to English:

1. las pilas _____

2. el foco _____

3. los órdenes _____

4. el detector de humo _____

5. las luces _____

6. la televisión _____

7. la cerradura _____

Translate the following to Spanish:

1. television _____

2. batteries _____

3. light bulb _____

4. lock _____

5. work orders _____

6. smoke detector _____

7. lights _____

GROUP II

MATCHING EXERCISE

Write the letter of each picture next to the Spanish word it matches below.

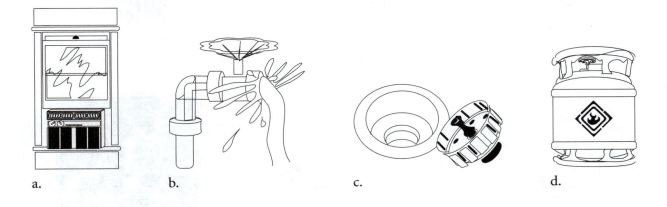

a.   b.   c.   d.

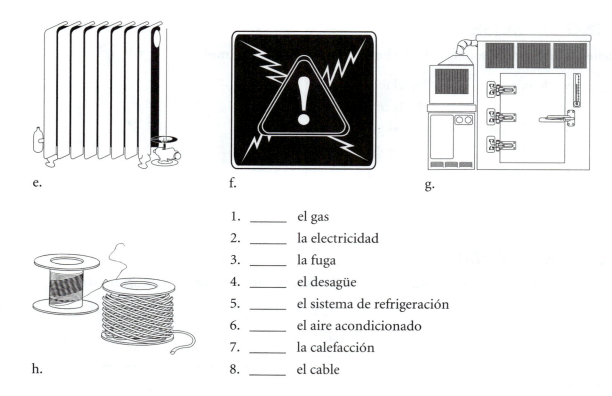

e.

f.

g.

1. _____ el gas
2. _____ la electricidad
3. _____ la fuga
4. _____ el desagüe
5. _____ el sistema de refrigeración
6. _____ el aire acondicionado
7. _____ la calefacción
8. _____ el cable

h.

VOCABULARY EXERCISE

Write the Spanish word for each picture in the space provided.

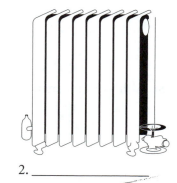

1. _____

2. _____

3. _____

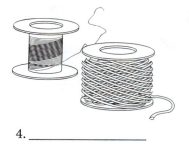

4. _____

5. _____

6. _____

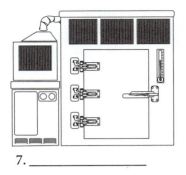

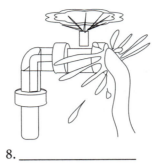

7. _____

8. _____

MATCHING EXERCISE

Write the letter of the Spanish word next to the English word it matches on the left.

1. _____ electricity
2. _____ wire
3. _____ air conditioner
4. _____ leak
5. _____ drain
6. _____ heater
7. _____ refrigeration system
8. _____ gas

a. el desagüe
b. la fuga
c. el cable
d. el sistema de refrigeración
e. el gas
f. la electricidad
g. el acondicionado aire
h. la calefacción

TRANSLATION EXERCISE

Translate the following to English:

1. la electricidad _____
2. el sistema de refrigeración _____
3. la fuga _____
4. el desagüe _____
5. la calefacción _____
6. el gas _____
7. el cable _____
8. el aire acondicionado _____

Translate the following to Spanish:

1. wire _____
2. leak _____
3. refrigeration system _____
4. heater _____
5. air conditioner _____
6. drain _____
7. electricity _____
8. gas _____

MULTIPLE CHOICE

Circle the letter of the correct answer.

1. lights
   a. las luces
   b. la fuga
   c. el foco
   d. las pilas

2. work orders
   a. las luces
   b. la fuga
   c. los órdenes
   d. las pilas

3. light bulb
   a. las luces
   b. la fuga
   c. el foco
   d. las pilas

4. lock
   a. el cable
   b. la cerradura
   c. la calefacción
   d. el acondicionado aire

5. batteries
   a. las luces
   b. la fuga
   c. los órdenes
   d. las pilas

6. air conditioner
   a. el cable
   b. la cerradura
   c. la calefacción
   d. el aire acondicionado

7. leak
   a. las luces
   b. la fuga
   c. el foco
   d. las pilas

8. heater
   a. el cable
   b. la cerradura
   c. la calefacción
   d. el aire acondicionado

9. cord, wire
   a. el cable
   b. la cerradura
   c. la calefacción
   d. el aire acondicionado

CROSSWORD PUZZLES

Across

1. sistema de refrigeración
5. órdenes
7. cerradura
8. fuga
12. pilas
13. luces
14. foco

Down

2. aire acondicionado
3. detector de humo
4. televisión
5. cable
6. desagüe
9. calefacción
10. gas
11. electricidad

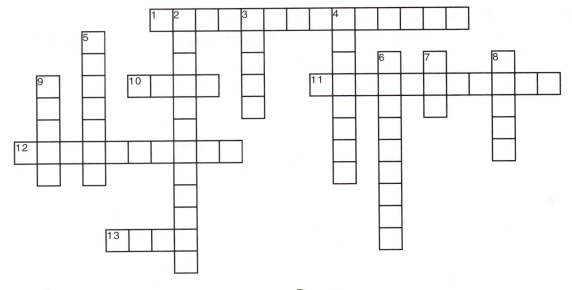

Across

1. smoke detector
10. light bulb
11. heater
12. television
13. leak

Down

2. electricity
3. wire
4. drain
5. work orders
6. lock
7. gas
8. batteries
9. lights

PART II—ACTIONS TO USE WITH BUILDING MAINTENANCE

repair	repara	**check**	checa
change, replace	cambia	**does not work**	no funciona
adjust	ajusta		

MATCHING EXERCISE

Write the letter of the Spanish word next to the English word it matches on the left.

1. _____ check   a. no funciona
2. _____ adjust   b. repara
3. _____ does not work   c. checa
4. _____ change   d. ajusta
5. _____ repair   e. cambia

TRANSLATION EXERCISE

Translate the following to English:

1. cambia _____

2. repara _____

3. ajusta _____

4. no funciona _____

5. checa _____

Translate the following to Spanish:

1. adjust _____

2. repair _____

3. does not work _____

4. check _____

5. change _____

MULTIPLE CHOICE

Circle the letter of the correct answer.

1. adjust
a. ajusta
b. cambia
c. checa
d. repara

2. does not work
a. ajusta
b. cambia
c. checa
d. no funciona

3. repair
a. no funciona
b. ajusta
c. cambia
d. repara

4. change
a. ajusta
b. cambia
c. checa
d. repara

5. check
a. ajusta
b. cambia
c. checa
d. repara

ROLE PLAY

Please fix . . . Pretend that you are the general manager in a very elegant, but old hotel. Things are breaking down. Ask your co-worker to repair certain items. When he asks *Where? (Dónde),* tell him. Pick and choose from the vocabulary below.

ESTUDIANTE A:	Checa la electrididad.
ESTUDIANTE B:	¿Dónde?
ESTUDIANTE A:	En la cocina.

Action	Item	Place
repara	el gas	el vestíbulo (lobby)
cambia	la fuga	la oficina (office)
ajusta	el foco	el comedor (dining room)
checa	el cable	el restaurante (restaurant)
	las pilas	la cocina (kitchen)
	las luces	el bar (bar)
	el desagüe	el cuarto (bedroom)
	la televisión	el baño (bathroom)
	la cerradura	la lavandería (laundry room)
	el calefacción	el sótono (basement)
	la electricidad	
	el detector de humo	
	el aire acondicionado	
	el sistema de refrigeración	

Translate the following to English:

1. Checa los órdenes. _____
2. La calefacción no funciona. _____
3. Ajusta las luces. _____
4. Cambia el foco. _____
5. Repara la cerradura. _____
6. Checa el detector de humo. _____
7. Cambia las pilas. _____
8. El aire acondicionado no funciona. _____
9. Repara la fuga. _____
10. Checa la calefacción. _____
11. Cambia el cable. _____
12. Checa la electricidad. _____
13. La cerradura no funciona. _____
14. Ajusta la televisión. _____
15. Repare el desagüe. _____

Translate the following to Spanish:

1. Repair the television. _____
2. Check the refrigerator system. _____
3. Adjust the heater. _____
4. The heater does not work. _____
5. Change the batteries. _____
6. Repair the smoke detector. _____
7. Change the light bulb. _____
8. Adjust the lights. _____
9. Check the work orders. _____
10. The electricity does not work. _____
11. Repair the leak. _____
12. Check the gas. _____
13. Adjust air conditioner. _____
14. The television does not work. _____
15. Change the lock. _____

Read the dialogue aloud in Spanish. Then translate it to English.

Jack:	Hola Miguel. ¿Qué tal?
Miguel:	¡Buenos días, jefe!
Jack:	Hay mucho trabajo hoy, Miguel.
Miguel:	Está bien.
Jack:	Planta los árboles.
Miguel:	¿Y las flores?
Jack:	Sí. Riega los árboles y las flores.
Miguel:	¿Y corta el zacate?
Jack:	Sí… y por favor… saca las hierbas.
Miguel:	Sí, está bien.
Jack:	Gracias. ¡Eres muy trabajador!

(más tarde, por la tarde)

Jack:	¿Qué tal, Miguel?
Miguel:	Bien… perfecto.
Jack:	¿Hay problemas?
Miguel:	No, no hay problemas.
Jack:	¿Plantaste los árboles?
Miguel:	Sí, jefe. Y las flores.

Read the dialogue aloud in English. Then translate it to Spanish.

Jack:	Hello Miguel. How's it going?
Miguel:	Good morning, boss!
Jack:	There is a lot of work today.
Miguel:	Okay.
Jack:	Plant the trees.
Miguel:	And the flowers?
Jack:	Yes. Water the trees and the flowers.
Miguel:	And cut the grass?
Jack:	Yes … and please … take out the weeds.
Miguel:	Yes, okay.
Jack:	Thank you. You are a hard worker.

(later that afternoon)

Jack:	How is it going, Miguel?
Miguel:	Fine … perfect.
Jack:	Are there any problems?
Miguel:	No, there are no problems.
Jack:	Did you plant the trees?
Miguel:	Yes, boss. And the flowers.

Jack:	¿Podaste los árboles?		Jack:	Did you prune the trees?
Miguel:	Sí y las ramas y los arbustos.		Miguel:	Yes and the branches and the shrubs.
Jack:	Gracias. Eres muy responsable, Miguel.		Jack:	Thank you. You are very responsible.
Miguel:	Sí, y organizado y cooperativo.		Miguel:	Yes, and organized and cooperative.
Jack:	Muy bien. Ven conmigo a la alberca.		Jack:	Very good. Come with me to the pool.
Miguel:	¿Te gusta nadar?		Miguel:	Do you like to swim?
Jack:	Sí, pero hoy hay mucho trabajo…		Jack:	Yes, but today there is a lot of work …
Miguel:	Está bien.		Miguel:	Okay.
Jack:	Por favor, limpia los muebles de alberca.		Jack:	Please, clean the pool furniture.
Miguel:	¿Recoje las toallas?		Miguel:	Pick up the towels?
Jack:	Sí. Examina el agua y añade el cloro.		Jack:	Yes. Test the water and add the chlorine.
Miguel:	Está bien.		Miguel:	Okay.
Jack:	Muchas gracias. Hasta manaña.		Jack:	Thank you very much. See you tomorrow.
Miguel:	Adiós. Hasta manaña.		Miguel:	Goodbye. See you tomorrow.

REVIEW

DIALOGUE

Translate the following to Spanish:

1. I like to read. _____

2. I like to be with my family. _____

3. I do not like to go to parties. _____

4. Do you like to play sports? _____

5. Man, woman, child _____

6. Bellhop, housekeeper, manager _____

7. The fork is to the left. _____

8. The napkin is on the plate. _____

9. Vacuum the carpet. _____

10. Dust the furniture. _____

11. Wash the fruit. _____

12. Prepare the cauliflower. _____

13. Bring the potatoes. _____

14. Slice the grapefruit. _____

15. Bring the ice bucket. _____

16. Clear the silverware and plates. _____

17. Sign the check. _____

18. Clear the table. _____

19. Bring the bread and butter. _____

20. Ketchup, mustard, oil and vinegar _____

CULTURE: TIPS FOR THE TRAVELER

Since culture shock is a very real phenomenon, it is important to be well prepared for a foreign trip. Buy and read several travel books about the country to which you are going. The books will tell you the local customs and answer many questions you may have about traveling, tipping, insurance, and so forth.

Begin laying out the items you want to bring several days before you actually pack. A few things to remember: your ticket, passport or birth certificate, a money belt or pouch, a dictionary or phrase book, your bathing suit, a hat and sunglasses, a camera and film, a novel, and a frisbee if you like. Do *not* bring anything illegal across the Mexican border. You will be a happy camper if you pack light!

If you are visiting people, don't forget a small gift from the United States. Something easy to carry but much appreciated may be t-shirts with sports logos, baseball caps, or lighters. Be creative.

Practice your new language. Especially with little children.

If you keep a few balloons in your pocket, you can blow them up and it will serve as a way to begin a conversation with them.

It is also important to have a list of all the important numbers you have in your wallet. Be sure to make a photocopy of the numbers and leave the list with a family member or friend. A list of safety numbers to have includes: your birth certificate, passport number, driver's license number, airline tickets, Traveler's checks, as well as any credit card numbers.

Before you leave, arrange for the post office to hold your mail until your return. Order foreign currency through your bank for your needs upon arrival ($50.00−$100.00). Make sure to buy a jug of bottled water before heading to your hotel.

Don't bury yourself in a guidebook. Ask the locals what to do. Get out and explore on your own. Be patient and have fun! *¡Buen viaje!*

RELATIONSHIP TIP

It appears, nationwide, that there is a relationship/ communication gap between Latino workers and many Anglo equipment technicians. Latinos have said that they are afraid they will be yelled at by the technician for breaking the equipment. They try and fix it by themselves, or worse yet, they don't turn it in at all. Several ideas to help this problem are: (1) have better equipment training at the start of each season; (2) make it safe to tell the truth; (3) number and assign the equipment to each crew; (4) use masking tape to outline an area where workers can drop off broken tools, and (5) assign a buffer person between the technician and worker to handle broken equipment.

add (to)	añade	bone	el hueso
adjust (to)	adjusta	boss	el/la jefe(a)
after dinner drinks	las bebidas después de la cena	bowl	el tazón
		bowl (to)	jugar al boliche
air conditioner	el aire acondicionado	branches	las ramas
airport transportation	el transporte al aeropuerto	bread basket	la cesta para el pan
		bread plate	el plato para pan
ankle	el tobillo	bread	el pan
appetizers	los aperitivos	breakfast	el desayuno
apple	la manzana	bring (to)	trae
arm	el brazo	broccoli	el brocolí
around	alrededor	broil	asa a la parilla
ash tray	el cenicero	broom	la escoba
asparagus	el espárrago	brother	el hermano
aunt	la tía	bucket	la cubeta
back	la espalda	busboy	el busboy
bacon	el tocino	butter	la mantequilla
bag	la bolsa	cake	el pastel
banana	la banana	candle	la vela
bar	el bar	carpet	la alfombra
bartender	el/la cantinero(a)	carrots	las zanahorias
basement	el sótono	cart	el carrito
bathmats	el tapete de baño	cauliflower	la coliflor
bathroom	el baño	celery	el apio
bathtub	la tina	clams	las almejas
batteries	las pilas	classroom style	el estilo salón de clase
be with family, to	estar con la familia	clean (to)	limpia
bed	la cama	clear (to)	quita
bedroom	el cuarto	cliente	el/la cliente
beef	la carne	closet	el closet
beer	la cerveza	coffee cup	la taza
behind	detrás	coffee	el café
bellhop	el botones	Come with me.	Ven conmigo.
between	entre	condiments	los condimentos
beverages	las bebidas	containers	los recipientes
blanket	la manta	cook	el/la cocinero(a)
bleach	el blanqueador	cook (to)	cocina
blood	la sangre	cord, wire	el cable
boil (to)	hierve	corn	el maíz

cousin	el/la primo(a)	eye	el ojo
crab	el cangrejo	family	la familia
crackers	las galletas	fat	la grasa
credit card	la tarjeta de crédito	father	el padre
cucumbers	los pepinos	feet	los pies
cut (to)	corta	fifty	cincuenta
chair	la silla	filters	los filtros
champagne	la champaña	fill (to)	llena
change	el cambio	Fine, and you?	Bien. ¿Y tú?
change (to)	cambia	fingers	los dedos
check	la cuenta	finish (to)	termina
check (to)	checa	fish	el pescado
cheese	el queso	fish (to)	pescar
chef	el/la chef	floor	el piso
chemicals	las químicas	flowers	las flores
chest	el pecho	fold (to)	dobla
chicken	el pollo	fork	el tenedor
child	el/la niño(a)	forty	cuarenta
children	los hijos	Friday	el viernes
chlorine	el cloro	fruit	la fruta
chop (to)	pica	furniture	los muebles
dance (to)	bailar	garbage can	el basurero
daughter	la hija	garlic	el ajo
decaf coffee	el café decaf	gas	el gas
dessert fork	el tenedor para postre	get (to)	consigue
dessert	el postre	give him, her	dale
dining room	el comedor	give me	dame
dinner plate	el plato	glass	el vaso
dinner style	el estilo comedor	glasses	los vasos
dinner	la cena	gloves	los guantes
dishwasher	el lavaplatos	go to parties (to)	ir a las fiestas
Do it like me.	Hazlo como yo.	Good afternoon	Buenas tardes
Do you like?	¿Te gusta?	Good morning	Buenos días
Do you speak English/	¿Hablas ingles/	Good night	Buenas noches
Spanish?	epañol?	Good work!	¡Buen trabajo!
Do you understand	¿Comprendes ingles/	Goodbye	Adiós
English/Spanish?	español?	grandparents	los abuelos
does not work	no funciona	grapefruit	la toronja
down, below	abajo	grapes	las uvas
drain	el desagüe	grass	el zacate
drink (to)	tomar, beber	ground beef	la carne molida
dry (to)	seca	groundskeeper	el jardinero
dryer	la secadora	guest	el/la huésped
dust (to)	desempolva	hallway	el pasillo
ear	el oído	ham	el jamón
eat (to)	comer	hamburger	la hamburguesa
eighty	ochenta	hand	la mano
elbow	el codo	head table	la mesa principal
electricity	la electricidad	head	la cabeza
elevator	el ascensor	heater	la calefacción
empty (to)	vacia	Help me.	Ayúdame.
entrees	los platos principales	Hi/Hello	Hola
Everything else is perfect.	Todo lo demás está perfecto.	hors d'oeuvres	los entremeses
		horseshoe style	el estilo herradura

host/hostess	la hostess
housekeeper	la camarista
How are you?	¿Cómo estás?
How much, many	Cuántos
How	Cómo
How's it going?	¿Qué tal?
How's your family?	¿Cómo está tu familia?
husband	el esposo
I don't like…	No me gusta…
I like…	Me gusta…
I live in…	Vivo en…
I love…	Me encanta…
I speak Spanish a little.	Hablo español un poco.
I'd like to introduce you to…	Quiero presentarte a…
I'm (from)	Soy (de)
I'm sorry.	Lo siento.
I'm studying Spanish.	Estudio español.
ice bucket	la hielera
ice cream	el helado
ice machine	la máquina de hielo
ice	el hielo
iced tea	el té helado
in front	delante
in, on	en
iron	la plancha
It's bad.	Está mal.
It's correct.	Está correcto.
It's good.	Está bien.
It's important.	Es importante.
It's necessary.	Es necesario.
It's not correct.	No está correcto.
It's so-so.	Está así así.
juice	el jugo
Keep trying.	Continua tratando.
ketchup	la salsa de tomate
kitchen	la cocina
kiwi	el kiwi
knee	la rodilla
knife	el cuchillo
lamb	el cordero
laundry room	la lavandería
leak	la fuga
leaves	las hojas
left	izquierda
leg	la pierna
lemon	el limón
lemonade	la limonada
lettuce	la lechuga
lightbulb	el foco
lights	las luces
lime	la lima
linen	la ropa

listen to music (to)	escuchar música
lobby	el vestíbulo
lobster	la langosta
lock (to)	la cerradura
locker room	el vestuario
lunch	el almuerzo
make (to)	haz
man	el hombre
manager	el/la gerente
matches	los cerillos
mattress pad	el protector de colchón
mattress	el colchón
mayonnaise	la mayonesa
meatball	la albóndiga
mechanic	el mecánico
melon	el melón
milk	la leche
mirror	el espejo
Monday	el lunes
money	el dinero
mop	el trapeador
mop (to)	trapea
mother	la madre
mushrooms	los champiñones
mustard	la mostaza
My name is…	Me llamo…
napkin	la servilleta
neck	el cuello
Nice to meet you.	Mucho gusto.
ninety	noventa
office	la oficina
oil	el aceite
on top	encima
one hundred	cien
onions	las cebollas
orange	la naranja
orders	los órdenes
oysters	las ostras
pamphlets	los folletos
paper towels	las toallas de papel
parents	los padres
parking	el aparcamiento
peach	el melocotón
pear	la pera
peel (to)	pela
pepper shaker	el pimentero
pick up (to)	recoge
pillow	la almohada
pillowcase	la funda
pineapple	la piña
pitcher	la jarra
plant (to)	planta
plants	las plantas
plates	los platos

play baseball (to)	jugar al béisbol	scrub (to)	restrega
play basketball (to)	jugar al básquetbol	seafood	los mariscos
play billiards (to)	jugar al billar	See you later.	Hasta luego.
play cards (to)	jugar cartas	See you tomorrow.	Hasta mañana.
play football (to)	jugar al fútbol	serve	sirve
	americano	server	el/la mesero(a)
play golf (to)	jugar al golf	set (to)	pon
play soccer (to)	jugar al fútbol	seventy	setenta
play sports (to)	jugar a los deportes	shake	el batido
play tennis (to)	jugar al tenis	sheet	la sábana
play volleyball (to)	jugar al volibol	shoulder	el hombro
Please	Por favor	shower	la ducha
polish	el lustrador	shrimp	los camarones
polish (to)	pule	shrubs	los arbustos
pool furniture	los muebles de alberca	sign (to)	firma
pool	la alberca	silverware	los cubiertos
pork chop	la chuleta	sink	la lavamanos
pork	el cerdo	sister	la hermana
potatoes	las papas	sixty	sesenta
prepare	prepara	skin	el cuero
prune (to)	poda	slice (to)	rebana
put, arrange (to)	coloca	smoke detector	el detector de humo
put away, store (to)	guarda	soft drink	el refresco
rag	el trapo	soiled linens	la ropa sucia
rake (to)	rastrilla	son	el hijo
read (to)	leer	soup spoon	la cuchara para sopa
receptionist	el/la recepcionista	soup	la sopa
red wine	el vino tinto	Speak slowly, please.	Habla más despacio,
refill (to)	rellena		por favor.
refrigeration system	el sistema de	specials	las especialidades
	refigeración	spinach	la espinaca
remove (to)	quita	sponge	la esponja
repair (to)	repara	spoon	la cuchara
restaurant	el restaurante	spray	la rociada
restroom	el baño	spread	la colcha
right	derecha	stain	la mancha
roast	la carne asada	stairs	la escalera
salad dressing	la salsa para la	steak knife	el cuchillón
	ensalada	steak	el bistec
salad fork	el tenedor para	stock (to)	surte
	ensalada	stomach	el estómago
salad plate	el plato para ensalada	strawberry	la fresa
salad	la ensalada	sugar	el azúcar
salmon	el salmón	Sunday	el domingo
salt and pepper	sal y pimiento	supervisor	el/la supervisor
Same to you.	Igualmente.	supplies	los suministros
sandwich	el sandwich	sweep (to)	barre
Saturday	el sábado	swim (to)	nadar
saucer	el platillo	table	la mesa
sausage	la salchicha	tablecloth	el mantel
sauté (to)	saltea	take out (to)	saca
scouring pad	el estropajo	taxi	el taxi
scrub brush	el cepillo	tea	el té

television	la televisión	washer	la máquina
ten	diez	Watch me.	Mírame.
test (to)	examina	watch television (to)	mirar la televisión
Thank you	Gracias	water	el agua
theater style	el estilo teatro	water (to)	riega
thirty	treinta	watermelon	la sandía
Thursday	el jueves	wax (to)	cera
tip	la propina	Wednesday	el miércoles
toast	el pan tostado	weeds	las hierbas
toilet paper	el papel de baño	Welcome	Bienvenidos
toilet	el inodoro	What	Qué
tomatoes	los tomates	What's your name?	¿Cómo te llamas?
towel	la toalla	When is	Cuándo es
towels	los toallas	Where are you from?	¿De dónde eres?
tray jack	la tijera	Where do you live?	¿Dónde vives?
tray	la charola	Where is Carlos from?	¿De dónde es Carlos?
trees	los árboles	Where is	Dónde está
Try it.	Trátalo.	Where	Dónde
Tuesday	el martes	white wine	el vino blanco
tuna	el atún	Who	Quién
turkey	el pavo	Why	Por qué
twenty	veinte	wife	la esposa
uncle	el tío	windows	las ventanas
up, above	arriba	wine glass	la copa
use (to)	usa	wine	el vino
vacuum	la aspiradora	With whom	Con quién
vacuum (to)	aspira	woman	la mujer
vase	el florero	work orders	los órdenes
veal	la ternera	wrap (to)	envuelve
vegetables	los vegetales	You are very kind.	Eres muy amable.
vending machine	el distribuidor	You are very patient.	Eres muy paciente.
	automático	You're a hard worker!	¡Eres muy trabajador!
vinegar	el vinagre	You're very strong!	¡Eres muy fuerte!
wash (to)	lava		

abajo	down, below	**Bienvenidos**	Welcome
los abuelos	grandparents	**el bistec**	steak
el aceite	oil	**el blanqueador**	bleach
Adiós	Goodbye	**la bolsa**	bag
adjusta	(to) adjust	**el botones**	bellhop
el agua	water	**el brazo**	arm
el aire acondicionado	air conditioner	**el brocolí**	broccoli
el ajo	garlic	**¡Buen trabajo!**	Good work!
la alberca	pool	**Buenas noches**	Good night
la albóndiga	meatball	**Buenas tardes**	Good afternoon
la alfombra	carpet	**Buenos días**	Good morning
las almejas	clams	**el busboy**	busboy
la almohada	pillow	**la cabeza**	head
el almuerzo	lunch	**el cable**	cord, wire
alrededor	around	**el café decaf**	decaf coffee
añade	add	**el café**	coffee
el aparcamiento	parking	**la calefacción**	heater
los aperitivos	appetizers	**la cama**	bed
el apio	celery	**la camarista**	housekeeper
los árboles	trees	**los camarones**	shrimp
los arbustos	shrubs	**cambia**	(to) change
asa a la parilla	broil	**el cambio**	change
el ascensor	elevator	**el cangrejo**	crab
aspira	(to) vacuum	**el/la cantinero(a)**	bartender
la aspiradora	vacuum	**la carne asada**	roast
el atún	tuna	**la carne**	beef
Ayúdame.	Help me.	**la carne molida**	ground beef
el azúcar	sugar	**el carrito**	cart
bailar	to dance	**las cebollas**	onions
la banana	banana	**la cena**	dinner
el baño	bathroom	**el cenicero**	ash tray
el baño	restroom	**el cepillo**	scrub brush
el bar	bar	**cera**	(to) wax
barre	(to) sweep	**el cerdo**	pork
el basurero	garbage can	**los cerillos**	matches
el batido	shake	**la cerradura**	lock
bebidas después de la	after dinner drinks	**la cerveza**	beer
las cena		**la cesta para el pan**	bread basket
las bebidas	beverages	**la champaña**	champagne
Bien. ¿Y tú?	Fine, and you?	**los champiñones**	mushrooms

la charola	tray
checa	(to) check
el/la chef	chef
la chuleta	pork chop
cien	one hundred
cincuenta	fifty
el/la cliente	cliente
el cloro	chlorine
el closet	closet
cocina	(to) cook
la cocina	kitchen
el/la cocinero(a)	cook
el codo	elbow
la colcha	spread
el colchón	mattress
la coliflor	cauliflower
coloca	(to) put, arrange
el comedor	dining room
comer	(to) eat
Cómo	How
¿Cómo estás?	How are you?
¿Cómo está tu familia?	How's your family?
¿Cómo te llamas?	What's your name?
¿Comprendes ingles/español?	Do you understand English/Spanish?
Con quién	With whom
los condimentos	condiments
consigue	(to) get
Continua tratando.	Keep trying.
la copa	wine glass
el cordero	lamb
corta	(to) cut
Cuándo es	When is
Cuántos	How much, many
cuarenta	forty
el cuarto	bedroom
la cubeta	bucket
los cubiertos	silverware
la cuchara	spoon
la cuchara para sopa	soup spoon
el cuchillo	knife
el cuchillón	steak knife
el cuello	neck
la cuenta	check
el cuero	skin
dale	give him, her
dame	give me
¿De dónde eres?	Where are you from?
¿De dónde es Carlos?	Where is Carlos from?
los dedos	fingers
delante	in front
derecha	right
el desagüe	drain
el desayuno	breakfast
desempolva	(to) dust
el detector de humo	smoke detector
detrás	behind
diez	ten
el dinero	money
el distribuidor automático	vending machine
dobla	(to) fold
el domingo	Sunday
Dónde	Where
Dónde está	Where is
¿Dónde vives?	Where do you live?
la ducha	shower
la electricidad	electricity
en	in, on
encima	on top
la ensalada	salad
entre	between
los entremeses	hors d'oeuvres
envuelve	(to) wrap
Eres muy amable.	You are very kind.
¡Eres muy fuerte!	You're very strong!
Eres muy paciente.	You are very patient.
¡Eres muy trabajador!	You're a hard worker!
Es importante.	It's important.
Es necesario.	It's necessary.
la escalera	stairs
la escoba	broom
escuchar música	to listen to music
la espalda	back
el espárrago	asparagus
las especialidades	specials
el espejo	mirror
la espinaca	spinach
la esponja	sponge
la esposa	wife
el esposo	husband
Está así así.	It's so-so.
Está bien.	It's good.
Está correcto.	It's correct.
Está mal.	It's bad.
estar con la familia	to be with family
el estilo comedor	dinner style
el estilo herradura	horseshoe style
el estilo salón de clase	classroom style
el estilo teatro	theater style
el estómago	stomach
el estropajo	scouring pad
Estudio español.	I'm studying Spanish.
examina	test
la familia	family
los filtros	filters
firma	(to) sign

el florero	vase	jugar al béisbol	(to) play baseball
las flores	flowers	jugar al billar	(to) play billiards
el foco	lightbulb	jugar al boliche	(to) bowl
los folletos	pamphlets	jugar al fútbol	(to) play soccer
la fresa	strawberry	jugar al fútbol americano	(to) play football
la fruta	fruit	jugar al golf	(to) play golf
la fuga	leak	jugar al tenis	(to) play tennis
la funda	pillowcase	jugar al volibol	(to) play volleyball
las galletas	crackers	jugar cartas	(to) play cards
el gas	gas	el jugo	juice
el/la gerente	manager	el kiwi	kiwi
Gracias	Thank you	la langosta	lobster
la grasa	fat	lava	(to) wash
los guantes	gloves	la lavamanos	sink
guarda	to put away (store)	la lavandería	laundry room
Habla más despacio, por favor.	Speak slowly, please.	el lavaplatos	dishwasher
		la leche	milk
¿Hablas ingles/epañol?	Do you speak English/Spanish?	la lechuga	lettuce
		leer	(to) read
Hablo español un poco.	I speak Spanish a little.	la lima	lime
hamburguesa la	hamburger	el limón	lemon
Hasta luego.	See you later.	la limonada	lemonade
Hasta mañana.	See you tomorrow.	limpia	(to) clean
haz	(to) make	llena	(to) fill
Hazlo como yo.	Do it like me.	Lo siento.	I'm sorry.
el helado	ice cream	las luces	lights
la hermana	sister	el lunes	Monday
el hermano	brother	el lustrador	polish
la hielera	ice bucket	la madre	mother
el hielo	ice	el maíz	corn
las hierbas	weeds	la mancha	stain
hierve	(to) boil	la mano	hand
la hija	daughter	la manta	blanket
el hijo	son	el mantel	tablecloth
los hijos	children	la mantequilla	butter
las hojas	leaves	la manzana	apple
Hola	Hi/Hello	la máquina de hielo	ice machine
el hombre	man	la máquina	washer
el hombro	shoulder	los mariscos	seafood
la hostess	host/hostess	el martes	Tuesday
el hueso	bone	la mayonesa	mayonnaise
el/la huésped	guest	Me encanta…	I love…
Igualmente.	Same to you.	Me gusta…	I like…
el inodoro	toilet	Me llamo…	My name is…
ir a las fiestas	to go to parties	el mecánico	mechanic
izquierda	left	el melocotón	peach
el jamón	ham	el melón	melon
el jardinero	groundskeeper	la mesa	table
la jarra	pitcher	la mesa principal	head table
el/la jefe(a)	boss	el/la mesero(a)	server
el jueves	Thursday	el miércoles	Wednesday
jugar a los deportes	(to) play sports	Mírame.	Watch me.
jugar al básquetbol	(to) play basketball	mirar la televisión	(to) watch television

la mostaza	mustard
Mucho gusto.	Nice to meet you.
los muebles	furniture
muebles los de alberca	pool furniture
la mujer	woman
nadar	to swim
la naranja	orange
el/la niño(a)	child
No está correcto.	It's not correct.
no funciona	does not work
No me gusta…	I don't like…
noventa	ninety
ochenta	eighty
la oficina	office
el oído	ear
el ojo	eye
los órdenes	orders
los órdenes	work orders
las ostras	oysters
el padre	father
los padres	parents
el pan	bread
el pan tostado	toast
las papas	potatoes
el papel de baño	toilet paper
el pasillo	hallway
el pastel	cake
el pavo	turkey
el pecho	chest
pela	(to) peel
los pepinos	cucumbers
la pera	pear
el pescado	fish
pescar	(to) fish
pica	(to) chop
la pierna	leg
los pies	feet
las pilas	batteries
el pimentero	pepper shaker
la piña	pineapple
el piso	floor
la plancha	(to) iron
planta	(to) plant
las plantas	plants
el platillo	saucer
el plato	dinner plate
el plato para ensalada	salad plate
el plato para pan	bread plate
los platos	plates
los platos principales	entrees
poda	(to) prune
el pollo	chicken
pon	(to) set

Por favor	Please
Por qué	Why
el postre	dessert
prepara	(to) prepare
el/la primo(a)	cousin
la propina	tip
el protector de colchón	mattress pad
pule	(to) polish
Qué	What
el queso	cheese
¿Qué tal?	How's it going?
Quién	Who
Quiero presentarte a…	I'd like to introduce you to…
las químicas	chemicals
quita	(to) clear
quita	(to) remove
las ramas	branches
rastrilla	(to) rake
rebana	(to) slice
el/la recepcionista	receptionist
los recipientes	containers
recoge	(to) pick up
el refresco	soft drink
rellena	(to) refill
repara	(to) repair
el restaurante	restaurant
restrega	(to) scrub
riega	(to) water
la rociada	spray
la rodilla	knee
la ropa	linen
la ropa sucia	soiled linens
el sábado	Saturday
la sábana	sheet
saca	(to) take out
sal y pimiento	salt and pepper
la salchicha	sausage
el salmón	salmon
la salsa de tomate	ketchup
la salsa para la ensalada	salad dressing
saltea	(to) sauté
la sandía	watermelon
el sandwich	sandwich
la sangre	blood
seca	(to) dry
la secadora	dryer
la servilleta	napkin
sesenta	sixty
setenta	seventy
la silla	chair
sirve	(to) serve
el sistema de refrigeración	refrigeration system

la sopa	soup
el sótono	basement
Soy (de)	I'm (from)
los suministros	supplies
el/la supervisor	supervisor
surte	(to) stock
el tapete de baño	bathmats
la tarjeta de crédito	credit card
el taxi	taxi
la taza	coffee cup
el tazón	bowl
el té	tea
¿Te gusta?	Do you like?
el té helado	iced tea
la televisión	television
el tenedor	fork
el tenedor para ensalada	salad fork
el tenedor para postre	dessert fork
termina	(to) finish
la ternera	veal
la tía	aunt
la tijera	tray jack
la tina	bathtub
el tío	uncle
la toalla	towel
las toallas de papel	paper towels
los toallas	towels
el tobillo	ankle
el tocino	bacon
Todo lo demás está perfecto.	Everything else is perfect.

tomar, beber	(to) drink
los tomates	tomatoes
la toronja	grapefruit
trae	(to) bring
el transporte al aeropuerto	airport transportation
trapea	(to) mop
el trapeador	mop
el trapo	rag
Trátalo.	Try it.
treinta	thirty
usa	(to) use
las uvas	grapes
vacia	(to) empty
el vaso	glass
los vasos	glasses
los vegetales	vegetables
veinte	twenty
la vela	candle
Ven conmigo.	Come with me.
las ventanas	windows
el vestíbulo	lobby
el vestuario	locker room
el viernes	Friday
el vinagre	vinegar
el vino blanco	white wine
el vino	wine
el vino tinto	red wine
Vivo en…	I live in…
el zacate	grass
zanahorias las	carrots